A MIRROR TO GENEVA

ITS GROWTH, GRANDEUR AND DECAY

A MIRROR
TO GENEVA
Its Growth, Grandeur and Decay

BY

GEORGE SLOCOMBE

Essay Index Reprint Series

BOOKS FOR LIBRARIES PRESS
FREEPORT, NEW YORK

INTERNATIONAL STANDARD BOOK NUMBER:
0-8369-1852-5

LIBRARY OF CONGRESS CATALOG CARD NUMBER:
70-121506

PRINTED IN THE UNITED STATES OF AMERICA

CONTENTS

v

CONTENTS

ILLUSTRATIONS

A MIRROR TO GENEVA

ITS GROWTH, GRANDEUR AND DECAY

Chapter I

LUNCHEON IN THE BOIS DE BOULOGNE

§ 1

ON a bright day in the spring of 1919, the first spring after the World War, four men sat down to lunch in the garden of a celebrated restaurant in the Bois de Boulogne. The scene was brilliant, the conversation gay, the food exquisite, the wines mature, for Paris during the four years of Armageddon had not forgotten how to stage a *décor*, talk wittily, eat wisely and preserve a palate for wine. Around them hovered venerable waiters with bald heads and trembling hands and gray mustachios clipped severely *à la Foch*, for the war generation of waiters was still mobilized on the Rhine. Around them rose the discreet clamor of voices in a dozen languages: voices grave and gay, cultivated, ironic, sententious, the voices of diplomats and high functionaries of state, of military officers, of stern and haggard old ladies of the Faubourg St. Germain, of actresses of the Comédie Française, trilling in liquid notes a laughter musical as water. And not infrequently broke in upon these carefully modulated and elegant voices the hoarse, sophisticated speech, rich in plebeian undertones, of a *cocotte* from the boulevards. For if the Peace Conference had been sitting for several months, and the great hotels and restaurants were crowded with the black-coated apostles of peace, the manners and morals of Paris were still those of wartime, and the wartime pro-

3

miscuity still lent an air of carnival and Mi-Carême to the most ordinary occasions.

The Peace Treaty was nearly complete. In less than five months the frontiers of Europe had been re-drawn; great nations had been destroyed or mutilated; other nations had been created. Shortly the draft of the Treaty was to be handed to the Germans, with the curt order to sign it or take the consequences. The four men were intimately concerned with one section of the Treaty—its Preamble. It had lived with them for days and nights. It was the charter of their future destiny. They examined it, in the secret of their hotel bedrooms, as a master-mariner gloats over his master's papers, or a newly liberated married woman contemplates her decree of divorce. They discussed it with outward calm, with a professional irreverence, adopting even towards the provisions of the famous Preamble the contagious attitude prevalent in Peace Conference circles, the peacetime projection of that breathless cynicism which haunted the dug-outs and trenches of the war of 1914-1918. And then, surrendering themselves to the magic of the spring sunshine in the Bois, rapt in the contemplation of pretty women and green leaves and the pattern made by the sunlight on white linen and smooth lawns, their nostrils gratified by the peculiarly French odors of burning brandy and melting butter and vintage wines, the four men forgot both Peace and Preamble in the delight of lunching long and leisurely in a Paris given up to the feverish exploitation of peace.

They were not conspicuous in a city full of conspicuous and vividly contrasted racial types. Two of the men were French. One was American. The fourth, and host of the party, was a Scotsman: bearer of an ancient Scottish name, heir to an ancient Scottish earldom and brother of the then earl. Royal blood, it was confidently believed by his intimates, ran in his veins. But in a city full of kings and statesmen, with reigning princes living in sixth-floor bedrooms and hereditary chieftains of Asiatic peoples paying extravagant rents for small furnished flats in Passy and Auteuil, with the proud melancholy features of the Emir Feisal flanking the stern figure of Albert of the Belgians and the grizzled head of Foch, with Renaissance Italians and *hospodars* of Wallachia and the Dobrudja at every street corner, royal blood did not count for much in Paris now that the Russian Grand Dukes were dead or ruined.

Moreover, the heir to the Scottish earldom was lean, unpicturesque, dejected-looking and unassuming. He wore, like the three guests at his table, the short black coat and gray-striped trousers of the functionary. He had a small head, a long neck with a prominent Adam's apple, a long nose and pale gray eyes. Clemenceau, seeing him at session after session of the Supreme Council of the Allies, alert, industrious, self-effacing behind the tall, dreamy figure of Balfour, to whom he acted as private secretary, had proposed him in a moment of ironic inspiration for the task outlined in the dull prose in which the dream of the visionary Wilson had been imprisoned. And in consequence Eric Drummond, precise, modest, unimaginative, the least elegant Foreign Office official who ever carried a neatly rolled umbrella in Whitehall, a man really happy only on his native heaths and trout-streams, and clad in loose and homely tweeds, found himself eating Sole à la Cardinal and Poularde de Bresse among the brilliant uniforms and vivid gowns of the first spring-tide in Paris since the war, a secretly despondent but loyal wire-haired Scots terrier with President Wilson's tin can tied to his tail.

§ 2

If the tin can was, appropriately enough, of American manufacture, its contents were largely and even peculiarly European. Periodically in earlier centuries the grandiose plan had moved the imaginations of men in Europe. After each great war the idea of the federation of the nations and of perpetual peace appeared like the Biblical vision of God moving upon the face of the waters. At the end of the religious wars of the sixteenth century Henri iv and his counselor Sully had laid the foundations of their Grand Design, which proposed the federation of the peoples of Christendom. A century later the Abbé de Saint-Pierre published his famous *Project for Perpetual Peace*. Kant, dreaming of a world state at Königsberg, outlined a league of nations and the basis of the modern Institute of Intellectual Co-operation in his secret article: "The maxims of philosophers on the conditions rendering peace possible should be consulted by the States armed for war." François de la Harpe, in 1767, won the prize of the Académie Française with a famous peace essay which concluded with the words: "You, whose right and talent it is to speak to mankind, great writers and eloquent philosophers, it is your task to plead for the peoples before their rulers in the interests of both." The revolutions in America and France had inspired Benjamin Franklin to the belief that Europe was now ripe for the plan of "good King Henri iv." And Joseph de Maistre had actually coined the phrase "Société des Nations," which is the official title, in one of its two official languages, of the modern League.

But the practical and political doctrine of the League, as distinct from its idealistic and humanitarian concept, came not from France or America, but from Russia. The real precursor of President Wilson was the Tsar Alexander I, and by a curious historic coincidence Russia has given the world the two great revolutionary ideas of modern times— the collectivist state and the super-state.

Alexander came to the concert of Napoleon's enemies young, naïve, courageous and full of generous illusions. He was the first Occidental to sit upon the throne of the Kings of Muscovy. He was sentimental, impulsive, ambitious, handsome and gallant. He loved the company of beautiful women and clever men, had been nourished by his tutor de la Harpe on the ideas of Rousseau, and had dreamed of leaving his name to posterity as that of a man who had liberated humanity. As counselors he had a small group of men curiously impregnated, for that period and that Court, with modern and liberal notions. The greatest of them, Czartoryski, was a Pole of noble birth and great intelligence, who saw in the Tsar's liberalism the means to the rebirth of Poland. Stroganoff, another familiar of the young Emperor, had been reared in accordance with the prescriptions of Rousseau's *Emile* and had been a member of the Jacobins' club in Paris. A third, Kotchoubey, had imbibed the dangerous political doctrines of the West in London and Geneva. To all three of them Alexander confessed enthusiastically that "he detested despotism wherever and however it ruled."

Czartoryski was hardly less devoted to Alexander than to his native Poland. He admired and loved the Emperor. He hoped, as he wrote later in his memoirs, "that Alexander would become in some sort the arbiter of peace for the civilized world; that he was the protector of the feeble and the oppressed, the keeper of justice among the nations." He suggested to the young Tsar the outlines of a new organization of the states of Europe and the establishment of a law of nations under the protection of the Great European Confederation. With his master's approval he sent the envoy Novossiltsov to London in 1804 to broach to a reluctant and skeptical Pitt a scheme for a federation of Europe which astonishingly anticipated the League of Nations. Pitt scoffed at the Utopian scheme, but ten years later it was revived by Alexander in the famous draft of the Holy Alliance. In the same year, 1814, Henri de Saint-Simon and Augustin Thierry published in Paris their treatise: "On the reorganization of European society, or, the Necessity and the Means of assembling the peoples of Europe in a single political body while preserving to each its national independence." And a few years later Napoleon himself, exiled on St. Helena, claimed the paternity of the idea: "I should have had my own Congress and my own Alliance. They were my ideas and they have been stolen from me."

In the meantime Alexander had succeeded in his plan of a Holy Alliance. Its manifesto, published in 1816, was read in all the churches of Russia. Its founder, in an access of mystic exaltation, saw himself as the Divinely inspired protector of public order and justice in Europe. "Providence," he wrote to a friend, "has not placed eight hundred thousand soldiers under my orders to gratify my own ambition, but to protect religion, morality and justice, and to secure the reign of those principles of order which are at the base of all human society."

His contemporaries shrugged their shoulders. If Goethe extolled the Tsar's proclamation as the "most beneficent thing ever attempted by mankind," Castlereagh dismissed it contemptuously as "a mixture of sublime mysticism and arrant absurdity." The Prince-Regent wrote politely that he approved so generous an engagement, but that the British constitution did not authorize him to append his signature to it. Louis xviii signed the treaty readily enough, but without attaching any importance to his signature, and prepared at any time to repudiate it. And the Austrian Emperor, who had, on the advice of his chancellor, already cut Alexander's prophetic references to the unity of Europe out of the first draft of the Treaty, only adhered to the final draft with reluctance.

Castlereagh, notwithstanding his skepticism, had contributed to the young Tsar's "confused medley of mysticism and absurdity" an idea of importance: the suggestion for periodical meetings between the Great Powers which resulted in the assembling of the first Congress. Article Six of the Treaty of the Holy Alliance, signed on November 20, 1815, incorporated Castlereagh's proposal in the following words: "To secure and facilitate the execution of the present treaty and to consolidate the intimate relations which today unite the four Sovereigns for the happiness of the world, the High Contracting Parties jointly agree to hold, at intervals to be determined, meetings which shall be devoted to their great interests in common and to the study of the measures which shall be judged most salutary for the repose and prosperity of the nations and for the maintenance of the peace of Europe."

But Metternich, whose rôle in the destiny of Alexander was strangely to prefigure that played by Clemenceau a century later in the last chapter of the public career of President Wilson, judged the project harshly and with a cynicism born of his early disillusionments. "Should the policy of Europe," he demanded in his *Memoirs*, "be at the mercy of a representative system of diplomacy? By any chance would the most complex affairs, the most delicate questions, gain by being discussed in assemblies of forty or fifty ministers, each independent of the other, voting by show of hands, and pronouncing by a majority often doubtful, often equivocal, upon matters that the intimacy and prudent experience of three or four ministries only succeed with the utmost difficulty in regulating to their satisfaction?"

The Holy Alliance nevertheless came into being. From Vienna the Congress of Europe moved its ponderous machinery to Aix-la-Chapelle, to Troppau, to Laybach and to Verona. It held together the but-recently dismembered fragments of Europe, the but-recently shattered dynasties and crumbling thrones. Formed to perpetuate the peace, the monarchical character, the new frontiers, the returning prosperity of a continent destroyed and devastated by years of war, it anticipated by a century the alliance of victorious Powers which under de Maistre's title of *Société des Nations* was to perpetuate and consolidate the new Europe of 1918. The Holy Alliance lasted fifteen years, from the second triumph of the Allies over Napoleon to the heroic insurrection of the Poles against Russia, the secession of Belgium from the Netherlands, the final expulsion of the Bourbon kings from France. By a second historic coincidence, roughly fifteen years were to elapse from the ratification of the Treaty of Versailles and the creation of the League of Nations to its humiliation at the hands of Italy, and the tragic and farcical failure to prevent the extinction of independent Abyssinia.

§ 3

But on this day of spring sunshine in the Bois de Boulogne there were no premonitions of that distant calamity.
Nor did the four men, to do them justice, dream of invest-
ing their infant creation with such magnificent trappings.
For them the apocalyptic vision of Wilson had already been
clothed in more modest and practical garments. They
were honest and unimaginative functionaries in black coats.
They saw the twentieth-century version of the Holy Alliance of Alexander 1 in terms of Peace Conference committees, jurists' drafts, typewritten reports, duplicating machines, hotel bedrooms transformed into hives of stenographers and interpreters, and such modest humanitarian or
economic activities as the co-ordination of railway time-
tables, the freedom of canals and waterways, the suppres-
sion of the traffic in arms, opium and women, the care of
refugees, the cleaning up of the confusion, disease, dirt and
chaos created by four years of war.

Of the four only the host had been trained in the school
of diplomacy. The others, and their immediate collaborators, subordinates and successors, were civil servants, journalists, professors of economics, philology or history. Their
only experience of international collaboration had been
gained in the Allied Revictualling Commission in London.
They had little experience, if much knowledge, of international affairs. They had not been encouraged, from the
harsh and sardonic utterances of Clemenceau, to place much
faith in the destinies of the organization committed to their
hands. The meetings of the League of Nations Commission in President Wilson's rooms at the Hôtel Crillon had
seen the early drafts of the League Covenant whittled down

to a dull and prosy impotence as the manifesto of Alexander had been whittled down by Metternich. The infant confided to them was the bastard of the Treaty, derided, neglected and scorned. For its maintenance they had been granted neither shelter nor money. Their first home was to be a drawing-room in an old house in a London square.

The first meeting of the Council of their newly born League approached and found its organizers still ignorant of the League's precise mission, duties and field of activity. The agenda of that first meeting was to be hurriedly improvised after a desperate search through the Peace Treaties for any vague reference to the League. That hastily contrived expedient was to yield them such apparently trifling subjects of discussion as the delimitation of the frontiers of the Saar, the charter of the World Court, the appointment of a High Commissioner in Danzig, the protection of minorities in Turkey and Armenia, a campaign against typhus in Poland and the repatriation of war prisoners. Their mission was to be that of the scavengers of the peace. They were to gather up the loose ends of the Treaties, the unconsidered trifles, neglected in scorn by the brilliant diplomats in the Hôtel Majestic, the Hôtel Crillon and the Quai d'Orsay, who were engaged in more dramatic activities —the dismemberment of Austria and Hungary, the creation of great new states in Central Europe like Poland and Czechoslovakia, the disarmament of Germany, the destruction of the Ottoman Empire and the expulsion of the Turks from Europe.

Being happily without imagination, the four men did not look beyond these minor tasks. They were grateful for the humblest crumbs dropped from the Supreme Council's table. They shared the modest enthusiasms, the disappointments, the fatigues, ardors and disillusionments which crowded thickly upon each other at the Peace Conference. They were secure in the illusory security of the bureaucrat who possesses a secretary, a filing-cabinet and a telephone. The charter of their future League held out before them no dangerous mirage of millennium. It was a severely practical document which reflected the midnight labors of many severely practical minds. It bore little resemblance, like the Peace Treaty itself, to the resounding promises made to the world in the Fourteen Points of President Wilson. It limited membership of the Society of Nations prudently in the first instance to the war victors and the complaisant or benevolent neutrals. It gave no hint of the generous exaltation, the momentary reconciliation, the high hopes and brief illusions to be aroused seven years later by the admission of the arch enemy to the League.

The apotheoses of 1924, 1926 and 1927, the handshaking of Herriot and MacDonald, the raptures of Locarno and Thoiry, the rhetorical flights of Briand and Stresemann, were as far from the thoughts of its creators as their tragic aftermath of failure and betrayal, the rape of Manchuria, the repudiation of Locarno and Versailles, the conquest of Abyssinia. In 1919 both the subsequent grandeur and the eventual decline of the League of Nations were as far from being conjectured as the manner and the method of its growth. It was still nebulous, a fantasy outlined on perishable paper, one of the many derided projects for the future organization of the world produced on demand by the talented young men in the Hôtel Crillon or the Hôtel Majestic. It was but a minor buttress in that vast tower of Babel which the delegates of the Paris Peace Conference built as a memorial to the World War: a tower built entirely of paper, a tower of resolutions, recommendations and reports, printed in many languages: the overtoppling tower of the chimera of peace.

That much, perhaps, but no more, our four men dimly perceived, as they appraised the beauty of the women, the warmth of the spring sunshine, the excellence of the food and wine, the gaiety and prosperity of post-armistice Paris, on this day in 1919. They may have divined, too, that this luncheon in the Bois de Boulogne with which the active history of the League of Nations commences was to be but the first of many political feasts. Luncheons and dinners henceforth were to follow each other with commendable regularity. The growing League and its army of diplomats, functionaries, secretaries, experts, interpreters and stenographers were to lunch and dine in London and Brussels, Madrid and Lugano, Paris and San Sebastian. It was to send missions and delegations, with an equal gastronomic zest, as far afield as the South Pacific and the Treaty Ports of China. But the early itinerant days were brief and soon forgotten. Vienna was to tempt them, with visions of imperial magnificence in the Hofburg, with memories of the Congress and of Alexander, Talleyrand and Metternich, and of ancient splendors in the Ballplatz, with all the seductions of a great capital, an opera and a ballet. But it was ordained that they were to be denied these privileges of statesmen and diplomats and condemned instead to the rigors and conventions of the city of Calvin. By the waters of Leman they sat down and wept.

Chapter II

THE PROPHET: WOODROW WILSON

§ 1

IN a village inn in Czechoslovakia I saw recently a photo-gravure portrait in the place of honor. Over it hung a faded sprig of laurel. The portrait was that of a man with lantern jaw, with high, narrow forehead and thin, compressed lips, and eyes that regarded the new Europe of his making sadly through rimless glasses: the most exalted, tragic and misunderstood figure of the twentieth century: President Wilson.

Woodrow Wilson was born in 1856, the son of Joseph Ruggles Wilson, a Presbyterian minister, and of Janet Woodrow. He studied at Davidson College, and later at Princeton; practiced law without success at Atlanta; took a degree of Doctor of Law at the Johns Hopkins University of Baltimore; and finally abandoned law for the profession of teaching. He was successively professor at Bryn Mawr, at the Wesleyan University, and at his own college of Princeton, where he was appointed to the chair of political science. In 1902 his reputation as historian and humanist was such that he became president of the university. Eight years later he entered the political arena as Democratic candidate for the governorship of New Jersey, and was elected. In 1912 he won the campaign for the presidency of the United States against Taft and Roosevelt, and sat in the chair of Lincoln and Cleveland.

The new President was a man in the earliest tradition of the founders of the American Republic. A Puritan by descent and early training, ascetic, disciplined in his habits of mind and body, knowing little of the world of politics or finance, judging men and their actions with the cold vision of the historian, he seemed totally alien to the oligarchical United States of 1912. Cold, unapproachable, impatient and intolerant of criticism, without friends and intimates, overriding both counsel and coercion from the Democratic Party bosses who had chosen him as their instrument, abhorring the rough joviality and shrewd opportunism of Theodore Roosevelt, and only reluctantly opening the barred shutters of his soul to the patient importunities of the Texan Colonel House, Wilson seemed immediately destined to anticipate the fate of other American presidents isolated from both party and public.

But in his first term of office he proved himself a politician of brilliant quality. He fought the financial magnates of Wall Street as courageously as his successor Franklin Roosevelt. He freed the Federal Treasury from the stranglehold of the great banks. He conciliated Mexico, gave a measure of autonomy to the Philippines and recognized the Chinese Republic of Sun Yat Sen. When the war broke out he found his instinctive pacifism strengthened by the natural and racial divisions of his fellow-countrymen. He proclaimed America's neutrality in the war, but he took measures to strengthen the American army and fleet. He proclaimed his country to be above the battle, and prepared to assume the rôle of arbiter when Europe should have exhausted itself in a senseless and fratricidal struggle. At the same time he conducted a long and vigorous diplomatic correspondence with both Great Britain and Germany in protest against the naval blockade, and the interference with the trading rights of neutrals.

In 1916 he was re-elected to the presidency on the slogan "He kept America out of the War." And within a year of his re-election, under the dual pressure of a Wall Street heavily committed to the Allies and of a public opinion gradually roused to indignation by the German submarine attacks on neutrals, he declared war on the Central Powers. But he was careful to distinguish, in his own rigidly departmented mind as well as in his public acts and speeches, between the responsibility of Germany and that of its imperial master. "We are not the enemies of the German people and they are not our enemies," he declared soon after America's entry into the World War.

§ 2

In the meantime the idea of a future League of Nations had been born on both sides of the Atlantic. Pacifists in both the Republican and the Democratic parties in the United States, among them ex-President W. H. Taft, had founded, in 1915, the American League to Enforce Peace. This League advocated, among other guarantees of international peace, the judicial settlement of disputes between nations, conciliation for disputes not so settled, and the periodical convocation of conferences to define or amend international law. At first Wilson had been skeptical of, and even openly hostile to, the program of Taft and his fellow-pacifists. But early in 1916 he was converted to their doctrines. At a banquet of the League to Enforce Peace, held at the Belasco Theatre in Washington on May 27, 1916, with the President of the United States as the principal guest, Wilson enunciated publicly the principles of the future League of Nations. "Henceforth," he proclaimed, "alliance must not be set up against alliance, understanding against understanding, but . . . there must be a common agreement for a common object, and . . . at the heart of that common object must lie the inviolable rights of people and mankind. The nations of the world have become each other's neighbors, it is to their interests that they should understand each other, it is imperative that they should agree to co-operate in a common cause, and that they should so act that the guiding principles of that common cause shall be even-handed and impartial justice."

Then came the enunciation of principles of the war settlement which were to obtain world-wide celebrity two years later—the first adumbration of the Fourteen Points: "Every people has a right to choose the sovereignty under which they shall live. . . ." "The small States of the world have a right to enjoy the same respect for their sovereignty and for their territorial integrity that great and powerful nations expect." And again: "The world has a right to be free from every disturbance of its peace that has its origin in aggression and disregard of the rights of peoples and nations. . . ." "If it should ever be our privilege to suggest or initiate a movement for peace among the nations now at war, I am sure that the people of the United States would wish their government to move along these lines: First, such a settlement with regard to their own immediate interests as the belligerents may agree upon. We have nothing material of any kind to ask for ourselves, and are quite aware that we are in no sense or degree parties to the present quarrel. Our interest is only in peace and its future guarantees. Second, *a universal association of the nations* to maintain the inviolate security of the highway of the seas for the common and unhindered use of all the nations of the world, and to prevent any war begun either contrary to treaty covenants or without warning and full submission of the causes to the opinion of the world, a virtual guarantee of territorial integrity and political independence."

On January 8, 1918, came the Fourteen Points. In them Wilson outlined his plan for a peace settlement founded upon equity and justice and the self-determination of peoples, the restoration of Belgium, the creation of an independent Polish state and the liberation of the oppressed nationalities of the Austro-Hungarian Empire. References to a future League of Nations were made in Points One, Three, Four and Five; and Point Fourteen ran: "A general association of nations must be formed under specific covenants for the purpose of affording mutual guarantees of political independence and territorial integrity to great and small states alike."

In essence the Fourteen Points of President Wilson were Democracy's reply to the double assault of Autocracy and Bolshevism. The second Russian Revolution of October, 1917, and the revelation of the secret archives of the Russian Court, of the agreements between the Allies (concealed from President Wilson) for the partition of Asiatic Turkey and of the Austro-Hungarian Empire and the attribution of Constantinople to Russia, had seriously undermined the allied governments' plea of honest defense against aggression and their pretensions that the war was being continued to achieve the restoration of Belgium and Alsace-Lorraine. The Bolsheviks had exposed the hollowness and the hypocrisy of the European democracies as they were shortly to expose, by their acceptance under protest of the peace of

Brest-Litovsk, the cynical and brutal aims of the then triumphant European autocracies. Wilson's trumpet-call was an attempt to marshal the disillusioned forces of democracy before it was too late: to recall the European allies to a sense of realities, if not to a sense of equity, to counter the fiery appeals to world revolution broadcast daily by Lenin and Trotsky from the Smolny Institute in Petrograd, and to appeal over the heads of the military masters of Germany and Austria to the stifled minorities and starving, war-exhausted masses.

§ 3

Eight months after the proclamation of the Fourteen Points, and six after the signature of the treaty of Brest-Litovsk, the military power of the Central Empires and their Balkan allies collapsed. In October, 1918, the German Chancellor made his first appeal for an armistice to the American President. Mastering his first impulse towards elation, Wilson received it coldly and suspiciously, fearing a trap. Disciplining himself, he ignored the protests of his colleagues. He regarded their opposition, in the words of his Secretary of State, Robert Lansing, as a personal affront. He closed his ears to counsel or comment. He conducted negotiations alone and unaided, tapping out, in the secrecy of his room at the White House, historic replies to historic communications on the typewriter he had brought with him from Princeton. In the exuberance of the Armistice Day celebrations, when all America celebrated the victory to which its eleventh-hour intervention had so largely contributed, the man who more than any single figure in the war had accomplished, controlled and justified that intervention, and had morally accelerated the collapse of the Central Powers, sat in the White House alone. His colleagues hated him. His party had abandoned him. Within a few weeks the victory of the Republicans was to rob his government of all save the fiction of power. The man who for over a year had dominated the councils of both associates and enemies, whose words had echoed throughout the world with the authentic ring of prophecy, whose summons had driven emperors into exile and had resuscitated historic corpses like Poland and Bohemia from the tomb of centuries, was shortly to leave American shores the most hated president since Lincoln, before death turned execration into eulogy and sneers into panegyric.

He left America a shattered image of clay. He arrived in Europe a demi-god. Rulers and statesmen regarded him with respect, with curiosity, or with concealed smiles of contempt or derision. But the people idolized him. He had a triumphal reception in London, in Brussels, in Paris. He slept in Buckingham Palace and in the Tsar's bed at the Quai d'Orsay. In Italy, before the Fiume incident turned him into an object of obloquy, he was hailed as a liberator. He signed the roll of freemen of Rome—a roll which began with Petrarch and has not ended with Mussolini. His portrait was sold by millions and cherished like an ikon in millions of peasant homes in Central Europe and the Balkans. His name was given to an avenue in Paris, a lakeside street in Geneva, a railway station in Prague. By the submerged nations of Europe the lean figure of the American President, tall, frock-coated, with the strange mechanical smile, the long teeth, the glassy eyes—a heaven-sent subject for caricaturists—was venerated like that of a Messiah. He was the Christ of the twentieth century. And his crucifixion was yet to come.

Chapter III

THE PEACE CONFERENCE AND THE LEAGUE

§ 1

THE Peace Conference assembled in Paris in January, 1919. The delegations of the victorious Powers, of the succession states and of the neutrals were crowded into the embassies, legations, hotels and furnished apartments of the capital. The representatives of the enemy Powers were isolated behind barbed wire in hotels at Versailles, closely guarded by police and detectives, and for long inaccessible to newspaper correspondents. Once his triumphal visits to the Allied capitals had been concluded, the United States President established his headquarters in the Hôtel Crillon, in a room overlooking the Place de la Concorde and the flower-crowned monuments to Alsace and Lorraine, the provinces lost and recovered by France. From his windows Wilson could see the captured German artillery parked in the historic Place, and on May 1, 1919, the flaming skeletons of the motor buses overturned and set on fire by a Paris mob. Across the Seine, and equally visible from the room which was to witness the last and most ineffectual of his struggles for world peace, rose the low pseudo-Greek profile of the French Chamber of Deputies. Adjoining it, on the Quai d'Orsay, was the handsome pile of the Ministry of Foreign Affairs. And there, in the gilded and Gobelins-lined Salon de l'Horloge, the public and private sessions of the Conference were held.

Wilson had come to Paris in the natural expectation that he would be unanimously offered the presidency of the peace deliberations. Germany had sought an armistice on the basis of his Fourteen Points. He was, among all the representatives of the Allied and Associated Powers, the solitary Chief of State. His country had emerged from the war with its army and navy practically intact, with its industrial and financial resources far exceeding those of the European Powers combined. Morally, politically and financially, as well as in unexhausted and still largely untapped military power, the United States was in a position to dictate the peace. Its President, by the mere fact of his country's renunciation of all part in the spoils of victory, felt himself to be the natural arbiter between the rival claims of both victors and vanquished.

But in this pretension he was sharply and rudely disillusioned. He found himself in immediate opposition to the personality, the mentality, the national and personal traditions and prejudices of two men—Georges Clemenceau and David Lloyd George. The French Premier was then over seventy. He presented a remarkable contrast, physically and spiritually, to the austere, monastic, high-principled pedant who held in his hands the destinies of the United States. Short, bald, gruff-voiced, with thick eyebrows that covered the fiercest and most sardonic eyes in the world, with a harsh mouth barely concealed by a scrubby white mustache, wearing a ready-made black string tie, a cloth hat of the kind worn by Irish farmers and cattle-drovers, a cape and a pair of leather gaiters which still bore traces of trench mud, and with his eczema-scarred hands eternally hidden under gray suède gloves, Clemenceau looked more like an old-fashioned country doctor than the President of the Council of Ministers.

He had nothing in his appearance or habits of the suave, cultivated and elegant Frenchmen, the Jusserands and Tardieus, whom Wilson had entertained at the White House. He was a fierce and unforgiving little old man who had seen the Prussians on the heights of St. Cloud in 1870, had practiced as a physician in Montmartre during the Franco-Prussian War and the Commune, had lived in the United States and married an American woman of whom he retained not the most affectionate memories, spoke English with a strong American accent, had lost all faith in both God and man, disliked and despised both his political adversaries and his followers, and had clung for fifty years to a life in which his only pleasure had been the downfall and discomfiture of his enemies and his only passion a passion of hatred for the country which had humiliated and mutilated his own. For nearly half a century, from 1871 until 1919, he had nursed his blind faith in the day of vengeance, and he was not to be cheated of his belated satisfaction by a rhetorical university professor from Princeton who posed as the arbiter of the world's quarrels and endeavored to dictate the settlement of France's ancient quarrel with Germany. "The trouble with Wilson," growled the old man over and over again, "is that he thinks he is Jesus Christ." He repeated this cynical accusation in Wilson's own outraged ears, and followed it up with comments even more blasphemous and occasionally obscene. When the chaste and unworldly idealist showed embarrassment or indignation, the Tiger merely chuckled in sardonic and contemptuous mirth, rubbing his gray-gloved hands together in his savage satisfaction at the revelation of the joints in the Arthurian knight's armor.

In blunt and abrupt language Clemenceau claimed and obtained France's right to preside over the Conference. Equally bluntly he intimated to the smaller Allies and the neutrals his intention to draft the principal Treaty without them. At the second plenary meeting of the Conference he invited them to preserve a discreet silence, adding that if it had not been for the prospective League of Nations their presence would have been dispensed with altogether. He overrode or ignored the protests of his colleagues. He provoked the gentle, courteous and elegant little Belgian delegate Hymans to bitter if impotent resentment, and did not even deign to reply when the Belgian indignantly reminded him of the Great Powers' wartime pledges to respect the rights of small nations. With the single harsh exclamation "Adopted!" or "Adjourned!" he rushed through the agenda of meeting after meeting at which the smaller nations were represented. All real business was done in the secret sessions—at first of a Council of Ten, which held 72 meetings; then of a Council of Five, which held but 39; and subsequently of a Council reduced to but four Great Powers, which met 145 times.

Of the Big Four the Italian representative, Signor Orlando, spoke no English. Wilson and Lloyd George spoke no French. To Orlando's frequent demands for the honoring of the secret engagements of the London Treaty of 1915, the French and British statesmen turned a deaf ear. The vital decisions of the Conference were frequently taken without the Italian delegate, or in spite of him, and the real responsibility for the peacemaking of 1919 belongs therefore to three men: Wilson, Clemenceau and Lloyd George.

§ 2

The British Prime Minister understood both Wilson and Clemenceau better than either of the two men understood the other. By his own religious and Nonconformist traditions Lloyd George was nearer to the Puritan American President than to the French freethinker. He had been reared, like Wilson, on the stern and lofty teachings of the Old Testament. Like him he could, on occasion, talk and think with the inspired conviction of a Hebrew prophet. But whereas Wilson's theology was largely intellectual, and his idealism academic, Lloyd George's theology was emotional, and his idealism rooted in material needs and practical knowledge of men and nations. Lloyd George's own political past, like Clemenceau's, had been radical, destructive and iconoclastic. He had less culture than either. Wilson had the book-learning of a professor of history and political science. Clemenceau had read philosophy, Greek and Roman history; collected books and pictures; and knew something of music and the drama. But the village-born and small-town-reared Welshman had more wisdom than the one, and more subtlety than the other. He understood and respected Wilson's sincerity and lofty idealism, if he was, like Clemenceau, irritated and amused by his pedantry and his affectations of omniscience. But also he understood and respected the patriotism of the Frenchman, his stubborn radicalism, his love of the soil of France, his determination to liberate his country from the recurring menace of aggression.

Nevertheless there were frequent and acrimonious disputes between the two Prime Ministers. Between Clemenceau and Wilson there was an unbridgeable gulf of mutual dislike and mutual suspicion. The American replied to the Frenchman's jibes by an attitude of cold disdain, withdrawing more and more within himself as the negotiations progressed, and only saved from blunders and embarrassments by the tact and resourcefulness of his familiar Colonel House. When his courtesy, his illusions or his patience had been worn to vanishing point, he issued his famous order to the battleship *George Washington* to make ready for departure. Lloyd George, of a more combative temperament, and secretly admiring the fierce and savage tenacity of the old Frenchman, replied to Clemenceau in kind. Once when the Tiger accused him to his face of mendacity he rose in anger and seized the old man by the collar, demanding and obtaining an apology. On another occasion, when Clemenceau charged him bluntly with having acted since the Armistice like an enemy of France, it is said that the British Prime Minister retorted imperturbably: "Surely that is our traditional policy?"

The result of this fundamental conflict of personality and of interest was the patchwork Peace. Anatole France, who had followed the negotiations with an ironic detachment in the serenity of his home in Touraine, said shrewdly at the time: "France is not strong enough without her Allies to make a peace frankly victorious; but not weak or resigned enough to accept a peace which will hasten the reconciliation of the peoples and permit of international co-operation. We fluctuate between two notions—an Imperialist peace, and a peace of reconciliation. Clemenceau wishes the former; our Allies hypocritically pretend to desire the latter. The Treaty of Versailles is a compromise badly constructed of both tendencies. It bristles with contradictions. It will not ensure peace. New wars will spring from it. . . . The most comic of all the delegates is Wilson. He knows nothing of Europe or its history, and he comes here to weigh the rights of nations in a chemist's balance. He hands out justice by the milligram. These Protestants are terrible. They mingle the principles of the Bible with the interests of finance: the result is odious."

Of Lloyd George the same skeptic observed: "He speaks the same language as Wilson, but he is utterly different. The other is a naïf. Lloyd George is a clever fellow. He reads the Bible and sings his Psalms, but he serves his country and himself. He is a great Englishman. He will abandon us before long, for at bottom he detests us. . . ."

§ 3

If the Treaty bristled with contradictions; if it was, on the admission of André Tardieu, one of its negotiators, "a compromise in the relative"; if it repeatedly renounced the principle of self-determination enunciated by Wilson (as in the case of the Germans in the South Tyrol, the refusal to permit the union of Germany and Austria, the attribution of the Chinese port of Shantung to Japan, the partition of Hungary), it retained, nevertheless, a greater substance of justice and wisdom than has been popularly credited. Today, eighteen years after its ratification, and shorn of its most bitterly criticized provisions, its penalties and disabilities, the Treaty of Versailles stands as a victory for Wilson and Lloyd George rather than as a monument to the vindictiveness or the vengeance of Clemenceau.

The restoration or creation of the states of Poland and Czechoslovakia, the independence of Belgium, the return of Alsace-Lorraine to France, stand as witnesses to the realization of one, and that not the least important, of the Fourteen Points. Of the excessive or arbitrary pretensions of Clemenceau in 1919, the most dangerous were steadily and successfully eliminated from the Treaty by the British and American delegates, and the others have since 1924 been one after another liquidated by peaceful negotiation or unilateral repudiation. Thus Wilson and Lloyd George refused to create a German Alsace-Lorraine problem by yielding to France's demand for the bridgeheads of the Rhine, and their offer of a military guarantee to France in compensation for this desired gage of security was only subsequently nullified by the American Senate's refusal to ratify the Treaty. They opposed all attempts to create an autonomous republic in the Rhineland. They equally refused to attribute the Saar to France, and the compromise then effected whereby the French were ceded the coal mines and the Saar territory was administered by the League for fifteen years has in spite of all prophecies of disaster been triumphantly vindicated. They refused to attribute Upper Silesia to Poland en bloc, without consultation of the populations concerned. They refused to hand over Danzig to the same state, and realized Wilson's original promise to grant to a restored Poland reasonable access to the sea by the expedient of the Corridor.

And finally they respected the territorial unity and sovereign independence of the German Reich, rejecting Clemenceau's suggestion that certain of the larger German states, notably Bavaria, should be invited to sign the Treaty. Wisely, if in cynical repudiation of the promises made by France and England to Italy in 1915, they prevented Italy from realizing her claim to the larger part of the Adriatic. The D'Annunzio adventure in Fiume was angrily denounced by Wilson, and Italy's occupation of the port was never recognized by her allies and associates, and came to an end in 1922 with the signature of the Italo-Jugoslav treaty of Rapallo.

There remains, as the most angrily debated relic of the Wilsonian incursions into world politics, the League of Nations.

§ 4

In Wilson's eyes the creation of the League was the pivot and foundation of his entire peace undertaking. It contained the germ of the emancipation of mankind from the burdens of war, injustice and oppression. It was greater and of more permanent utility than the Treaty whose first Article was to become its charter. By it the contradictions, the injustices and the weaknesses of the Treaty could eventually be remedied. And to salve the League from the abyss of confusion and conflict in which his great design seemed to be foundering, he made concession after concession to his European and Far Eastern associates, persuading himself that such concessions would ultimately be justified by the greatness of the end towards which he labored.

He had landed in Europe to discover that the concept of the League had made notable headway since his speech at the banquet of the American League to Enforce Peace in 1916. Pacifists of all the political parties had seized upon the idea with enthusiasm. In England Mr. Henry N. Brailsford had published, in 1917, a treatise with the prophetic title, A League of Nations. In France the Socialists, and in the neutral countries the peace societies, had applauded the notion. Even the autocratic and militaristic Germany offered its collaboration, Chancellor Bethmann-Hollweg declaring before the Reichstag in November, 1916: "The first condition preliminary to international relations based on arbitration and the peaceful settlement of disputes should be the abolition of offensive alliances. Germany is ready at all times to join a league of peoples, and even to place herself at the head of such a league formed to subdue the disturbers of peace." In 1918, after Wilson had incorporated his proposal in the Fourteen Points, the British Government had appointed a commission to report on the project under the presidency of Lord Phillimore. The Phillimore Plan, issued on March 20, was sent to Washington for the examination of the American President, who read it with interest and passed it on for detailed criticism to Colonel House. The Texan Colonel revised the draft of Lord Phillimore and returned a text to the White House which became known as the House Plan. This document, after revision by the President, was subsequently issued as the Wilson Plan.

In December, 1918, on the eve of the opening of the Paris Peace Conference, two important contributions to the League concept were made by General Smuts and Lord Robert Cecil. Smuts published a pamphlet outlining the system of administering ex-enemy colonies under League mandates which was later to be adopted in the Peace Treaties. And Lord Robert Cecil proposed, among other features of the future League charter, the creation of a permanent court of arbitration. Wilson accepted both suggestions.

On January 25, 1919, the Peace Conference, at its second plenary session in the Salon de l'Horloge of the French Ministry of Foreign Affairs, appointed a commission to draft the constitution of the League and supplied it with terms of reference in the following uninspired and uninspiring resolution:

"It is essential, in order to ensure the maintenance of a state of peace in the world, that the associated nations here assembled should undertake as from today the creation of a League of Nations. Alone such an institution will encourage an international co-operation likely to ensure the carrying out of international obligations freely accepted and required to furnish full safeguards against war.

"This League should be created as an integral part of the Peace Treaty. It will be open to every civilized nation fully determined to promote its ends.

"The members of the League shall assemble from time to time in an international conference. The League will be supplied with an organization and a permanent secretariat in order to permit it to continue, in the intervals between such meetings, the business already in hand."

The committee appointed by the Peace Conference to draft the charter of the League was placed under the chairmanship of President Wilson, and it met for the first time at the Hôtel Crillon on February 3. It consisted at first of fifteen, and later of eighteen members. A photograph taken of the Commission after one of its earlier sittings preserves for posterity the features of the founders of the League. It is one of the most remarkable documents of our time. The pioneers of the future world organization wear an air of melancholy unusual in that atmosphere of cynical exultation or facile enthusiasm. It is as if the camera eye had surprised them collectively in a mood of disillusionment. They look out sadly on a world of mutual envy, distrust and hatred—the two Japanese delegates, Viscount Chinda and Baron Makino; the pale, haggard Lord Robert Cecil; the Italian Orlando and Pessoa; the Greek Venizelos with his enigmatic mask; the Frenchman Larnaude; the amiable old peace fanatic Léon Bourgeois, eternally preaching a League armed in tooth and claw; the square-headed Czechoslovak Kramar; the Serb Vesnitch; the South African General Smuts, grave and erect like a Dutch pastor; the Chinese Wellington Koo, with his diamond-bright eyes in an expressionless face; the Roumanian Diamandy, and handsome white-haired Paul Hymans of Belgium. Only Wilson, standing in the middle of the group, well-groomed and clean-shaven and alert as the principal of a Middle-Western business college, self-assured, measuring with calm eyes behind his gleaming nose-glasses his chances of immortality, seems to challenge the prevailing air of calamity.

His chance had come at last. In other rooms of other hotels in Paris, in the narrow dusty corridors of the Quai d'Orsay, in a thousand bedrooms and sitting-rooms carpeted in red and furnished with real or imitation pieces of the period of Louis Seize, the army of diplomats, jurists, experts, generals and admirals of the Peace Conference might labor over the delimitation of frontiers, over the strategic railways, roads and rivers of Europe, over the disarmament of Germany, the campaign to exterminate the equally perilous epidemics of Bolshevism and typhus in Eastern Europe. Marshal Foch might stump up and down the ante-chambers of the Supreme Council grumbling to all and sundry that without a frontier on the Rhine France must fear the révanche of a re-armed Germany. Clemenceau might rub his gray-gloved hands together in terrible mirth, uttering blasphemies and obscenities in that strange, staccato American voice of his. But here, in the first-floor room of the Crillon, the author of the Fourteen Points, the prophet of world peace and reconciliation, the moral arbiter of the war and the peace, the representative of the greatest democratic nation in the world, was free at last to build, four-square and solid as the rock upon which the Christian church was founded, the new temple in which humanity might worship without fear.

§ 5

His religion, which was to have been universal, and founded upon the equality of all races, states and nations, was not, however, applicable to all men equally. Surrendering once more to the demand of France, Wilson excluded the ex-enemy Powers from the privileges of the new faith. Under pressure from his own countrymen, he struck two blows even more deadly at his own concept of universality. He refused to accept the Japanese proposal to insert a declaration of racial equality in the Covenant. And he insisted on a reiteration of the intangibility of the Monroe Doctrine in Article Twenty-one of the League Covenant, thus expressly excluding from the jurisdiction of the League the greater part of the American continent. Both the British and the American delegates agreed in opposing the French demand for an international force to impose respect for League principles.

The Covenant finally drafted was largely Anglo-Saxon in inspiration: a mosaic of the ideas contributed by Lord Phillimore, Lord Robert Cecil, General Smuts, Colonel House and Wilson himself. Its actual text was the work of an American and an English jurist, David Hunter Miller and Sir Cecil Hurst. In four months the committee had finished its work, and on April 28, 1919, a plenary meeting of the Peace Conference gave its blessing to the Covenant. The occasion was more solemn than was wont in those cynical days. The delegates caught from the emotion of Wilson, from the unexpected earnestness of the spectators, diplomats, and journalists alike, possibly from the resounding periods of the Covenant itself, a sense of drama and of history in the making. Colonel House, writing of the scene years later, referred to the sudden realization men had that the advent of the League of Nations would change the face of the world. Mr. Wickham Steed, not yet the enthusiastic if critical partisan which he was to become, reported the sense of something new and irrevocable which overcame all present in the Salon de l'Horloge. For the principal character in the scene it was a moment of spiritual exaltation that he was never to know again. He stood before the nations as Moses stood before Israel, the prophet and leader, pointing from the peak of his moral isolation to the land of promise. But if he was to lead them to its gates, he was, like Moses, not destined to enter therein. Before the year was out his work had been repudiated by his own country. The Treaty of Versailles, and the League Covenant which was its Preamble, had been rejected by the United States Senate. Wilson was ruined politically and physically. His death rang down the curtain on the last act of the greatest individual tragedy of modern times.

Not even his disappearance from the stage on which for five years he had played so preponderant a rôle caused the tide of public opinion to run again in his favor. He had excited too much resentment, too much distrust, had disappointed too many hopes, had wounded too many vanities. Derision is harder to destroy than hatred. In his failure in Europe he had incurred both resentment and scorn. He had lowered the prestige of a proud nation. Seventeen years after his death Americans still speak of Wilson with the resentment that under the Restoration and the Third Republic succeeding generations of Frenchmen felt towards Napoleon. But in Napoleon's case the posthumous tide of popularity has ebbed and flowed and ebbed again. History has rehabilitated him. Modern dictators have donned his mantle and their smaller stature has lent added glory to his own. But Wilson's legend has not yet grown to heroic dimensions. His name shares the vicissitudes of his creation. A world destroyed by war, or rejuvenated by the long enjoyment of peace, may well have cause to remember it.

Chapter IV

THE CITY OF CALVIN

§ 1

IT is not generally known that Wilson had intended the first Assembly of the new League to be held in Washington. It was to have been convened by the President of the United States in person as an earlier conference of the world's governments, summoned to assemble at The Hague, had been convoked by another Chief of State, the ill-fated Tsar Nicholas II. An official of the recently created and still skeleton League Secretariat even went to Washington in 1919 to make a preliminary survey of convenient assembly halls, and actually leased a residence for himself and another official. When the United States Senate refused to ratify the Peace Treaty, and it became clear that America for a long time to come would have nothing to do with the League, Washington was abandoned as the meeting-place of the first Assembly, alternative sites were one after the other rejected as inconvenient and the League, whose temporary headquarters had been established in Sunderland House, London, decided reluctantly to hold its first assembly in Geneva, which had been fixed by Wilson, romantically influenced by vague notions of Calvin and Rousseau, as the seat of the new organization.

Other minds than Wilson's had been attracted, during the course of the nineteenth century, to the Swiss city on the shores of Leman. Byron and Shelley; George Sand with her close-cropped hair and student's pipe and boy's clothes; Liberals, Social Revolutionaries, Nihilists and other political exiles from Germany and Russia; a host of romantic tourists from Northern Europe, had all fallen victim to the spell of its beauty, its blue-green lake, its gray or white or green houses overhanging the Rhône, the arrow-like spire of the cathedral of Saint Pierre darting heavenwards from the cluster of old houses on the hill, the vision of distant Mont Blanc, often obscured by cloud and mist, but never forgotten when once seen, its snowy peak rosy in the evening light across a valley already filled with a magical and melancholy green, the green reflected from the lake, from the tall houses on the quays, the green and white dancing boats, the rushing waters of the Rhône below the dam.

In summer the city gleamed a dazzling white, and the lake mirrored a sky of unchanging blue. The thick plane trees along the quays made a green roof of cool foliage over the heads of pedestrians. The gardens of the University offered a grateful silence to shabby students of philosophy of both sexes, the men bearded, thin, undernourished, with feverish eyes and hollow cheeks, the women inelegant, unbeautiful, with shortsighted eyes peering through glasses and dry colorless hair twisted stiffly into a defiant bun. Where the lake ended in a rushing torrent of green foam, low stone bridges spanned the noisy gulf. On the little island named after Jean Jacques Rousseau, in the shade of giant poplars, a kiosk spread iron tables at which one drank milk or beer or the thin white wine of Fendant. The town was full of clocks, and shops which sold watches and clocks, and men who made clocks and watches in the days before they made a better living by selling time-pieces of uncertain accuracy imported from Japan. Great white and gilt steamers paraded importantly up and down the lake, calling at all the towns on its shores from Geneva to Nyon and Ouchy and Montreux and Evian. The sun danced from a myriad points of light on the green waters, and sent reflections down to the great boulders of ancient glaciers in the lake bed, boulders undarkened by weed, clear and sharp as when they were first splintered from the mother rock, between whose brilliant facets the fish played, clear as goldfish in a bowl. On days of wind the glass-smooth surface of the lake was plowed into a million furrows of a blue as hard as steel. The sails of boats made a brilliant curve against the blue, as harsh and brilliant as bleaching linen on a lawn in April.

Sometimes a sudden storm made havoc of the scene. An evil wind came down from the mountains. The great arch of the sky came down low and black and threatening over the lake. The shores, but lately so green and smiling in the brilliant sun, were blotted out by a driving rain. The black waters heaved angrily, swamping small boats, drowning spluttering engines, foundering untried yachtsmen and travelers. Then the sky cleared as if magically. The treacherous waters subsided. The hidden shores reappeared. The white-capped mountains, from which the dark fury had come, reared their peaks imperturbably and innocent of malice into a sky empty of wrath. And for the rest of the long, hot, languorous spring and summer Geneva and its lake basked in a peace without guile, a city seemingly without blemish, with neither flaunting wealth nor shameful poverty, exposing its calm, unhurried life to the gaze of strangers as tranquilly and as without coquetry as its girls sunned themselves all day on the shores of the lake.

But in winter the city wore another aspect. The sky shut down upon the valley like a lid. The distant peaks were invisible. The lake was a dark gray, fretful and menacing. The geometrical houses and hotels along the quays, whose greenish stone or cement façades had glistened a brilliant white under the sun, loomed sullenly against the sky. An icy wind, known locally as the *bise*, swept down the mountain passes and churned the lake into a menacing monster of jade. The *bise* howled through the streets, swept the gritty dust from the harsh granite pavements into the pedestrian's eyes, nose and ears, and made the passage across one of the unprotected bridges of the city, between a wintry lake and a roaring torrent, a Wagnerian adventure.

The town itself, which in the long summer had lain open and hospitable to the stranger, its steamers and sailing boats, its cafés and restaurants, its kiosks and kursaals, its gardens and promenades smiling, bright with color, brilliant with light and warmth and activity, suddenly presented a bleak, closed and sullen face. It had gone into hibernation. Its café terraces were abandoned, and the cafés themselves, decorated in a style more German than French, dark, uncomfortable, ill-ventilated and overheated, offered opaque, steamy and forbidding windows to the street. The wide, stone-paved streets were deserted. The hotels were empty. The Kursaal had closed for the winter. The steamers were shuttered, silent, the forest of little brown and white motorboats and canoes moved restlessly against its mooring ropes. The cab-drivers had abandoned the leafless plane trees on the Quai de Mont Blanc and spent their idle days huddled over the stove in one of the steamy little cafés.

The citizens of Geneva retired into their silent and secretive châlets on the hill of Champel, or into the small, dark, old-fashioned apartments in the steep narrow houses of the old town.

§ 2

Such then was the Geneva to which the search for a neutral city within convenient distance of London, Paris, Madrid, Rome and Brussels, the Calvinist traditions of Wilson and its own historic associations with international works of peace and goodwill—the International Red Cross had been established there since 1864—had condemned the League. It was at once a town of a treacherous climate, of an illusory hospitality, of a calculating welcome; and a town of Roman relics, of frontier wars, of tyrannous medieval dukes, of Renaissance republics, of sanguinary struggles, of harsh intolerant religions, of intrigue, cruelty and ripe learning. The breath of Liberty had been blown upon the lake; the trumpet of independence had been sounded upon the city walls. But the life-breathing spirit had long since departed. The descendants of the burghers who resisted the Escalade of the archers of Savoy were bald, sallow, spectacled men who owned banks and factories and maintained in their pseudo-Gothic and pseudo-Renaissance villas along the lake a sullen and suspicious attitude to all social classes below them and all foreigners. The bourgeoisie, which had been arrogant and supreme in France and Germany during the later years of the nineteenth century, which martyred Dreyfus and shot down working-class strikers, had retired upon its last citadel in Switzerland. It feared and hated Socialism and Communism. It secured the acquittal of the assassin of the Soviet delegate Vorovsky at Lausanne. It called for the rifles and machine guns which mowed down an unarmed crowd in Geneva in 1935. For long, if impotently, it resisted the invitation to the U.S.S.R. to send delegations to the disarmament, economic and health conferences organized by the League, and threatened to withdraw when the Soviet Union was finally admitted to membership. It belied its own undertakings under the League Covenant by taking shelter under a traditional and illusory neutrality.

For all its proximity to France and its long traditions of association and friendship with France, Geneva has as little of the modern French spirit as Quebec. It is an outpost of the defeated bourgeoisie on the French borders as Coblenz in the revolutionary wars was an outpost of the defeated French monarchists. It harbors the League, but has never been of the League. Its adherence is but lip service, its partisanship perfunctory, its loyalty suspect, its aid without meaning. Geneva lived by the League, in the years of depression, and unceasingly grumbled that the League had driven out the traffic in tourists, a traffic already killed stone-dead by the war and not likely to revive during the many post-war years in which Switzerland was the dearest country in Europe and its currency exchange the highest. It offered its hotels, its climate, its view of Mont Blanc, its few cinemas, its single theater, its indifferent cooking, its expensive wines grudgingly and at extortionate prices. It complained incessantly of the embarrassments created by the League's presence, only to sue for a continuation of its patronage when a movement began for the transfer of the League to more hospitable and more stately Vienna.

For seventeen years the several thousand foreigners of culture and distinction associated with the various international movements with headquarters in Geneva have lived on the fringe of a small, dull and conservative society which at first affected to ignore their very existence and later made clumsy and transparent attempts to create social relations with them.   When the Secretariat had been established in Geneva nearly a year without any sign of recognition from the sham-Gothic châteaux, the wooden châlets and concrete villas of Geneva's aristocracy, an awkwardly worded invitation was received in the higher degrees of the League hierarchy to meet *quelques dames de Génève*. No lady having cared or dared to take the initiative in bridging the widening gulf, refuge had been found in a collective invitation.   The frail bridge thus tentatively thrown over the abyss of ostracism and contempt which separated the League officials from the descendants of the embattled burghers of Calvin proved insufficient.   No real contact was ever established between the League and Geneva.   At the end of seventeen years the cosmopolitan body of men and women of the world's first civil service are as far as ever from any real intimacy with the citizens of their adopted capital, are as much resented, envied and disliked by them, as remote from their secret world of religious and social bigotry, Renaissance vendettas, feuds and intrigues, prudery and concealed perversions, commercial cupidity, exaggerated thrift, political bias, religious intolerance, reactionary zeal and fanaticism, and periodical outbreaks—as for instance during the annual celebration of the Escalade—of repressed sexual impulses.

§ 3

At heart Geneva is the most secretive, and the most mysterious city in Europe.   Its calm exterior, its air of candor, good-will, and commercial integrity, its innocent delight in the summer beauties of lake and mountains, its orderliness, its appearance of civilization, intellectual tolerance and large humanity are deceptive. The handsome bas-reliefs of the Wall of the Reformation in the gardens of the University celebrate the greatest revolution in the history of thought. The rough stone memorial on the heights of Champel makes generous, if belated, admission of the bigotry which sent Servetus to the stake. But the monument to the martyred heretic Servetus is small and insignificant: a stone tablet in a wall in a quiet suburb. The arrogant figure of Calvin, twice life size, in red marble, dominates the lakeside and the town. The stern, theocratic figures of Calvin, Bèze, and Cromwell break in upon the meditations of quiet loiterers in the University gardens. There has been little freedom of thought in Geneva since the *Contrat Social* of Rousseau, who had fled the city as a small boy, was publicly burned and a warrant issued for the arrest of the author if he should dare to return.

Since Rousseau's day the town has contributed neither philosophy, literature nor art to the world's culture. Its history is an eternal enigma. It alternately charms and repels the stranger. It looks askance at the man of unconventional or subversive theories; it persecutes the revolutionary; it offers a chilly welcome to mild and peace-loving cranks and fanatics; to apostles, like those of the Oxford Group, of comfortable and new and unembarrassing religions, exponents of revision of currency, railway time-tables and calendars, statisticians of all sorts (for the Swiss, like all book-keepers, love figures) and, naturally, financiers. The greatest regret of the Genevese is that they are required to harbor the unpractical idealists of the League of Nations, instead of the glossy-hatted, smooth-faced, well-groomed bankers of the International Bank of Settlements, which inconsiderately chose for its headquarters the rival Swiss city of Basle.

Chapter V

THE HEROIC DAYS

§ 1

THE Hôtel Victoria in Geneva occupies the greater part of one of those strange green cubes of concrete and masonry which line the quays of the lake on both sides of its outflow into the Rhône. Its windows look out on the English Garden, on the gray hall of the central markets and on the façades of the more aristocratic hotels of the Quai de Mont Blanc across the lake. The fourth side of the hotel block is blind. The hotel backs up against the end of a long, narrow, rectangular building with small windows high up in its ugly walls and an air of neglected piety: a Calvinist conventicle, neither entirely sanctuary nor entirely secular, the Salle de la Réformation. In this drab building, ill-ventilated, a furnace in the heat of September, without design or acoustics, without color or character, the Calvinist obsession of Wilson was gratified a second time, and with it the cautious Scottish utilitarianism of the loyal servant to whose hands the sacred tablets of the covenant had been entrusted for safe keeping: Sir Eric Drummond.

The Hall of the Reformation became the early scene of the Assembly of the League of Nations and remained so for nearly a dozen years. A door was pierced in the back of the conventicle, to permit of communication with the hotel adjoining it, and the entrance of the Hôtel Victoria

—with the aid of palms in pots, a few yards of thick red cord, a great strip of white bunting with the inscription crudely printed on it: *Assemblée de la S.D.N. Entrée des Délégués*, and half a dozen Swiss police in blue and red uniforms—became the official entrance to the first ten Assemblies of Wilson's League. The small, old-fashioned lounge rooms of the hotel, with their creaking parquet floors, their old-fashioned curtained windows, their Victorian furniture of faded red rep and green Utrecht velvet, their round occasional tables, their bits of discolored lace, their last year's magazines and tourist propaganda, provided the ludicrous *décor* for the greatest assembly of races and nations ever seen, the statesmen and diplomats of half a hundred countries.

At one or other of the small tables covered with a nameless lace—tables with spindly legs, and littered with cigar and cigarette ash, with typewritten copies of speeches, with copies of the reports of the Opium Committee, the Committee on Mandates, the Committee on the Traffic in Women and Children, with reports of inquiries into Manchuria, into the Saar and into Danzig—Briand and Stresemann sat during the heroic years of the League, each with his crowd of acolytes. The tall restless figure of Titulescu, lithe and dangerous as a leopard, paced hungrily from group to group. The high squeaky voice of Stresemann rose above the hubbub of conversations, the clash of teacups and cocktail glasses, the rustling of the stiff satins of old ladies staring through their gold-rimmed *face à main* at the weary profile of Briand, and even above the loud, cheerful, sardonic accents of the Victoria's porter, Philippe, big, bloodshot-eyed and red-faced like one of the Pomeranian grenadiers at the price of whose bones Bismarck would not have purchased the whole of the Balkans.

Behind the broad shoulders of Philippe stood huddled the anxious and awed figures of tourists, gazing uncomprehendingly at the statesmen in silk hats and morning coats as they walked out of the stuffy lounge into the sunlight of the street. They saw defile under their noses, within elbow reach and whispering distance, the spokesmen of the white race, the yellow and the black; bearded Ethiopians; little brown Japanese; a brilliant, handsome gigantic Negro from Haiti speaking the French of the École des Sciences Politiques and of Voltaire; a German baron from Liberia; the bland, enigmatic face of Wellington Koo; the stout, smiling, well-groomed figure of the Aga Khan; a couple of Indian maharajahs; a Persian ambassador, with the face of a Khan of Tartary; and the monocle and high glossy stare of Sir Austen Chamberlain.

In the upper rooms of this hotel, which was for ten years the antechamber of the League, the lobby of the first World Parliament, sat League officials, stenographers, journalists and the fanatics of the many world leagues for the promotion or the abolition of as many diverse causes. On the third and fourth floors of the hotel were the rooms of the correspondents of the French, British and American newspapers; correspondents shrewd and farsighted enough to establish their typewriters and working quarters within the very citadel of the Assembly.

By day the hotel was a babel of strange sounds: the squeaking of the old wood floors, the complaints of the ancient lift, conversations in many languages, the machine-gun rattle of typewriters, the shrilling of telephone bells, and the whine of the mimeograph machines multiplying copies of speeches just made in the drab hall beyond the faded plush and rep of those Victorian sitting-rooms. But by night, when the statesmen and the secretaries and the detectives and the curious public had departed, a strange peace fell upon the hotel. The squeaking floors which earlier had been trodden by the slow, dragging feet of Briand, the quick impatient step of Stresemann, the light and panther-like tread of Titulescu, which had been struck by high wooden heels and brushed by silk skirts, were silent. The ancient lift was still. In his office the jovial, red-faced, sardonic Philippe slumbered in his chair. And in the little writing-room behind him, filled with the stale smoke of cigars and the odors of whisky and beer and ham sandwiches, long into the night and well into the morning, in a grim silence only occasionally punctuated by sounds of surprise, relief or discontent, sat the veterans among the special correspondents, playing poker or *chemin de fer*.

§ 2

The League came into existence heavily handicapped in the matter of publicity. It was born in a world still shaken by the reverberations of the war. It claimed the attention of newspapers whose front pages and headlines were given up to sensational reports of the great war's brood of little wars. Eastern Europe was in chaos, Eastern Asia in confusion. The Poles and the Bolsheviks were at war, the Greeks and the Turks were at war, the Poles and the Lithuanians were at war. Wilson had collapsed. Clemenceau had been defeated in his effort to be elected President of the French Republic. His victorious rival, Alexandre Millerand, had just acknowledged Wrangel as the head of the Russian government. Landru, the Bluebeard of the twentieth century, accused of the murder of many foolish and love-stricken women whose remains could not with any certainty be identified among the ashes of a kitchen stove, was being tried and would shortly be guillotined. France, England, Germany were full of industrial revolt. The metal workers of Italy were in successful occupation of the steel foundries, and would have created a Socialist Republic in Italy if an intellectual named Serrati had not just been snubbed by Lenin in the Kremlin and returned to Italy to wash his hands of a mere industrial upheaval. The Coalition government in Downing Street was threatened with revolt in India, unemployment and economic collapse at home, and civil war in Ireland. The triple specter of typhus, famine and revolution threatened Western Europe from the Urals.

Lloyd George, fresh from his victory over the dark, hectoring figure of the German coal magnate Stinnes at the Conference of Spa, was preparing to browbeat Briand and Doumer at the approaching Reparations Conference in Paris in 1921. Nationalist assassins in Germany, the forerunners of the Nazi headsman of 1933, the incendiaries of the Reichstag and the gunmen of the Nazi purge of July, 1934, were lurking in wait for Kurt Eisner, for Rosa Luxembourg and Karl Liebknecht, for Erzberger and Walther Rathenau. The world's press was full of social and political scandals, of resounding crimes, of sadistic orgies of murder and assassination, of denunciations of Bolshevism, of diplomatic duels between Paris and London, London and Washington, Paris and Berlin. The wealthy, omnivorous and immensely powerful newspapers of America had replaced the obscured and ridiculed figure of the former President as the arbiter of world affairs: triply arbiter and commentator and historian; the news-hungry, neutral, and objective recorder of world history.

Its correspondents ranged the five continents and the seven seas, indefatigable, imperturbable, cigar-smoking, typewriter-punching, cocktail-drinking men of all ages who reported wars and revolutions and strikes and famines and mutinies and murder-trials with zest, cynicism and an unappeasable hunger for travel, excitement, work, gambling, cabaret girls, the stimulation of alcohol and the unexplored mysteries of the Tenderloin quarters of Europe, Africa and Asia. They had reported the war and they were now engaged in reporting the peace. They moved in marauding bands from London to Paris, from Paris to Madrid and Rome, from Rome to Vienna, from Vienna to Constantinople, where for some years the adventurers of the world assembled in night clubs run by authentic grand duchesses, and the victims of the revolution in Russia danced with the victors of the revolution in Turkey. They settled down with their assistants and secretaries in the capitals of Europe, spending an ambassador's salary on the entertainment of cabinet ministers, minor diplomats, prima donnas and cabaret artists, and another ambassador's salary on cable tolls to America. They traveled luxuriously between Paris and Vladivostok in trains crowded to the roof with fleeing refugees or returning exiles. They lived in the best hotels, at their newspapers' expense, and drank the best champagne at their own. With a spendthrift's contempt of money and a miser's economy of time they hired the largest and fastest cars, aeroplanes and speedboats. They were familiar with every great restaurant in Europe, from Larue's and Foyot's and the Tour d'Argent in Paris to the cigar-smoking and aristocratic Madame Sacher's decaying establishment in Vienna. They moved with the world's military leaders, diplomats and statesmen from conference to conference, from casino to casino, from the Kaiser's wartime villa in Spa to the casino of San Remo, the glitter of San Sebastian, the Cercle Nautique at Cannes and the medieval bankers' guilds of Genoa, sunny and beflagged in April.

They followed the lure of the big headline and the trail of the front-page news wherever it led them. They had the nose of hounds for a fresh scent. They followed it in full cry: eager, joyous, skeptical, enthusiastic, tireless in work and in play, the journalistic soldiers of fortune. They sought news everywhere with the patience and the curiosity of a seeker after new religions or after buried treasure. But they could not be persuaded that it was to be found, in those early days of Wilson's defeat and of European disorder, in the infant League of Nations. All the wiles of the American Arthur Sweetser and the French Pierre Comert, both former newspaper correspondents and now League pioneers, could not tempt them to Geneva. But on the path on which they had refused to follow the blandishments or the pleas of League officials, it was destined that a little girl should lead them.

§ 3

In 1920 and 1921 Geneva was a third-rate European city of little international importance. It was a small town in a small state, and not even its capital. Nothing happened there. Sometimes in midwinter the rumor percolated through the icy mists and bleak, lowering skies of the city that a ski-ing accident had occurred in the mountains, an avalanche or other disaster. The hotel porters concealed or minimized the loss of life. A paragraph would be telephoned or telegraphed to the newspapers of London or Paris by Swiss correspondents, frequently casual, sometimes unprofessional. There were no resident foreign journalists in Geneva. One or two leading British newspapers received publicity paragraphs and occasionally advertisements from tourist agents and hotel-men. Of Americans there were, in the first year of the League, practically none.

Then a staid, hard-working, conscientious and unadventurous American newspaper man strolled up from Rome. He had been sent to report some activity of the League. He was the representative of an American newspaper which was not greatly interested in the rejected progeny of Wilson. He came up to Geneva for a few days, wrote his brief and unepicmaking story and was about to return. On the night before he caught his train to Rome, being idle, bored and friendless in Geneva, he went to a cabaret. In those days some reflex of the post-war jazz fever was still visible in Geneva. There were half a dozen night cabarets in the town, cabarets of the international type, uniform from Paris to Constantinople, with Negro orchestras, small squares of polished dance-floor, red-plush seats, tables with a bottle of expensive and inferior champagne in a pail of ice, and a dozen or so girls of all nationalities —facile, often beautiful, French, Russian, Hungarian, Italian, with the French predominating.

The cabarets invariably bore the titles of Ciro's or Maxim's, or Florida, or Eldorado, or Eden. Europe in those days was full of Edens. Years afterwards the choice of name might have seemed significant. The cabaret chosen by the American newspaper man was probably

Maxim's. It was the best known *boîte de nuit* in Geneva. Some years later, when the jazz fever had subsided, and the wandering race of diplomats, demobilized soldiers and newspaper men had exhausted their pocketbooks or their palate for champagne, Maxim's became a melancholy haunt for a handful of faded and jaded dance-hall queens and for the dipsomaniac Conradi, assassin of the Soviet ambassador Vorovsky. But in 1920 Switzerland was still spending its war profits. Maxim's was gay, garish and noisy with saxophones and popping corks and the shrill laughter of girls. The lonely American, prim and highly respectable and hard-working, found himself in conversation with an attractive little girl who later gained merited applause by performing a dance *solo*. The journalist was sentimental and impressionable. He regretted that he was leaving for Rome. The next day he went to his friend Sweetser and told him he would like to become a resident correspondent in Geneva if it could be arranged with his chief. The matter was arranged. Shortly afterwards the American was transferred to Geneva and became the first correspondent formally assigned to the League of Nations. Ten years later the number of such accredited correspondents was to swell to two hundred. But in those days the League was the Cinderella of the world's newsmarket. The appointment of a resident correspondent was greeted with the joy aroused by the return of the Biblical prodigal. Only the little dancing girl received no official recognition of her efforts. She joined the long procession of unrewarded and uncomprehended League of Nations enthusiasts, a series which began with Wilson and ended with Briand.

§ 4

Another anonymous cabaret artist figured in the early history of the League. In the small hours of a June morning in 1921, during a session of the League Council, half a dozen newspaper correspondents, French, English and American, left the noise and smoke and heady atmosphere of Maxim's for a moonlight excursion in a motorboat on the lake. Among them was the late Lincoln Eyre, then correspondent of the *New York World*, a tall, handsome man with a romantic air, a brilliant flair for journalism, and an inextinguishable curiosity in matters of sex. He had covered the war, had interviewed Lenin in blockaded Russia, had been with me inside the barricaded steel foundries in Italy, and had retained undaunted by years of travel and experience all the candor, naïveté and enthusiasm of a Harvard freshman. He was impressionable, vital, eager, avid of experience, throwing himself with the same exuberant energy into work and pleasure, and magnificently paradoxical in all he undertook, even the most puerile things. To conquer the facile heart of a midinette he employed the tactics of a young *flâneur* of the New York of O. Henry. He besieged prima donnas and midinettes with the same persuasive and powerful batteries—hired Rolls-Royces, boxes at the opera, caviare, flowers, champagne. Women loved him and deceived him. But they all invariably admired his good looks, his height, his strength, his clothes, his generosity and his love of gallantry.

On the night in question, as upon many other nights, Lincoln Eyre was accompanied by a young woman, his latest conquest. For some reason, however, perhaps his over-polite attentions to another girl in the cabaret they had just left, she was not in the best of tempers. She entered the motorboat unwillingly, and repulsed him from her side. Eyre attempted to conciliate her, but she refused to be conciliated. Suddenly he rose in alcoholic dignity and climbed to the covered fore-deck of the boat. His companions shouted to him to return, but he ignored their warnings. He stood there poised for a minute, six-feet-four of handsome masculinity, very handsome and elegant in his black clothes and shining white shirt in the moonlight, then plunged into the lake. The girl, now repentant and hysterical, stood up and shrieked. Another journalist prepared to strip off coat and shoes and dive in after him. But when the boat's engine had been stopped the romantic man could be seen swimming effortlessly to the shore. The boat followed him. The weeping girl embraced him as he climbed out of the water. The two, now reconciled, departed in a taxi for their hotel. A Frenchman in the boat, greatly moved by the sentimental scene, expressed his sense of the American's gesture in the admiring words, "Ah ça, c'est chic!"

§ 5

Such incidents enlivened the dull, tentative and timorous early proceedings of the League. They were not confined to the gay, cynical and irresponsible newspaper men visiting Geneva. In one year a Chinese delegate, excitable, witty and intemperate, created some scandal by violently interrupting a speech of Sir Austen Chamberlain and then, after accusing the British government of encouraging the opium traffic in China, suddenly falling sound asleep. The same delegate added to his reputation for eccentricity by falling asleep at Sir Eric Drummond's dinner-table. And at the height of the Manchurian dispute of 1932, Mr.

Matsuoka, the leader of the Japanese delegation, a convert to Christianity and a man of great charm and intelligence, signaled each crisis in the League negotiations by appearing in the lounge of the Hôtel Métropole in Geneva wearing a brown kimono and bearing in his hand a bottle of cognac.

No such scandalous incident has ever marred the League history in Geneva as that which occurred during the Lausanne Conference, when the young correspondent of a London newspaper, irritated at the attentions paid by a Roumanian diplomat to a pretty film actress from Berlin in whom the journalist claimed prior interests, burst into the Roumanian's bedroom at midnight and struck him over the head with an electric reading-lamp. The matter might have been diplomatically if not amicably settled if the journalist had not ignored the Roumanian delegation's request that he should not be permitted to use the dining-room, and if he had not violently resisted the entreaties of hotel manager and head-waiter at a moment when the august figure of Lord Curzon was about to make a solemn entry on the scene. As it happened he was ejected from the hotel, violently protesting, and expelled the same day from Switzerland on the charge of resisting the police. His editor, after inquiring into the incident, promptly dismissed him, and the hero of this unfortunate undiplomatic incident shook the dust of Fleet Street from his heels to seek other newspaper fortunes in other countries.

The only known violent encounter between a newspaper correspondent and the police in Geneva, until the demonstration made by the Fascist journalists against the defeated Emperor of Abyssinia in 1936 caused their expulsion from the Assembly and subsequently from the canton of Geneva, was a much more banal and innocent matter.

The offending journalist, a brilliant if occasionally irresponsible writer, was found by gendarmes in the small hours of a summer morning sleeping off the effects of the previous day's potations on a bench on the lakeside. The Swiss police, like the police of other small European countries, are more zealous than discreet. They awakened the sleeper somewhat rudely, taking him for a common tramp or a malefactor lurking in the innocent byways of Geneva with intent to do mischief upon a visiting statesman. The journalist, resenting their attentions, and not wholly aware of his surroundings, struck one of the gendarmes and was promptly arrested and dragged off to the police station. There he stayed until morning, when telephone calls to the League Secretariat and to friends in Geneva established his identity, and he was discharged with a warning.

§ 6

But even these minor disturbances of the peace in Geneva are rare. They are the light airs which ruffle the surface of a lake and serve but to emphasize its placid calm. The real conflict in Geneva is not one of personalities but of principles, of national interests, of rival ambitions and contradictory policies. The little world of international officials, diplomats, journalists, interpreters and secretaries is a microcosm of the great world. It lives in a curious atmosphere of detachment, reflecting a little belatedly, feeling a little less acutely, the sensations and the passions of the world of which it is the slightly distorting mirror. The visitor from another country, even from the smallest in Europe, has the curious experience of finding himself in a state smaller still, a state with a population no larger than the membership of a London club, of a régime neither monarchical nor republican, despotic nor democratic, a state without an army or navy, without a police force, without uniforms, social traditions, commerce, industry or amusements, without judges, criminals or litigation, without sports, newspapers, theaters, literature or music, without scandals, corruption or vices, a state composed entirely of civil servants, but not without its hierarchy, social orders, and degrees of privilege. Hitherto the sovereign states of the world have been governed by priests, by soldiers, by lawyers, by men of birth and men of wealth. The super-state of the future may possibly be governed by scientists. The timid compromise between nationalism and internationalism which is the League of Nations is governed by bureaucrats and secretaries. And in a state of secretaries the Secretary-General is king.

Chapter VI

SIR ERIC DRUMMOND

§ 1

THE Concert of Europe of the early nineteenth century held its conferences, its secret negotiations, its diplomatic conversations and its passionate intrigues in a setting appropriate to the times and the characters. It was an assembly of monarchs and their ministers of state. It met in royal or imperial palaces. It moved against a glittering background of court etiquette, royal dignity and archaic ceremonial. In its solemn manifestoes, its dynastic disputes and reconciliations, its pageant of stars and jewels and uniforms, its state balls and banquets, its military parades and reviews, its religious ritual, the monarchical and despotic systems of the old world celebrated their apogee in a great fanfare of colored fires. When, a hundred years later, the triumphant democracies of the new world, republican or monarchical, decided to stage a similar spectacle, their efforts resulted in the sheerest anticlimax.

To replace the rich décor of imperial Vienna and Renaissance Verona they had the banal hotels of a Swiss city of banks and touring agencies and watchmakers and Protestant pastors. Instead of the palace of Charlemagne at Aix-la-Chapelle as assembly hall, they had the drab Salle de la Réformation and the Hôtel Victoria. Another hotel, the National, assumed the historic rôle of the Ballplatz in

Vienna. For the palaces of kings and emperors and hereditary nobles which had witnessed the rise and fall of the Holy Alliance, the dispute between the Tsar Alexander and Metternich for the favors of the same lady, and the patient intrigues of Talleyrand, the modern Concert of Nations could find no substitute but a string of hotels with the same view of Mont Blanc behind a picture-postcard lake, with the same red and green plush furniture, the same imitation of French cooking, the same polished pinewood floors and white ripolined doors and lace curtains and German-Swiss managers and creaking lifts and double windows against the dreaded bise—hotels without history and without character, with symmetrical green or greenish gray façades, with cumbrous, old-fashioned motor buses making three times a day the same monotonous journey to the Cornavin station, bringing back old ladies and cigar-smoking businessmen from the Middle West of America intent on doing the grand tour on American Express checks and a single language; hotels with such names as Beau-Rivage and Beau-Sejour and Carlton Parc and Bergues and Russie and Paix and Métropole and Terminus and Bellevue and Richemond, and last, and probably least, the enigmatically named Hôtel Touring et Balance.

Of all the lakeside hotels with the eagerly sought if but occasionally granted view of Mont Blanc, the farthest from the center of the town along the quay named after President Wilson is called the Hôtel National. It was first opened in 1875, was rated in the pre-war Baedeker as a first-class hotel, and was described as having two hundred and thirty beds with rooms from four to twelve Swiss francs, and as providing breakfast for two francs, luncheon for four francs fifty, dinner for six, and full pension for fourteen.

The hotel is separated from the lake front by a lawn planted with magnolia trees, and ornamented with a statue of a Negro girl who lifts an unlit lamp in her arm; and a white stone balustrade encloses the lawn and against it, during the past few years, has been visible a marble tablet with the inscription: "To the memory of Woodrow Wilson, President of the United States, Founder of the League of Nations." Overlooking the Negro girl and the magnolia trees was a glass-walled and glass-roofed restaurant, subsequently transformed and enlarged, in which the guests of the hotel drank tea in summer and listened to music and danced in the evenings in an atmosphere of Swiss cigars and lavender and the rich, sickly scent of magnolia blossom. Among the pre-war guests of the hotel whose names have been reverently preserved were such celebrated personages as the Khedive Abbas Hilmi of Egypt, the Duke of the Abruzzi, Prince George of Greece, the Grand Duchess of Mecklenburg-Schwerin, the Duchess of Devonshire, the Arch-Duchess Gisèle of Austria, the Maharajah of Kapurthala, the Serbian Prime Minister Pashitch, the American Ambassador Myron Herrick, and the newspaper magnate, William Randolph Hearst. Three distinguished women also signed the hotel register—the Princesse Chimay, the American prima donna Mary Garden and the great actress Eleonora Duse. A morganatic marriage famous in the history of European courts—that between the Duke of Croy and Miss Nancy Leishman of the United States—was celebrated in the hotel drawing-room. And a member of an ill-fated imperial house, Countess Mathilde von Trani, a Bavarian Duchess, and sister of the tragic Empress Elizabeth of Austria, had her suite on the first floor, and slept in the sunny corner room with the big windows overlooking the lake.

In the autumn of 1919 the hotel was closed for internal reconstruction and redecoration. Eighty-two new bathrooms were added to the modest plumbing arrangements installed in 1875; hot and cold running water was conveyed to all the bedrooms; a loggia and a hall on the ground-floor were built. In the summer of the following year the hotel was ready to reopen in expectation of the tourist revival, the universal prosperity, the rush of war-interrupted travelers to enjoy the mild pleasures, the chaste and pastoral distractions of peace-loving Switzerland. But early in August, 1920, before the hotel reopened, a scion of the ancient Scottish kings arrived with a draft on an English bank of almost equally respectable antiquity. The hotel changed hands for the sum of five and a half million Swiss francs. The new baths, wash-basins and hot-water pipes were torn out. The bedroom furniture was removed. The manager of the hotel, the discreet and experienced Herr Hottop, trained to distinguish at a glance between blue blood and plebeian, parvenus and princes of the Holy Roman Empire, abandoned his respectable and well-remunerated profession of hotelkeeper for that of international official. The glass pavilion became the council chamber of the League of Nations. And the bedroom of the sister-in-law of the Emperor Francis Joseph became the office of Sir Eric Drummond, first Secretary-General of the League, and creator of the world's first international civil service.

§ 2

The appointment of Sir Eric Drummond was not the least of the sardonic jokes perpetrated by Clemenceau at the Peace Conference. The great scheme of Wilson called for an idealist, a visionary, a man of imagination and initiative. The International Labor Office, its humbler companion, a mere hack in the stable in which the fiery League charger waited, had been handed over to a rider of mettle, the scheming, impatient, eloquent Albert Thomas, a Celt of fire and imagination, both realist and dreamer. With a grim chuckle Clemenceau handed the reins of the nobler steed to the shy, silent, unimaginative and severely practical Scotsman whom he had seen whispering in Balfour's ear in the Salon de l'Horloge, supplying him with notes and figures and references, sitting behind his chief unobtrusively, alert, patient and efficient, the perfect secretary— a tall man with a small head, with fair hair and small, stubbly mustache, a small pointed chin, a shy, diffident smile, a slow, well-modulated voice, a long neck with a low collar, a short black coat, gray-striped trousers, a watch-chain, a tightly rolled umbrella and a Foreign Office despatch case.

James Eric Drummond was the younger brother of the Earl of Perth. At the time of his designation by name in the Annexe to the Covenant as first Secretary-General to the League of Nations he was forty-three years old. He had been in the Foreign Office for nineteen years, since April 12, 1900. His career had been blameless and unsensational; his advancement had been slow but steady. For four years, from 1906 until 1910, he had been private secretary of the Parliamentary Under-Secretary of State. In 1911 he had been appointed private secretary to Sir Edward Grey, the Foreign Secretary. In 1912 until 1915 he had been private secretary to the Prime Minister, Mr. Asquith. From 1915 until 1919 he was again private secretary to the Foreign Ministry, first Sir Edward Grey and then Mr. Arthur James Balfour. He had attended the Peace Conference as secretary to Balfour. His rank at the Foreign Office gave him, at most, the first claim on a fairly important British Legation abroad. His salary was something under £1,500 a year. It pleased Clemenceau that this modest, efficient Scotsman, who after nineteen years of patient work in Downing Street could not expect more than a legation in Vienna or Athens, at £2,000 a year, should be offered over the heads of the expectant ambassadors and under-secretaries of both Downing Street and the Quai d'Orsay and Washington a job worth £10,000 a year and a place in history—if the newly-born League survived its birth pangs and its infantile maladies long enough to gain the notice of posterity, which the Tiger did not think probable. In any event the appointment angered Clemenceau's compatriots and disappointed Wilson, who had hoped it might go to an American. And both results gave the old man exquisite pleasure.

§ 3

Sir Eric Drummond, who had been made a Knight Commander of the Order of St. Michael and St. George for his work at the Peace Conference, accepted the offer without enthusiasm, but also without apprehension. He may not have believed, at the outset, in the prospects of the League, but his chief believed in them, and had urged his acceptance. Balfour was that rare phenomenon in British politics, a Scotsman with imagination. He was endowed with wit, an intelligence and reasoning power of high order, and a high serenity of mind. At once more subtle and more practical than Wilson, a better judge of human character, a

great statesman and a greater diplomatist (had he not, with
a disarming candor, told Wilson in Washington of the
existence of secret treaties between the Allies without seem-
ing to attach any real importance to them and thereby provoking the President to demand their embarrassing dis-
closure?), he had no excessive respect for the personality of
Wilson but he respected his enthusiasm for the League
of Nations.   He was himself an unexpectedly warm and
eager partisan of the League.   He had no illusions concerning its powers and its limitations.   On June 17, 1920, in a
speech before the House of Commons of great persuasive-
ness and sound sense, he defined both with almost prophetic accuracy:

"You cannot, and no rational man would, suggest that
the League of Nations is constituted to deal with a world
in chaos, or with any part of the world which is in pure
chaos. . . . The League of Nations may give occasional
assistance, frequent assistance, effective assistance, but the
League of Nations is not and cannot be a complete instrument for bringing order out of chaos.

"Those who would throw upon it that burden in the
name of peace and in the name of the League of Nations
and in the name of co-operation amongst civilised peoples
are doing the greatest dis-service they could to the League
of Nations.

"The League of Nations will serve you well if you do
not overload it; at least that is my hope, my faith, my belief.   If you overload it you will assuredly break it down.
. . . If you either allow the League of Nations to be used
as an instrument by the free nations of the world in their
own party warfare, or if they try and throw upon it bur-

DRUMMOND

dens which it is ill-fitted to bear, on them will be the responsibility of destroying the most promising effort in the direction of the renewal of civilisation which mankind has ever made."

Balfour had not been a member of the League committee of the Peace Conference, and had no direct part in framing the Covenant. But he gave the new organization his blessing and his highly efficient private secretary. Modestly, and with characteristic Scots caution and economy, Sir Eric Drummond entered upon his new office and its responsibilities. In 1919, after the signature of the Treaty of Versailles, he installed himself in a back drawing-room at 23 Manchester Square with one assistant—Lord Colum Crichton-Stuart—one shorthand-typist, and one office-keeper. Later, when he had recruited the nucleus of a Secretariat— among them Jean Monnet, the son of a well-known French brandy-distiller, Pierre Comert, a former correspondent of the *Temps*, the American Arthur Sweetser, and the industrious British economist Arthur Salter—he transferred his headquarters to Sunderland House. In the summer of 1920, when it became clear that America was not coming into the League, preparations were made to transfer the organization, subject to the approval of the first Assembly, to Geneva. The Hôtel National was purchased. On October 27, 1920, Sir Eric Drummond and his staff left London for Geneva. The first assembly of the League, held in the following month, approved the choice. And for the next sixteen years the Secretary-General of the League of Nations occupied Countess von Trani's old room in Herr Hottop's Hôtel National.

§ 4

The success of Sir Eric Drummond's fourteen years' tenancy of the highest post in the League may be measured by the efforts made by his successor, M. Joseph Avenol, to imitate his methods, to model himself upon his personality, to reproduce even his gestures and idiosyncrasies. Clemenceau had chosen more wisely than he had known. The Scottish private secretary of Arthur James Balfour had little of the Biblical inspiration of Woodrow Wilson, probably for the reason that he is a Roman Catholic, and Roman Catholic laymen are rarely familiar with the Old Testament. But what he lacked in imagination, in prophetic fire, in intuition, in the genius of personality and the exaltation of spiritual conviction he more than possessed in powers of organization. He had been a perfect private secretary. He became a perfect Secretary-General. He created an entirely new organization of over six hundred men and women of all races and nationalities and religions, individuals highly varied and distinct in type, culture and profession, many of them without previous bureaucratic experience, aptitude or inclination, and made of them an international unit, the first in the world's history. He not only succeeded in transforming them into an international civil service, he achieved the much more difficult task of infusing into them the zeal, the detachment, the objectivity and the corporative spirit of the Civil Service of his own country.

He did this without haste, without the brilliant logic and intuitive foresight which distinguished his colleague Albert Thomas, the creator of the neighboring International Labor Office; and, in the early days, almost without money. In the uncertainty and sense of impermanence of the early days of the League the organization lived almost literally from hand to mouth. A Secretariat had been created, but no funds had yet been guaranteed by the members of the League in process of formation. The Allied governments contributed sums on account of their first year's probable dues. When these were exhausted Sir Eric Drummond called a meeting of the higher officials at Sunderland House and told them they would have to go without their salaries in order that the junior members of the staff might be paid in full. The day was a Monday, and the spirits of the officials, already influenced by the traditional Monday dejection of London, were at their lowest. The financial director of the League, Sir Herbert B. Ames, a cautious middle-aged Canadian from Montreal, had to find six hundred pounds for salaries, another five hundred pounds for a committee working in Brussels, and had in all exactly one thousand pounds in the bank. The League seemed fated to expire before it actually saw the day. The new President of the United States had already announced its death. And for years afterwards the American Consul in Geneva was ostentatiously to cross to the other side of the street as he approached the League offices in case America should be suspected of entertaining secret relations with the unhallowed infant. Suddenly, as the officials sat gloomily in Drummond's room, a ring was heard at the door, and the stolid British office-keeper announced "a gentleman to see the Financial Director." It was the representative of the Central American republic of Guatemala, and he brought with him a check for £1,948, the full amount of his government's first year's contribution to the League. The prudent Canadian treasurer gave his swarthy visitor a cigar and engaged him in conversation while his clerk hastened to the bank to have the check verified. It was reported to be authentic. The caller was handed a receipt and the salaries and the expenses of the Brussels committee were paid on time.

Subsequently money flowed in more or less regularly to the League treasury, but the Scottish Secretary-General was not relieved of the secret preoccupation of insecurity. Hence the modesty of his early efforts at stage-production —the cheap conventicle, the rigid economies in the furnishing, decoration and function of Herr Hottop's transformed hotel, the close scrutiny over staff salaries, pensions, and other expenditures. He had little vanity and no sense of the theater. Farther along the lakeside the black-bearded Albert Thomas sat in a luxurious little room paneled from floor to ceiling in rare woods, a room rich and gleaming and secretive as the Frenchman's own darting brown eyes. The International Labor Office had a council chamber like a medieval banqueting-hall, and its staff was accommodated in a building as modern, as expensive and as efficient as a New York bank. But half a mile away the head of the larger world organization—who was a modern Moses, to plan but never to occupy the present grandiose palace of the League—sat uncomplainingly in his transformed hotel bedroom with its bare walls and cheap curtains and banal radiators, and pressed the tips of the fingers of his brown, muscular hands together over his plain office desk, and smiled at his visitors with his shy diffident smile, and looked up at the ceiling and then down at his blotting-pad with the air of pleasant abstraction he had caught from his year of secretarial intimacy with Sir Edward Grey and Herbert Henry Asquith and Arthur James Balfour. And on Saturday afternoons he played, conscientiously and with keen pleasure, his weekly round of golf. And during his annual vacation in Scotland he played more golf on his native courses and fished in his native streams, and like all business men at play, reached a satisfactory solution of annoying office problems as he walked from green to green or adjusted a new fly to his trout line. For if to the Socialist freethinker Albert Thomas the problems of world organization were as the problems of a personal theology, to the Scottish Roman Catholic Sir Eric Drummond, whose church competently took care of his religious interests, they were merely aspects of a large and important business. And Clemenceau, whose jests were usually more shrewd than other men's sermons, was to see himself, long after he had ceased to take interest in the affairs of a world which he scorned, justified of his sardonic prescience.

Chapter VII

THE VISIONARIES: SMUTS, CECIL, NANSEN

§ 1

W ILSON was in disgrace: a defeated and a dying man. But the League he had founded had nevertheless in its earliest years, the enthusiastic support of a handful of remarkable men who shared the convictions of Wilson and endeavored, within the limitations of their nationality, their birth and traditions, to translate his Apocalyptic vision into reality. These men were the Boer farmer Smuts, the Norwegian explorer Nansen, the veteran French Radical senator Léon Bourgeois, the English Tory aristocrat Lord Robert Cecil, the Swedish Socialist Branting, the Czech conspirator against the Habsburgs, Edward Benes, the Greek lawyer-diplomat Politis and the Belgian politician Hymans. Of them all the most remarkable and the most powerful in their influence on the growth of the infant League were the South African, the Englishman, and the Czech. Let us consider the case of General Smuts.

§ 2

He had come to England in March, 1917, to represent South Africa at the Imperial Conference. A critical stage had been reached in the World War. The first Russian Revolution had driven the Tsar from his throne. A mutiny had broken out in the French army, and had been followed by a change in the ministry and a change in the high com-

HYMANS

mand. The cause of the Allied governments seemed almost lost, and the military value of the intervention of the United States was still problematical. The war might be won by Germany on the Western front before American reinforcements could change the unfavorable balance of man-power into overwhelming advantage for the democratic powers. Suddenly, from the farthest end of Africa, came a middle-aged, bearded farmer-statesman, modest as Cincinnatus, laureled indeed with his victories over von Lettow-Vorbeck in German East Africa, and even wreathed, in the memories of an older generation, with the more ancient if now faded laurels of his victories over the British in the South African War; but, nevertheless, a strange and alien figure in a darkened London full of khaki-clad women, clean-shaven, pink-cheeked, red-tabbed generals, and worried luncheon-table conversations in Whitehall in which monotonously recurred the ominous words *blockade, attrition, salient, submarines, minelayers, Zeppelins,* and *Passchendaele.*

The newcomer brought with him an atmosphere of otherworldly calm. He was unhurried, unapprehensive, reflective and serene. In a moment which seemed to many in England the darkest in her history he spoke cheerfully and optimistically of the permanence and the power of the British Empire, which in a happy inspiration he rechristened the British Commonwealth of Nations, describing it as "a system of states, and not a stationary system but a dynamic, evolving system." He recalled to a despondent nation its own victory over the Boer farmers at the beginning of the century, and the wisdom which had turned that victory not into bitterness and the hope of revenge, but the foundation for a loyal and friendly association. To audiences which had seen in the collapse of Tsarism but the collapse of a powerful Ally and the imminent defeat of the Western democracies he proclaimed on a note of unperturbed confidence that the spirit of freedom was on the wing, and that "the great Creative Spirit was once more moving among the nations in their unspeakable anguish."

He insisted that the war was a war of ideals and that it must be fought until it ended in a victory of the spirit. And a nation which had heard similar if less simply and happily phrased declarations *ad nauseam* from the lips of Herbert Henry Asquith and David Lloyd George took new heart in the saying, returned to its war tasks and war burdens with less weariness, and cheered the speaker with something of the religious enthusiasm with which over a year later Europe was to greet the oracular pronouncements of President Wilson.

Jan Christian Smuts was then forty-seven years old, and looked older than his years. His scanty hair revealed a high and broad brow, the brow of a thinker and philosopher rather than that of a soldier or statesman. His tanned cheeks gave him an air of incongruous and rude health. His eyes were pale, deep-sunk and melancholy, and looked through men instead of at them. The mouth under the heavy farmer's mustache was firm. A short blond beard, already showing signs of gray, completed his appearance of a rural philosopher. In France he would have passed for a small-town notary, a professor of a *lycée*, or possibly a radical senator. In wartime England he fell naturally into no social or professional category. His beard, his khaki uniform with its general's tabs, his air of tanned health but military unprofessionalism, made him a figure to be stared at in Whitehall. Augustus John, then official painter to the

Canadian army, was, with the single exception of King George v, the only other known bearded Britisher in khaki.

Smuts had been born and reared on the farm of his father, who was also a member of the Cape Legislative Assembly. At twenty-one, after taking his degree at a South African university, he travelled to England with a scholarship to study law, took a double first at Cambridge, wrote an essay on Walt Whitman, returned to the Cape a mystic, was admitted by the Supreme Court, practiced law first in Cape Town and later in Johannesburg, and was appointed by President Kruger, in spite of his youth, to the post of State Attorney. When the Boer War broke out he fought with distinction, had several escapes from death, suffered privations with equanimity, and once rode more than seven hundred miles across bad country in under five weeks. After the peace he helped Botha to form the national association known as "het Volk," was elected to the Assembly, became Botha's Colonial Secretary, and worked equally enthusiastically for the union of the South African states and friendly association with Great Britain under a common crown. Subsequently he served as Minister for the Interior, for Mines and for Defense, and when at the beginning of the World War the rebellion broke out in Southwest Africa he helped Botha to extinguish it. Two years later, in German East Africa, at the head of a heterogeneous and ill-assorted force of Swahilis, Hindus, Englishmen and Cape Dutch, he carried to a triumphant conclusion the campaign already mentioned against von Lettow-Vorbeck.

The subtle politician whom his friends and enemies in South Africa knew admiringly as "Slim Jannie," and who had been first a resolute adversary and later a firm friend of British rule, now enjoyed celebrity on a wider stage and influence in the world beyond Africa. He had been sent in 1917 by Lloyd George to Switzerland on a secret mission to confer with an emissary of the new Austrian Emperor, eager to sue for peace, and had reluctantly reported unfavorably on the intentions of Austria. He had already conceived the juridical and moral structure of the system later to be known under his own admirable title of British Commonwealth of Nations. He was shortly to assume, with Woodrow Wilson, the moral and political responsibility for a larger and more ambitious system, of which the British league of nations he believed was but the embryo. In the summer of 1918, a few months before the end of the war, he published a work entitled *The League of Nations: A Practical Suggestion*, in which he outlined many of the principles which were subsequently incorporated in the League Covenant. When the Armistice was signed he insisted that the primary and fundamental task of the impending Peace Conference must be the creation of a real League of Nations—that league towards which, he declared, all civilization had consciously or subconsciously been working.

When the Peace Conference opened he pleaded in memorable words for the use of "pity and restraint" towards the defeated enemy. He fought hard for the principle of non-annexation. He spoke, like Wilson, in the simple language of the Bible, a language with which the Protestant communities of England, America and Germany had been familiar almost from birth. He spoke as a humanist, urging that "civilization is one body and that we are all members one of another." He urged the generous treatment of Germany as a vital factor in the restoration of European civilization. When the Peace Treaty was drafted, it confirmed his worst apprehensions. It was, he declared, far worse than the Treaty of Vienna. It perpetuated the war spirit. As a result of it Europe was still "seeing only red through a blinding mist of tears and fears—almost a mad continent, more fit for Bedlam than for the tremendous task of reconstruction." Nevertheless he signed the Treaty because he felt that in spite of its follies and deficiencies the war must be liquidated, and the Treaty did at least achieve two things—it destroyed Prussian militarism and established a League of Nations. These alone justified, in his cool, appraising eyes, the bitterly criticized act of Versailles. He has since referred in his book, *Holism and Evolution*, to the League of Nations as the chief constructive outcome of the Great War, and the "expression of the deeply felt aspiration towards a more stable holistic human society."

Since the early years of the League Smuts has made but infrequent visits to Europe. He has not once attended, as delegate of the Union of South Africa, an assembly of the League at Geneva. He is content at a distance to fill the rôle of prophet and creator. Since the death of Wilson no statesman speaks more eloquently than Smuts of the destiny of mankind. Since the rise of the dictatorships in Europe his has been almost a solitary voice in defense of democracy. "No better alternative as a basis of government has yet presented itself," he proclaims. Although "liberty as a form of political government is a difficult experiment," it is "probably the only political system that promises to endure. The consent of the governed is the only secure and lasting basis of government, and liberty is the condition of consent."

Soldier although he is, and a general who has commanded an army with distinction in two wars, Smuts has no particular respect for a career which he assumed reluctantly. He has robustly condemned nationalism as the glorification of war, and war itself as the "great weapon of kings . . . the child of an inflamed, unwholesome mentality, springing from groundless or exaggerated fears or ambitions, usually from both combined." Before the advent of Hitler he regarded the Great War of 1914-18 as "the last supreme effort of the national system," and he passionately urged disarmament not merely in the sense of eliminating the more inhuman instruments of war, but of outlawing it altogether, making it difficult and finally impossible. "What is the good of all the wealth and comfort and glamor of the Victorian age," he exclaims indignantly, "when the next two decades bring us to the graves of ten million young men slain because of the base passions of greed and domination which lurked below the smiling surface of that age?"

Smuts is perhaps the only man associated with the League ideal since its inception whose career has been neither made nor marred by the League. A sincere and almost fanatical devotion to the League of Nations ultimately destroyed Woodrow Wilson, who sacrificed one after another of his Fourteen Points in its interests, and sacrificed them, and himself, in vain. Briand and Stresemann rose to international celebrity through and by the League. Sir Austen Chamberlain's career as Foreign Minister will be remembered chiefly for his activities at Locarno and Geneva. Lord Cecil gave up a ministerial career to become a crusader for the League. A host of continental statesmen—Benes, Titulescu, Politis, Hymans, among the most notable of them—rose to world stature by their

SMUTS

speeches in League Assembly or League Council. But Smuts alone, although the League Covenant will ever be associated with him, and he has consistently fought the battle of the League, owes little of his unique prestige as man, warrior and statesman, to his association with that much-criticized body.

Yet if he neither sought nor gained laurels in the glorious days of the League of Nations, he might well have shared in the humiliations of its days of decline. For Smuts has consistently believed in the furtherance of collective security by the League, and in the League as almost the only possible instrument of collective security. He believed that Geneva would create "new machinery" for the maintenance of peace, machinery "less directly under the pressure of public opinion than the politicians are, and needs must be, in a democratic state." He advocated the appointment of expert scientific commissions to deal with complicated national and international issues, and urged the adoption of "the cool, serious, gentle spirit of science" in the direction of world affairs.

If he has been disillusioned by the turn of affairs in Europe since the destruction of the democratic republics in Germany and Austria, and the Italian conquest of Ethiopia, he has not betrayed his disillusionment to the world. He remains, at the age of sixty-eight, an unrepentant idealist, but an idealist whose hope for humanity rests upon a knowledge of humanity's needs and shortcomings. "Human government," he admits, "can be no better in the end than human nature." He believes that progress is a matter of experience through trial and error. Bolshevism and Fascism in his mind are but "temporary expedients." Hitlerism is merely a form of that nationalism which he condemned for its glorification of the childish instrument of war. Few minds in Europe have preserved his peculiar and brilliant sanity. He owes his sense of the unity of mankind to his own primitive religion, although paradoxically enough he does not admit that unity in his dealings, as a South African statesman "directly under the pressure of public opinion," with the black races in South Africa. And he owes to the good fortune of having been born at a distance from the shores of Europe the more singular paradox of being almost the only good European in the world since the death of Briand.

§ 3

Between General Smuts and Viscount Cecil of Chelwood there is a curious resemblance, both spiritual and intellectual. Both men are notable for a certain simplicity of mind, a natural modesty and gentleness of habit. Both men are ascetics. The Boer general gained the austerity of his character from early life on his father's farm, in the silence of the veldt. The English patrician acquired his own in the Victorian piety of the household of his father, Lord Salisbury. Boer and Briton seem equally remote from the modern world. They would have been happier in the sixteenth century. Smuts might have been set down without incongruity in the seat of William of Orange, who was, like himself, a warrior, a liberator and a rebel. Lord Cecil would have been admirable as one of his own ancestors, the famous godfearing ministers of Elizabeth. He has retained, almost alone among his generation of politicians, a good deal of that singular and characteristically sixteenth-century mixture of shrewd statecraft and religious zeal. Place a beard on his chin and a ruff about his neck and he is his own kinsman Burleigh, or even more exactly that patient Dutch emissary at the Court of the Valois kings, Ouden Barneveldt; although the high forehead, the nose of a bird of prey, the long ascetic lip, the intent and curiously smoldering eyes are also those of the Duke of Alva in the great portrait by Antonio Moro. Yet not Burleigh, not Barneveldt, and certainly not Alva is his prototype in history, but Sir Philip Sidney. For his career since 1916, when in the high tide of war he first drafted for the British Cabinet the proposal for the organization of peace which he subsequently sent to Colonel House, has been one of chivalrous devotion to an ideal.

Lord Cecil is now seventy-three years old. He belongs, like the late Sir Austen Chamberlain, to that seemingly ageless category of British politicians whose names, faces and idiosyncrasies have been a part of the familiar fare of newspaper readers since the beginning of this century. Age does not wither them nor custom stale. . . . They bring with them into a Westminster full of dapper business men and industrial lawyers in short black coats, wing collars and gold watch-chains something of the more leisured, more urbane and more rhetorical parliamentarism of the nineteenth century. Their Toryism or Liberalism is of an older school; their eloquence is more studied and rotund; their manner is that—deliberate, faintly ironic, melancholy and aloof—of men who have sat at the feet of Gladstone and Disraeli, and in their youth caught echoes from the speech of even remoter gods.

But Lord Cecil enjoys another distinction. Having been reared in that rare atmosphere of men to whom the almost mystical concept of a party was the mainspring of their political lives, who daily sacrificed personal ambition and private principles in the party's hallowed name, he had in 1927 the courage to break with his most intimate associates when he felt that their interest in the cause of disarmament was purely perfunctory, less all-absorbing than his own. The clue to the mental attitude which decided that breach with government and party might have been found in a speech he made eight years earlier, in a debate at the Cambridge Union, with the late Duke of Northumberland. The subject of the debate was the League of Nations, then in process of creation. Northumberland had attacked the Wilsonian concept with his habitual blunt vigor. Lord Cecil replied to him in a speech which at first differed little in matter or manner from the average House of Commons debate. At its end the speaker abruptly changed his ground of approach. His measured, slightly ironic, well-modulated debating style dropped from him, and he said with unusual earnestness and unusual directness: "I am not satisfied to leave the condition of the world as it is. The whole system of armaments and counter-armaments, of alliances and counter-alliances, is wrong and bad. The League of Nations may be idealistic, but [*here he raised his right hand above his head, with its long forefinger pointing at the ceiling*] it is a preference of spiritual to material things."

At Geneva his reputation for courtesy, sincerity, intelligence and honesty stood, and still stands, higher than that of any British delegate to the League since its inception, not excluding the late Arthur Henderson and Sir Austen Chamberlain. The incongruity between his hawk-like appearance and his gentleness of character provoked the witty Comtesse de Noailles to compare him one day in Geneva to "a vulture chasing butterflies." Although almost totally deficient in the wit with which a Scialoja or a Briand en-

LORD CECIL

livened the proceedings of dreary Council meetings, and averse from, if not incapable of, those sparkling intellectual passes *d'armes* which Paul Boncour and the late Soviet Commissar Lunacharsky occasionally diverted the Preparatory Disarmament Commission, Lord Cecil has always been one of the most popular and most successful members of both Council and Assembly. For if he has little or no wit, he has a dry humor equally telling on occasions, and his humor, modesty and charm in both public and private intercourse make him an effective and attractive figure in assemblies where rhetorical flourishes are at the mercy of the interpreter and are accordingly discouraged.

Ironically enough, in spite of his dramatic resignation from the British government over disarmament, and his long and ardent championship of the League in England, Lord Cecil has figured in few great public controversies in Geneva. It is for quiet work on the Council and on the Committees of the League that he is remembered. His more sensational career in connection with the League began after he ceased to be an official delegate to its meetings. The one verbal duel in which he took part in Geneva as a spokesman of the British government occurred at a Council meeting in 1923, when the administration of the Saar, then much criticized as being more pro-French than pro-League (it was during the occupation of the Ruhr), had come up for discussion.

The government of M. Poincaré was anxious that the discussion should be secret. Its representative on the Council, the late Gabriel Hanotaux, objected to a proposal by Lord Robert Cecil (as he then was) that he should present the British case in public. Lord Robert argued that the violent criticisms uttered against the Saar administration, many of which were without justification, made it important to avert any fresh charge that the affair was being hushed up by the Council. Both men stood on their positions. M. Hanotaux rejected a suggestion by the Italian president, Signor Salandra, and the Swedish member Hjalmar Branting, that both the British statement and the French rejoinder should be made public, but the discussion thereon remain private. Lord Robert Cecil argued that the matter was of importance both to the governments and to the peoples concerned. He insisted that it was necessary to inform the democracies of the matters at issue. "When we make the people our masters," he quoted, a trifle sententiously, "the next duty is to educate our masters." A Japanese delegate suggested the Machiavellian compromise that the discussion should be in secrecy, but that Lord Robert should be free to make any communication he liked to the press afterwards. But the British delegate rejected this suggestion, and insisted that the Council decide by vote whether or not to admit his original demand for a public session. The vote was taken, and the British spokesman won his point. But when it came to his speech on the Saar, it was delivered so judiciously and with so much urbanity that M. Hanotaux publicly felicitated Lord Robert on his tact and good sense.

When so much regard was manifested by a British delegate for the principles of democracy and popular rights as far back as 1923, it is of interest to speculate what would have been the attitude of the present Lord Cecil if he had represented Great Britain on the League Council during the Manchurian dispute in 1933, or during the Abyssinian dispute of 1935?

Yet even if one has a reasonable conviction of the kind

NANSEN

of action Lord Cecil would have taken on those fateful occasions, it may be justifiably objected that a better instrument would have made little difference in the execution of a bad policy. Since 1920 the League of Nations has been a battleground between the realists and the idealists in international affairs. It was, in its early years, almost entirely abandoned to the idealists. The realists then in control of British and French foreign policy had little use for Geneva, except as a futile debating chamber. The French were the first to realize, with the defeat of Poincaré in 1924 and the abandonment of the ultra-nationalist and encirclement-of-Germany policy of Poincaré and Millerand, that the League offered them and their new allies in Central and Southeastern Europe a system of mutual protection against isolationist Britain and America on the one hand and against Habsburg restoration and German revisionism on the other. And some years after their entry in force on the Geneva scene, under the banners of Herriot and Briand, the spirit of League idealism seems to have taken hold of a Conservative British government, and the Tory Sir Austen Chamberlain vied with the Radical Aristide Briand for the laurels of League champion. That was the moment, ironically enough, chosen by the most ardent League idealist of them all to break with his party and his colleagues, and go out into the wilderness to preach the pure gospel of the Covenant.

§ 4

A third of the knights errant of Geneva deserves mention here: perhaps the noblest, the most solitary, the most disinterested of them all, Dr. Fridjof Nansen.

Nansen came to the League of Nations straight out of the Norse mythology. In the early years of this century he was already an almost legendary figure. In the history of Arctic exploration his two expeditions to the Pole in 1889-91 and 1893-96, the first of them conducted when he was not yet thirty, and the second in his early thirties, had made of him a hero of the Victorian age. From that epic and remote past of action and adventure the old Viking suddenly emerged after the World War as a Norwegian delegate to the first Assembly of the League of Nations. His political disinterestedness, his honesty and his talent for organization inevitably suggested him as the organizer of relief for the great fugitive populations from the war or civil war-torn countries of Eastern Europe—the Hoover of the peace. He was appointed League High Commissioner for Refugees in 1921, and his work for the émigrés or exiles from Soviet Russia gained him the Nobel Peace Prize in the following year. In 1923 he successfully organized the settlement of the million and a half expatriated Greeks from Asia Minor, and thereafter he stood as a living symbol of the humanitarian efforts of the League of Nations.

Geneva knew him as a lean, modest and reticent man with a bronzed weather-beaten face, a deep sad voice, and patient, melancholy eyes. He seemed to have left any personal ambition he may once have had behind him in the frozen wastes of the Pole. And with ambition his capacity for personal happiness. I have known only one other man who had Nansen's look of an incurable melancholy: Alexander Kerensky. By a curious coincidence Kerensky, like many thousands of other Russian exiles, now travels on a Nansen passport.

Chapter VIII

THE ARTISAN: BENES

§ 1

IF Geneva is immutably hostile to all revolutionary doctrines, it has, nevertheless, played a curious part in the history of revolutions and their leaders. It has given reluctant hospitality to many proscripts in exile. It has seen the same proscripts return, crowned with honors, as the official representatives of the countries which once condemned them to prison or banishment. Of the many European statesmen who have looked down from the windows of their hotel apartments, in moments of ennui or of reverie, at the plane trees on the Quai Wilson, not a few have occasionally been tempted to recall with pride or with irony the circumstances of their first visit to this town, of their early lives as shabby, impoverished and nervous fugitives from the police, among the cosmopolitan crowd of students in the university library and the idlers on the lakeside. Among such revisitants to the Geneva scene I have known Russians, Poles, Greeks, Letts, Lithuanians, Czechs, Serbs and Italians. Not Mussolini, for whom the Swiss city of his early humiliation and subsequent triumph was not Geneva but Lausanne. But among the Czechs one hero of an adventure that the historians of his country will without exaggeration describe as romantic; an adventure that began in a professor's study in Prague and ended in the collapse of the empire of the Habsburgs:

the small, modest, unromantic-looking Edward Benes, now president of the republic of Czechoslovakia.

Benes is past fifty. When the war broke out he was just thirty. He had been born the last of a family of twelve children, the son of a Czech peasant, whose ambition it was that his son should become an intellectual, one nevertheless who would never forget the taste of bread laboriously earned. He studied philosophy at the University of Prague, and there he met the man who was to lead the movement for the independence of the Czechs and Slovaks: Thomas Garrigue Masaryk. Benes was then a thoroughgoing Marxist, agnostic and convert to the materialist conception of history. After a year at Prague, on Professor Masaryk's advice he went to Paris and to Dijon, spent the summer vacation of 1906 in England, and almost the whole of the following year in Germany, and when a year later he resumed his studies in Prague he brought with him the diploma of Doctor of Law of the University of Dijon. In 1909 he became Doctor of Philosophy of the University of Prague. In the meantime he had studied the technique of revolution at first hand among the political exiles in Paris, London and Berlin. He returned from his life abroad a less orthodox Marxist, and a less fanatical agnostic. He remained anti-clerical, but was no longer anti-religious. He had abandoned the materialist conception of history, and wrote (in 1908) articles in refutation of that famous Marxist principle. He had exchanged international socialism for a socialism strongly imbued with the spirit of nationality, if not of nationalism. Politically he was nearer the strange ameliorist and characteristically insular philosophy of the British Labour party than that of any of the continental revolutionary parties.

§ 2

The outbreak of the Great War gave him his historic opportunity. When he learned that Austria-Hungary, contrary to his predictions, had committed the disastrous act of folly of provoking war, he had no illusions concerning the end of the Dual Monarchy. Its ultimate collapse was now certain. The only doubt that existed in his mind was whether the collapse would come during a disastrous war or in the internal disorder, social and political revolution which would follow the war. When he learned that Great Britain had entered the war, he expressed his conviction that Germany's defeat was now certain, and that the break-up of the Habsburg Empire would accompany it. His own decision was taken immediately: unhesitatingly to devote himself, his freedom, his life, his married happiness with a young wife, to the Czech cause against Austria.

He spent the first year of the war in Prague, the intimate confidant and collaborator of Masaryk in the little group of Czech conspirators which now formed. At the end of 1914, when Masaryk, who had left Austria on a short visit to Italy, was threatened with arrest on his return to Austria, Benes intercepted the order of arrest, warned his leader in time, and during Masaryk's continued absence assumed the leadership of the insurrectionary movement inside Austria. He took amazing risks, organized a secret courier service between Austria and Switzerland, and repeatedly crossed the border into Germany and Switzerland in disguise. And he enjoyed equally amazing good fortune. In Vienna the secret correspondence of the Austrian Minister of the Interior was regularly read by the Minister's Czech valet, who surreptitiously abstracted important documents from his master's desk, copied them at midnight on a type-writer, and sent the copies by a trusted hand to Benes.

When the war had been in progress a little over a year, and the time had come for a public campaign on behalf of Czech independence, Masaryk urged his lieutenant to join him outside Austria. Benes quietly destroyed all incriminating evidence, established a secure system of secret correspondence with his friends in Prague, bade his wife a farewell that both knew might be the last, and armed with a forged Austrian passport in the name of Herr ——, who purported to be a traveler in optical instruments, imperturbably crossed the Austro-German frontier, traveled through Bavaria on foot, and crossed the German border into Switzerland. On the evening of that day he joined his chief in Geneva.

Henceforth he was an open enemy of the Habsburgs. He arrived in Paris at the end of September, 1915, a lonely little man without a country, with little money, few friends and no influence. Five months later he had founded the National Council of the Czechs, which was ultimately to be transformed into the first Czechoslovak government. He became Secretary-General of the Council, and when Masaryk and Stefanik, respectively the philosopher and the warrior of the conspiracy, left Western Europe for Russia, and ultimately for America, Benes became the responsible leader of the Czech revolutionary movement in Europe. He was still practically unknown to the governments of the Allied countries. But he had become an assiduous lobbyist, a haunter of the antechambers of Foreign Offices, and one of the *bêtes noires* of busy or pretentious ministers. He worked all day and half the night, slept little, wrote and talked incessantly. He wore at that time a lean and hungry look, a Cassius-like air which has never left him. His own wants were easily provided for. His own scanty savings from his pre-war professional salary, eked out by journalism, were sufficient for his own purposes. The generous subsidies which were available in those miraculous years for any and every revolutionary effort directed against the Central Powers were eventually offered to him, but were employed exclusively for purposes of propaganda and organization. On his arrival in Paris Benes had resumed his student habits and mode of life, and these he maintained until his cause had triumphed.

§ 3

His first success was the insertion, at his instigation, of a demand in the Allies' War Aims, communicated to President Wilson on January 10, 1917, for "the liberation of the Italians, the Slavs, the Roumanians and the Czecho-Slovaks" from foreign domination. The phrasing of this article of the Note betrays the confusion then existing in the minds of the Allied governments and their advisers regarding the ethnical character of the Slavs and the Czechoslovaks. And it is possible that the drafters of the Note did not realize that in the use, for the first time in history, of the term "Czecho-Slovaks," they were asserting the national unity of two races of which one then formed part of Austria and the other of Hungary, and that the fulfillment of their demand automatically implied the destruction of the Dual Monarchy.

The next diplomatic achievement of the young Czech leader was the creation in France and Russia, by agreement with the governments of those countries, of Czech legions under the authority of the National Czech Council; and the first victory of the Czech legionaries in Russia resulted in further signs of Allied recognition of the Czech cause. In March, 1918, when the Central Powers seemed on the verge of victory, Benes was one of the few men in the Allied camp who did not give way to despair. Exhausted although he was by nearly four years of unremitting and anxious effort, his nerves frayed by night after night of labor at his desk, he had not given up hope of success. Some of his French friends told him of their intention of taking refuge in America if Germany should win the war. Benes replied to them smilingly, and without any trace of braggadocio: "I shall go to Switzerland for a six months' cure for my nerves, and then I shall begin all over again."

His struggles had not ended with the victory of the Allies, the break-up of the Habsburg Empire, the Treaties of St. Germain and Trianon, which consecrated the creation of the new state of Czechoslovakia with its fifteen million inhabitants, and its strategic position in the heart of Europe, astride Napoleon's road to Austerlitz and the great Moravian gateway which had been the historic path of migration and invasion in Europe for twenty centuries. Successively Prime Minister and Foreign Minister of the new republic, he realized that its security was precarious, that it was surrounded by enemies on all sides, and that at the first threat to European peace Czechoslovakia's security and independence were inevitably in danger. His foreign policy remained constant, and immutably based on two cardinal points: the maintenance of European peace; and the prevention of the restoration of the Habsburgs.

He had from the beginning to face the enmity of Austria and Hungary, the dislike of Germany, the suspicion of Italy, the doctrinal hostility of Soviet Russia, and the distrust of Great Britain. During the first ten years of his long career as Foreign Minister, Benes was regarded with an unreasoning and unreasonable suspicion by the British Foreign Office. For that he had partly to blame his own zealous and sincere, if imprudent, efforts to bring about a reconciliation between France and England after the breaches made in the Entente Cordiale by the quarrels between Lloyd George and Millerand, Lord Curzon and Poincaré; and partly the fact that he was, or seemed to be, a protégé of France in Central Europe, and a pivot in the French post-war system of continental alliances. That he succeeded in living down this British suspicion is due in part to his own patience, modesty and freedom from vanity, and in part to the fact that the estrangement between France and Great Britain, which he rightly saw endangered the stability of Europe, was at last ended.

§ 4

As a revolutionary Benes owed much to Marx, however violently he may since have disagreed with the prophet. As a statesman Benes owes almost everything to Geneva. He is at once a child of the League and one of its parents. If a political or natural cataclysm swept away the entire League of Nations tomorrow, and with it its Secretariat, its archives, the text of the Covenant, the history of its Councils and Assemblies, Benes is one of the few men in the world, perhaps the only man in the world, who could reconstruct the League overnight, himself impersonate the Secretary-General and the more important heads of departments, rewrite the Covenant from memory, and write in a week an accurate and astonishingly detailed record of the League's most important discussions and decisions. He has had a hand in every League negotiation and every debate, and the drafting of almost every resolution. The famous Protocol of 1924 was largely his work. It has been claimed by, or attributed to, a great many other statesmen, diplomats and officials, but fundamentally it was of his conception and his inspiration. This was but one of many grievances held against him by British ministers, although when the main features of the rejected Protocol of 1924 were later incorporated in the Briand-Kellogg Pact of 1928, the diplomatic hue and cry raised against Benes and the Protocol in 1924 was discreetly forgotten.

Since then Germany has rearmed, and the fanciful danger of a French military hegemony in Europe, so loudly denounced by Liberals and Socialists in England in the early post-war years, has been succeeded by the very real danger of a hegemony based on the much-discussed axis of Rome-Berlin. The active, industrious, much-traveled, often-suspected, but loyal and far-sighted Foreign Minister Benes of the pre-Locarno years has become the respected, sympathetic, admired President of the Czechoslovak Republic, the head of a state directly threatened by the revival of Pan-German imperialism, the potential Belgium of the next European war. His colleague Krofta has succeeded him in the post of Foreign Minister, as head of the department which he held unchallenged for seventeen years. But Benes, it may be suspected, still retains active direction of Czechoslovak foreign policy. In his sixth decade he is still the indefatigable conspirator of thirty-one. He has had the longest uninterrupted diplomatic experience of any statesman in the world. He knows Europe and its leaders intimately. He speaks Russian, French, German, English, Czech and a little Italian, and all in that strange, harsh accent of his which emphasizes the consonants and ignores the vowels, so that the venerable Lord Balfour was once startled in a League Council meeting to hear the youthful Czech Foreign Minister address the distinguished delegates in words which sounded like "*mes enfants*," when in reality he had wished to say "*mais enfin.*"

§ 5

Benes is probably the most successful as well as the most skillful diplomatist of the post-war generation. He has had almost as great physical difficulties to overcome as the Soviet Commissar Maxim Litvinoff. Without distinction of appearance, short, diffident, completely ignorant of the art of histrionics, without which no diplomat or politician is immediately successful, Benes has nevertheless achieved a position in international diplomacy almost unique in modern history. The secret of his success probably lies in his complete indifference to that fatal stumbling-block of rulers and governments, *prestige*. The constitutional monarchies and republics and totalitarian states of the twentieth century are not less sensitive on the score of vanity and reputation than were the absolute monarchies of the seventeenth and eighteenth centuries. It was, both directly and indirectly, Serbia's fear of loss of prestige which led her to reject the most humiliating terms of the Austro-Hungarian ultimatum of July, 1914. It was Austria-Hungary's fear of losing prestige in Europe as a first-class power, as much as the desire to avenge the assassination of the heir to her throne, which inspired her refusal of all compromise with Serbia. The rise of democracy has increased, and not decreased, the vanity of governments, and especially that of their silent and unseen collaborators—the permanent officials. Parliamentary institutions do, indeed, provide a check where none existed in the case of the absolute monarchs of other days, but parliaments have become comparatively ineffectual in comparison with the control of public opinion now wielded by the more powerful and less responsible press. In the case of the dictatorships, where both parliament and press are merely docile organs of the dictator, the democratic check on the governing power is totally lacking.

It is characteristic of Edward Benes that in the spirit of realism with which he faced the issues raised by the outbreak of war in 1914 he has resolutely eliminated all questions of national prestige from discussions affecting his country. He has a peasant's shrewdness, and a peasant's disdain for mere verbal finesse. He is utilitarian, practical, pragmatic. He has a very undiplomatic horror of insincerity. When he was felicitated on his success in Paris during the war he replied ingenuously: "The only reason is that I have never said anything but the truth." And years afterwards he told an interviewer: "I never feel sure of myself except when I am speaking the truth. Then I am certain of my arguments." In many years of contacts with him I have not had occasion to doubt this assertion. He talks freely and frankly, if rarely for publication. His candor has sometimes seemed brutal; his self-confidence, or rather his belief in the destinies of his country, a trifle too assured. He has not feared to warn the statesmen of the Great Powers of the dangers or the difficulties which lay in their path, and his warnings, if resented at the time, have rarely proved unjustified.

In 1920, when Austria was anxious to create the *Anschluss* with Germany, he said to the Austrian representatives bluntly: "Create the Anschluss if you are set upon it. But have no illusions. It will involve you in war." He said to the leaders of the small Czechoslovak Communist party: "Gentlemen, be logical and courageous. My business is to defend order, but I do it effectively. If you are revolutionaries, start your revolution. It is your duty. And I shall do mine, which will be to crush you." He said to the Germans in pre-Hitler days, in reply to reproaches of his Francophilia: "I am France's ally because in the first place I like France, and in the second place because France is necessary to us and to our freedom. If I were the ally of Germany, Czechoslovakia would not be protected, but submerged."

He is not merely the spokesman of Czechoslovakia, he is the spokesman of all the little nations. One feels in discussing Europe with him that he thinks less of the frontiers of his own country than of the common frontier of the small Powers against the Great Powers. Probably his own early experiences of revolutionary agitation and conspiracy have left deeper traces on his character than he is aware. The Habsburgs to him are not merely the past and possibly the future rulers of Austria-Hungary. They are the eternal symbol of the oppressor.

§ 6

There is no more curious spectacle in Europe than that of the little peasant-professor-President in his official residence in the Hradcany, the palace of the kings of Bohemia and of the emperors of Austria, on its crag above the River Moldava. The greater part of the palace, with the glittering Spanish ballroom, the beautiful Gothic hall of Vladislas, has now become a museum. Five small rooms in one wing of the building suffice for the simple tastes of the President. From his windows he looks over the wide curve of the river with its many bridges, the great city of Prague on the farther bank, the gunpowder tower, the townhall, the churches, and the oldest university in Europe.

His capital is in the center of that ancient kingdom of Bohemia which Bismarck, who had, like Clemenceau, a weakness for epigrammatic description, once described as "a fortress built by God in the heart of Europe." It lies strategically across the path of Germany southeastwards to the Balkans, to Hungary and to the Ukraine. The conqueror who assures himself possession of Bohemia has an open road eastwards or westwards through Central Europe. Czechoslovakia is the northern wing of a federation of states with an aggregate population of fifty millions, and a peace-time army of sixty divisions. She has hitherto had to face enemies on three of her four frontiers. Germany on the west, Austria on the south, Hungary on the southeast. Behind Roumania on the eastern frontier stood, until 1933, a Soviet Russia with which the Czechoslovaks maintained but barely polite relations. Today Russia is their ally, and the only obstacle to the German invasion and conquest of Czechoslovakia is the fear of a joint Franco-Russian air fleet. The peasant Benes may well have learned his statecraft in a harsh and dangerous school. His days of struggle are possibly not yet over.

Chapter IX

THE CRITICS: POINCARÉ, CURZON, MUSSOLINI

§ 1

RAYMOND POINCARÉ reigned at the Quai d'Orsay from the fall of Briand during the Cannes Conference in January, 1922, to the victory of the Bloc des Gauches at the French elections in May, 1924. A little over two years, during which that redoubtable but sincere little man managed to drive a wide breach in the friendship between France and Great Britain, to invade the Ruhr, and to unveil, Sunday after Sunday, and after an appropriate libation of measured rhetoric, many hundred war memorials in French villages. Since his death no biographer has arisen to do justice to Poincaré. Possibly because Poincaré has done himself such ample justice, in his voluminous war memoirs. The fact remains that no Frenchman of this century has been more maligned, and with less reason.

Poincaré was not loved, but few of his contemporaries, if pressed, could have given reasons for their lack of affection. "I do not love thee, Doctor Fell. The reason why I cannot tell." He was kind-hearted, and could at times show generosity to a friend, if rarely or never to an enemy. He was honest, loyal, industrious, painstaking. He had all the bourgeois virtues. But his exterior was cold and forbidding. His voice was harsh and metallic. His little eyes smiled rarely. He had neither wit nor humor: only at times a dry irony redeemed his interminably long and prosy speeches, his hard, didactic, fact-crammed and precise efforts at conversation. If he had love in his heart for any creature, it was probably lavished on his wife's Belgian griffon, a dog which figured somewhat incongruously in his memoirs and in the President of the French Republic's much-criticized departure for Bordeaux in the early months of the war. If he could display moral courage he was, like many men of sedentary habit, physically timid. Anatole France said paradoxically of him once: "*Il est tellement lâche qu'il est capable de tout acte de courage.*" (He is such a coward that he is capable of any act of courage.) The real passion of his life was his love for France. And even that was transmuted, in the strange alchemy of his harsh, unforgiving nature, into a sterile hatred of Germany.

He was a Lorrainer, had seen the German invasion of 1870, and had had his country house at Sampigny, near Bar-le-Duc, sacked and burned by the Germans in 1914.

He had raged impotently at the failure of his attempts to discuss policy and military strategy during the war. He had raged impotently at Clemenceau's studied insults, neglect and indifference during the Peace Conference. He had bitterly criticized many features of the Peace Treaty, and had shared Foch's discontent at the failure to annex the left bank of the Rhine. But paradoxically enough, no sooner was he freed from what he subsequently described as his seven years' term of imprisonment in the Elysée than he became the self-constituted champion of the Treaty of Versailles, the most pedantic, the most unrelenting, the most ardent of all its defenders. He was a lawyer, and the Treaty seemed to him like the Mosaic covenant. It became the mainspring and motive of his life. If his death-bed thoughts could have taken lyrical form, they would undoubtedly have intimated that the words "*Traité de Versailles*" would be found graven on his heart, as the word "*Calais*" seemed to the dying Mary Tudor to be inscribed on her own.

§ 2

The fall of the Briand government in January, 1922, gave Poincaré his long-coveted opportunity to direct France's foreign policy. The failure of Germany, wilful or unavoidable, to complete her coal deliveries to the Allies gave him his equally awaited opportunity to cast aside the velvet glove and display the mailed fist. Not without precise and often-repeated warnings to Germany, he marched into the Ruhr and occupied the German mines. He had previously defeated all efforts to have Germany's economic situation discussed dispassionately, at an international conference. At Genoa the French spokesman, Louis Barthou, under daily telegraphic instructions from Poincaré, rejected all the overtures of the German delegate Walther Rathenau, and equally refused to sanction any agreement with Soviet Russia except on condition that the claims of the French holders of Tsarist bonds were recognized. The result was that Germany, in despair, signed the Rapallo Treaty of Alliance with Russia, an act which precipitated the end of the Genoa Conference and gave a new weapon to the French nationalists in their campaign for the integral execution of the Treaty of Versailles.

The Ruhr adventure gave the German ministers the moral courage they lacked to begin systematic evasion of the provisions of the Peace Treaty. They did nothing to prevent, if they did not in fact secretly encourage, the fall of the mark. The secret rearmament of Germany, the creation of the Reichswehr as an army of cadres, the nucleus of the great army of Hitler's Third Reich, dates from the Ruhr. The murders of Rathenau and Erzberger by German nationalists, the renascence of the Junker spirit, the ferment of German nationalism humiliated but not destroyed by the Republic of Weimar, and finally the emergence of Hitler, may be traced to the same event. They would probably have occurred in any event, without the provocation of Poincaré's harsh policy towards Germany. It is a fact that they proceeded at a greatly accelerated pace during the period of conciliation ushered in by his successors at the Quai d'Orsay. But it seems fairly clear that Poincaré provided the anti-republican elements in Germany with a rallying-cry, and that the already feeble and spiritless republic received a blow in the Ruhr occupation from which it never really recovered.

§ 3

The relentless little Lorrainer had in the meantime given British statesmen several shrewd thrusts from his rapier. He had not come to blows with Lloyd George directly, having left the honors of diplomatic combat with that formidable adversary to his colleague Barthou, witty, urbane, smooth and treacherous as quicksand. But in the autumn of 1922 he had had a sharp skirmish with Lloyd George's majestic Foreign Secretary, the Marquess Curzon. The British government was alarmed and irritated by the friendly overtures made by Poincaré and his envoy, Franklin Bouillon, to the victorious Mustapha Kemal, then at war with Mr. Lloyd George's protégés the Greeks. Lord

Curzon went to Paris to expostulate with the French Premier. He was received, together with the then British Ambassador in Paris, Lord Hardinge, in the handsome room of the Minister at the Quai d'Orsay, a room brilliant with the blue and rose tints of Gobelins tapestries, the clear autumn sunlight of Paris entering by the tall windows overlooking the garden, the warm gold of paneling, and the gilded curves of the great desk of Vergennes, the Foreign Minister of Louis the Sixteenth.

The conversation between the two statesmen was direct and disconcerting. Instead of waiting to be reproached, Poincaré passed immediately to the offensive. His fierce little eyes gleamed. His voice was shrill, his beard aggressive. He accused Curzon of having used intolerably hectoring language in his Notes to France regarding the Chanak incident. Before the sudden and unsuspected brutality of the attack the proud marquess wilted. The arrogant mask of the ex-Viceroy of India collapsed. The voice that had called unruly princes to order faltered. The pride that had done battle with the equal pride of Lord Kitchener and emerged triumphant from the clash of wills was humiliated, at last. The Foreign Secretary betrayed himself as only his closest intimates knew him, a vain but sensitive man, kind-hearted and courageous, but unequal to an occasion such as this. Lloyd George had once seized Clemenceau by the collar. The majestic Curzon could hardly have stooped to shaking the little Frenchman as a terrier shakes a rat. In his rage, in his humiliation, in his sense of injustice, in his sense of impotence, there was only one way out; and Curzon seized it. Curzon wept.

He was hurried out of the room by Lord Hardinge, and allowed to compose himself. Before he returned, the

British ambassador ventured to rebuke Poincaré for his aggressiveness. He found the Lorrainer entirely unrepentant. "He should not have written to me in such a tone!" protested Poincaré indignantly.

A few weeks later it was Poincaré's turn to experience humiliation. The rebuff was administered to him not by a British statesman, but by an Italian, not by Lord Curzon, but by Mussolini. It was the eve of the Lausanne Conference, called in the autumn of 1922 to revise the Treaty of Sèvres, as a result of the victories of Mustapha Kemal and the military renascence of Turkey. The British and French Foreign Ministers had been invited to meet Mussolini, then newly installed as dictator of Italy, for a private discussion before the Conference opened. Curzon and Poincaré expected to find the Italian waiting for them at Lausanne. Instead of which, when the train on which both ministers had private saloons—saloons prudently separated by several coaches of the train—arrived at Lausanne, a message awaited them that Mussolini had gone to Territêt, on the other side of the lake, and there hoped to have the pleasure of their company at dinner.

Irritated, perplexed and suspicious, the British and French statesmen finally agreed to follow Mussolini to Territêt. There they dined with him alone, embarrassed by their contiguity at the same table after so recent a dispute, and uncomfortable at the absence of their secretaries, whom Mussolini had very pointedly not invited. After dinner Curzon and Poincaré returned to Lausanne, and there, on the next morning, Mussolini smilingly joined them. The conversation was resumed in a small music room of the Hôtel Beau-Rivage, and on this occasion it was Poincaré who uttered recriminations, and Mussolini who replied to them. He retorted so vigorously, and with such a complete disregard for diplomatic convention, that Poincaré was reduced to silence. Curzon emerged from the interview with a bland smile of satisfaction on his massive and imperial features. Poincaré returned to Paris, and never again consented to meet the Italian dictator.

§ 4

In Poincaré's eyes the Treaty of Versailles was primarily an instrument of constraint and chastisement, and only secondarily the legal charter of the new Europe. He was not indifferent to that section of the Treaty which created the League of Nations and provided it with a permanent organization, a Council, an Assembly, and a set of principles in the Covenant. But he regarded the League as an association of the war victors. It provided a stage and an audience for occasional declarations of French policy. It reminded the neutral states of their eternal obligations to the Western Powers, which had saved for them the principles of justice, nationality and freedom. When the League threatened to run off the rails, as, for instance, on that unfortunate occasion in 1920, at the first Assembly, when one state raised the question of the admission of Germany, French orators like René Viviani existed to recall the assembled states, amid a thunder of applause, to their sense of reality. Apart from such occasional incidents, the Geneva organization attracted little attention in France outside of the early post-war years, outside the parties of the Left and the Senate, whose President, the veteran Léon Bourgeois, exhibited an enthusiasm for the infant League which amounted in the eyes of his nationalist critics to nothing less than a sign of approaching senility.

Poincaré himself did nothing to deprive his fellow senators of their amiable foible. He did not, like his adversary Lord Curzon, regard the League of Nations as "a good joke." Poincaré was not in the habit of jesting about institutions legally created. But he had no intention of transferring the control chamber of French diplomacy from Paris to Geneva. So long as he remained at the Quai d'Orsay France was represented at the League by second-rate men. Even his predecessor Briand, who was later to discover the uses of Geneva as a magnificent sounding-board for his own appeals to the world, gave no sign during his brief period of office in 1921-22 that the League interested him. Then and later Philippe Berthelot, the Secretary-General of the Foreign Ministry, and Briand's closest adviser on foreign policy, was in the habit of proclaiming that "the League of Nations would never be anything more than a colossal *fumisterie*." For Poincaré the League represented the spirit of demagogy. And whatever his virtues or his failings, Poincaré had nothing in him of the demagogue. In 1922 and 1933, therefore, Geneva was practically abandoned by France—French diplomacy, entirely absorbed as it was in the question of German reparations and the occupation of the Ruhr.

The revenge of the demagogues came in the following year. The elections at the end of 1923 had brought Mr. Ramsay MacDonald's first Labour government to office, if not to power, in Great Britain. And a few months later, despite an unfortunate letter of good wishes sent to him by Mr. MacDonald, as Foreign Secretary, on the eve of the French election in May, 1924, a letter evidently written in the foolish belief that the victory of M. Poincaré's supporters of the Bloc National was almost certain, Édouard

Herriot and the Bloc des Gauches were triumphant in France, and the Poincaré government had fallen. At the League of Nations Assembly of September, 1924, the leaders of the two left-wing parties met dramatically. The stout French Radical Herriot shook hands with the lean and elegant Ramsay MacDonald on the floor of the Assembly in the Salle de la Réformation. The Ruhr occupation had been liquidated by the Dawes Plan. The nationalist policy of Poincaré and his supporters had been defeated in France. In Great Britain the more temperate nationalist policy of the Conservative party had been modified in respect to Germany, if it was soon to break out in more exasperated form against Soviet Russia. The war spirit had been defeated, if not destroyed. Democracy was on the march, and the little democracies at Geneva applauded the symbolic encounter of French radicalism and British socialism with eager hands.

Chapter X

THE DEMOCRATS: HERRIOT AND MAC DONALD

§ 1

EDOUARD HERRIOT, the new French Premier, aroused much curiosity and speculation on his arrival at Geneva. He came of plebeian stock. His father had been a sergeant in the army. His aunt, who reared the son, had been a housekeeper to the French nationalist, Maurice Barrès. He had had a brilliant academic career. He had been one of the most successful professors at the university of his native city of Lyons. He wrote graceful essays—on Goethe, Beethoven, Madame Récamier. His lectures were followed by hosts of admiring women. He had entered the Chamber just before the war, but had made no especial mark in the political field. His real genius seemed to have been shown as an administrator. He was mayor of Lyons, the second city of France.

His personality presented something of a paradox to observers. Physically he seemed of the phlegmatic type. He was corpulent, with a square head, a stiff mane of black hair, a fleshy jowl, a rotund belly, short thick legs and broad shoulders. His thick hands were thrust in the sagging pockets of his coat, or were clasped around a bulging and shabby leather portfolio. A short, heavy pipe was almost perpetually stuck in his heavy jaw. His overcoat in winter, creased and unbuttoned, was as carelessly and

HERRIOT

negligently worn as that of Lord Baldwin. Yet for so stout and placid-looking a man he was strangely active. He wrote all night in the train that carried him twice a week between Paris and Lyons. He wrote rapidly and interminably at his desk in the Chamber or in his mayoral office in Lyons, in a quick, graceful, facile professor's hand. Despite his phlegmatic air he was impressionable, nervous, emotional, over-sensitive to criticism, alternately the prey of exaltation and despondency. Later, when he became President of the Chamber of Deputies, he gave frequent exhibitions of his lack of self-control. He could easily dominate that tumultuous assembly by the sheer power of his voice, but he had little confidence in himself. He rang his President's bell too agitatedly. He was on his feet too often, vainly shouting for order. A man of more wit and quieter manner, like his predecessor Fernand Bouisson, had more control over the Chamber.

Despite all their physical dissimilarities, there was much in common between Herriot and Ramsay MacDonald. Both had a secret inferiority complex. Both were painfully conscious of their humble origins. Both expanded visibly, like a flower in the sun, in the warmth of flattery and admiration, and particularly under the attentions of women admirers. Both had a certain facile demagogic eloquence. Both collapsed under direct attack, were discouraged and despairing in defeat. But there the resemblance ended. Intellectually and culturally the Frenchman was far superior to the Scotsman. Herriot had a sound and logical mind. He was a brilliant product of the university, the École Normale, and the École des Sciences Politiques. His speeches were cast in a literary form, and bore the test of newspaper reproduction. His thought was clear and limpid, his ideas were intelligent and connected. His only deficiencies as a statesman were an excessive vanity, a certain stubbornness in persisting in error when the error had long since become patent and dangerous, and, paradoxical as it may seem, too obstinate a loyalty to his friends.

Whatever his failings, Herriot inspired affection. Even those who derided him most savagely admitted his personal charm. His simplicity was disarming; his good nature boundless. On the morrow of the discovery of the body of Philippe Daudet, mysteriously shot in a Paris taxicab, the son of the Royalist leader Léon Daudet, one of the most violent political enemies of Herriot, the Radical approached the Royalist in the lobbies of the Chamber and spontaneously offered his sympathy, and expressed his indignation at the crime. The gesture would have seemed normal enough in England or America. But in a country where political feuds make personal relations difficult if not impossible between men in rival camps the action of Herriot surprised and touched the Royalist.

§ 2

The capacity to inspire affection, so redeeming a feature of the character of Herriot, was notably lacking in that of Ramsay MacDonald. No man was more wont to bewail his need of friendship, the emotional sterility of his life, his loneliness, his desire for friends. No politician of our day made more claim on the sympathy of his supporters, his audiences, his colleagues. No man inspired more respect and admiration and aroused more hopes than Ramsay MacDonald in the days before the collapse of the second Labour government in 1931. Yet even in his heyday as leader of the Labour Opposition, when the votes of the rugged and suspicious Clydesiders had elected him to the leadership over the head of the staider if more stable J. R. Clynes, even in the glowing moment of his return to power at the head of the second Labour government in 1929, Mr. MacDonald could never bridge the gap of reserve, aloofness, which separated him from his followers.

He was admired, but he was not liked. The enthusiasm which he inspired in the rank and file of his supporters came rather from the electorate than from members of his party. His handsome appearance, his silver voice, his command of the technique of public platforms, his air of earnestness and sincerity, and even that slightly evangelical manner of his, charmed and convinced vast audiences of working-folk. He was a born demagogue, and contact with the people seemed always to bring out in him the simplicity and austerity and also the idealism of his early youth. But in the House of Commons, or in a party meeting, and above all in the daily contacts with his Labour colleagues, his inspiration deserted him. He was too accessible to flattery, too sensitive to criticism. His speeches were vague; his thought was troubled, inconsequential; he lacked resolution; he also lacked constructive ideas, forethought and even—rare in a Celt—imagination.

Towards the end of his second administration he became more and more detached from his Cabinet colleagues. With one of them, the late Arthur Henderson, Secretary and real architect of the Labour party, his relations had never been good. In the end they never spoke except in the Cabinet and on business. His only intimate among the Labour ministers was Mr. J. H. Thomas, who followed him into the National government, and observers often speculated on the common ground for the friendship be-

tween the jocular, cynical, bridge-playing, race-going ex-
railway porter, full of the slang of Ascot and Brighton, and
the proud, sensitive, esthetic Scotsman, who boasted of
his love of the fine arts and collected water-colors by Wilson Steer. The real reason for this intimacy, which enabled Mr. Thomas to push his way familiarly past horrified
secretaries into the Prime Minister's room at 10 Downing
Street when other and more important members of the
Cabinet, with state business in hand, were obliged to cool
their heels in ante-chambers, was possibly that the astute
Welshman had long since seen through the defensive mask
of his leader; that the leader responded eagerly to the very
aggressive joviality in his colleague which was most deficient
in himself; that he liked, as most men do. the qualities he
envied in others.

Most men, too, are capable of at least one act of courage
in their lives. Mr. MacDonald's opportunity came to him
in August, 1914. Inspired possibly by the memory of Mr.
Lloyd George's opposition to the Boer War in 1900, which
had not notably interfered with the then Chancellor of
the Exchequer's subsequent political career, or more probably, by the moral conviction that the war, any war, was
wrong, the then leader of the Labour party in the House
made his celebrated protest. He suffered for his act in
silence and in dignity. He was humiliated, attacked, and
vilified during the war. In the khaki election after the
armistice he was overwhelmingly defeated in his own constituency of Leicester. Three years later, in 1921, he was
beaten in Will Crooks's old seat at Woolwich; a hitherto
almost solid Labour constituency. Mr. MacDonald wrote
to the late Charles Masterman after this defeat that his
political career was at an end. He made the same confes-

MAC DONALD

sion to an American friend, William C. Bullitt, the present
United States Ambassador to France. He was destined,
like Mr. Bullitt, who had resigned from the American
Peace Commission as a protest against what he described
as President Wilson's betrayal of the Fourteen Points, and
whose public career was not resumed until Roosevelt's victory in 1932, to make a spectacular re-entry on the political
scene. Little over two years after his defeat at Woolwich
he was not only elected to Parliament as member for Aber-
avon, but became Prime Minister in the first Labour government.

But his successes, after the days of adversity, had not the
expected effect of strengthening the stoic element in him.
They seemed rather to make him more and more disin-
clined to risk his late-found political security on any quix-
otic issue. He had made his gesture once, and it had
brought him years of defeat and humiliation. When the
next great turning-point in his career arrived, over the
financial crisis of 1931 and the question of cuts in the dole,
inevitably he must have been secretly reminded of the last
historic division in the Labour party, that division, so fatal
to himself, which was occasioned by the war. Then a
part of the Labour party had joined the Liberal and Conservative parties in the common cause of the national
struggle. He had opposed national unity, and had been
defeated. Politically he had backed the wrong horse. On
this occasion, when the danger to the country might be
thought to approach that in 1914, he would not risk defeat
a second time. In 1914 he had been with the minority in
the country. In 1931 he would not only join the majority,
but lead it.

There was, he possibly reasoned to himself, a kind of

ironic justice in the thing. It was his secret revenge for the mistake of 1914, and the affronts and humiliations of the war. Some of those in his second Labour Cabinet who now denounced him as traitor to the Labour case—the Arthur Hendersons, the Clynes, the Tom Shaws—had been associated during the war with the men who denounced him as traitor to the national cause. They were now paid back in their own coin. From his new vantage-point at the head of the stairs in Londonderry House, white-haired, gracious and urbane between his hosts, Lord and Lady Londonderry, as the members and supporters of the National government filed by on an eve-of-session reception-night, he could look down with a certain melancholy, martyr-like air of forgiveness at the bitter Labour ex-ministers at Transport House. Often, in the new and friendly security of his intimacy with the Baldwins and the Simons of the Old Parties at whom he had so often and so impotently railed across the floor of the House of Commons, his Labour career in opposition or in office seemed remote and almost forgotten.

But to do him justice, he could not forget the humble folk in the industrial North whose faces were now so desperately set against him. Courageously, patiently, he attempted to justify himself. He won Seaham Harbour against a hostile population of miners who greeted him with savage shouts of "Traitor!" In spite of rebuff after rebuff, he made friendly overtures to former friends and followers. In the Member's Lobby one day he met a Labour member of one of the mining divisions of Yorkshire and, reminding him of their old friendship, offered him his hand. "You are no friend of mine!" exclaimed the Yorkshireman roughly, and pushed his hand away.

The then Prime Minister sighed, shrugged his shoulders, and walked off with bowed head as if the cross were indeed too heavy to bear.

§ 3

But in September, 1924, these days at once of triumph and disillusionment lay far ahead. Not many months earlier Mr. MacDonald had kissed hands at Buckingham Palace on his first appointment as His Majesty's principal Minister and Secretary of State for Foreign Affairs. He sat in Pitt's room in Downing Street and enjoyed the old-world charm, peace and tranquillity of the country retreat but lately provided for Britain's Prime Ministers by the generosity of Lord Lee of Fareham. He had done the honors of Chequers and made the *tour du propriétaire* in company with the new Radical Premier of France, and the stout, square-headed, stubbly-haired Herriot had been photographed sitting with his host in plus-fours and smoking his pipe affably on the lawns of Chequers. The Dawes Plan had been launched, the occupation of the Ruhr had been liquidated, and MacDonald and Herriot, the Castor and Pollux of the new skies dawning over Europe, came to Geneva to share the plaudits of the little nations and solemnly to inaugurate the new era of peace.

The British Prime Minister was accompanied by two colleagues, Mr. Arthur Henderson and Mr. J. R. Clynes. The French Premier was supported by the Socialist lawyer and future Radical Prime Minister M. Paul Boncour, and by M. Léon Jouhaux, in pre-war days the anarcho-syndicalist secretary of the union of match-makers, later pacifist secretary-general of the General Confederation of Labor, then war Jingo, and ultimately to become, under the Pop-

ular Front government of M. Léon Blum, a regent of the
Bank of France and leader of a belligerent C.G.T. with
five million members.

M. Herriot became immediately popular in Geneva. He
walked across the bridge from the French delegation headquarters in the Hôtel des Bergues, his pipe strongly
clenched between his wide jaws, his hat on the back of
his head, his hands in his pockets, his coat flapping open
in the light autumn breeze over the lake, his friendly,
naïve, trusting eyes opened wide in curiosity, in pleasure,
in wonder. He walked into the Assembly hall in the Salle
de la Réformation as he was accustomed to walk into the
Chamber of Deputies, shaking hands with his left hand
and with his right, or with both together, affable, simple,
and informal. Mr. MacDonald drove up from the Hôtel
Beau-Rivage in one of the British delegation's hired Swiss
cars, posed graciously for the photographers, and entered
the sunny doorway of the Hôtel Victoria amid a flurry of
secretaries. When he came into the Assembly hall Herriot rose from his seat, hastened towards him and took both
hands in his own. The moment was well chosen. Both
men were clearly visible to the seated delegates, to the
crowded press tribunes and public galleries. The incident
was cheered; the first informal act to provoke applause in
the hitherto sedate and undemonstrative League Assembly.
The next occasion to create spontaneous demonstrations of
enthusiasm was the entry of the Germans in September,
1926.

But thereafter the illusion of novelty and change was
soon exhausted. Herriot addressed the Assembly; a speech
full of generous ideas, one of the best he had uttered; a
speech warmly cheered. But Mr. MacDonald disappointed

the audience. He had adopted an unfortunate combination of his election platform technique and his House of Commons debating manner. He hectored like a prosecuting attorney. He preached like a Dissenting minister. He expounded like a schoolmaster. He seemed to have forgotten, or to be indifferent to, the fact that he was addressing the foreign ministers, statesmen and diplomatists of forty-eight states. He harangued them as if they were members of a refractory section of his own Labour party. He provoked resentment, disillusionment and not a little derision. His speech, for all the peremptory tone and drama of its manner, was singularly disappointing and deficient as to matter.

Mr. MacDonald took little subsequent interest in the proceedings of the Assembly. He liked to receive important foreign statesmen at his hotel. He liked to lecture the ministers of less important states on their nations' shortcomings, on the magnanimity, grandeur and generosity of Great Britain, on his own immense burdens. He took pleasant drives in Switzerland and the Jura, admiring the mountains and the lakes, and discoursing agreeably out of his own fairly extensive experiences of travel. He listened intently to the counsel, suggestions and comments of his intimates of the moment, chief among whom were Mr. Wickham Steed, Dr. Alfred Zimmern, and the late Sir Robert Donald, a fellow Scotsman who had risen to the editorship of the great Liberal *Daily Chronicle* from humble beginnings as a gardener in Aberdeen, and who had encouraged Mr. MacDonald's own early efforts in journalism. Mr. MacDonald was, characteristically, more accessible to these unofficial advisers than he was to his own fellow Socialists and Cabinet colleagues, Mr. Henderson and Mr. Clynes. And he left to them the delicate negotiations regarding the draft Protocol of Geneva, and was therefore in a better position to disown that compromising document (or at least to hint that when in due course it came to him to be examined in detail, it would certainly be accepted with important reservations) when Conservative and even Liberal opposition seemed to be increasingly violent.

He left Geneva in some irritation. His earliest memory of the town was of a visit in 1920, when he had been a delegate to an international Socialist congress, a delegate still separated from his own fellow British delegates by the divisions of the war. The present Assembly had not, he felt, realized his real greatness. It had given warmer and sincerer applause to Herriot. When he revisited Geneva in 1929, again as head of a British Labour government, it was to find that again a Frenchman had stolen his thunder. On this occasion the usurper was not Herriot, but Briand.

Chapter XI

THE ORATOR: ARISTIDE BRIAND

§ 1

BEFORE the end of 1924 the Protocol of Geneva was dead.

By the following year Sir Austen Chamberlain had succeeded Mr. Ramsay MacDonald as Foreign Secretary and Aristide Briand had followed M. Herriot at the Quai d'Orsay. In the autumn of 1925 Briand made his first appearance as leading French delegate at Geneva, which was to become the scene of the greatest triumphs of his career.

We are still too near him to take his full measure. He has been dead but six years, and in the meantime much of his work has been undone. Over his grave in the little Normandy village of Cocherel lies a great roughly hewn block of granite, brought there from the coasts of his native Brittany. But a rock was never his symbol. He may have had its steadfastness, but he had none of its rigidity. Nevertheless that recumbent mass of stone impresses by its sheer mass and inertia. The dimensions of the buried man may thus have seemed to his contemporaries. At Geneva during the 1936 Assembly of the League, the French delegate, M. René Cassin, permanent representative of the French associations of ex-servicemen, and a man who had known Briand since the war, said to me: "Do you remember the exclamation of Henri III when he stood looking down at the murdered figure of his rival, the Duke of Guise: '*Qu'il est grand!*' Well, that is how one feels at Geneva today, in regard to the dead Briand."

No man was more thoroughly French, or more thoroughly representative of the lower middle class—peasant, functionary, artisan or small tradesman—which is the backbone of France. He had been born at Nantes on the banks of that river Loire which flows through the heart of France and which for centuries saw the greatest events in that country's history enacted on its banks. His father was a small innkeeper. He was reared at St.-Nazaire, on the coast of Lower Brittany, and from his earliest years had the sea in his nostrils and in his heart, if not, as in the case of deep-sea sailors, in his eyes. His uncle was a river pilot on the Loire, and one of the earliest of the young Aristide Briand's experiences of tragedy in humble lives was the sight of his uncle's body brought home. "He had been drowned," he said, long afterwards. "I can see him still. There he was stretched out. I couldn't take my eyes off his big boots, which were dripping water. Those heavy boots . . . I could see them filling with water and dragging him down. . . . My parents would never again listen to my ambition to become a seaman. It was then that I gave up the idea, and often have I regretted it. Never since have I been able to watch a boat clear the harbor without wishing I could be aboard. . . ."

A chance meeting with an old professor in St.-Nazaire, named Genty, led to a lifelong friendship. From the old man the youth gained a rudimentary knowledge of the classics. On the quays of the Breton port the professor recited entire passages from the Iliad or the Odyssey to him, reconstructing in voice and gesture the combats of the heroes and the siege of Troy. "When you grow up," he told him, "you will go to Marseilles, to the shores of the Mediterranean, where our civilization was cradled. You will listen carefully to the laborers in the port, as they insult and threaten each other. And only then will you get an idea of the flavor of the conversation of Homer's Greek heroes." But Briand in after years had no need to seek the modern version of Homer's dialogue in Marseilles. In Paris, in the Chamber of Deputies, he was to find a Trojan war in mimicry—the posturings, the threats, the vanity, the sublimity and the pettiness of Homer's characters.

Another friend of his childhood was Jules Verne, who took young Briand for walks on Sundays and used him as a character in one of his lesser-known books. Verne made a very considerable impression on Briand. "He was a good soul, a good, calm little bourgeois with a benign expression and a beard. I have a very vivid memory of his home. Its atmosphere was unimaginably provincial and ordinary . . . and there it was that those tales of marvelous voyages and glorious adventures were written. His rooms were very simple, very neat and shipshape. I recall he had a number of blackboards on the walls. On these he had written many formulae. All these figures and algebraic equations were being made for the inventions that would later appear in his books of fantastic exploits. You know, Verne really worked with the utmost scientific and mathematical precision. All his calculations were exact. They have since been verified, and now the wonders that were worked out on those blackboards are matters of actual occurrence."

When he left his school in Nantes Briand went to Paris to study law. To earn the money for his board, lodging and law-school fees, he who in after years could scarcely be persuaded to put his pen to paper, so greatly he disliked the labor of writing, worked at nights copying briefs, writs and pleas for an attorney. The Latin Quarter was then in its romantic heyday. He was admitted as a member of one of the most famous clubs of the Quarter, the Hydropaths, many of whose members subsequently became famous. There he met Guy de Maupassant, the novelist Paul Bourget, the poet Jean Richepin, the medievalist Huysmans, the poet Albert Samain, the future Goncourt academician Lucien Descaves, the actor Coquelin and Sarah Bernhardt, who frequently recited for them. On the *impériale* of one of the old-fashioned horse-buses he met Victor Hugo. He was one of the little group of writers, artists and students who founded the famous cabaret of the "Chat Noir" in Montmartre, at which the *chansonnier* Aristide Bruant afterwards gained celebrity.

He returned to St.-Nazaire with his diploma as advocate. There he threw himself into political work, Socialist and Syndicalist propaganda, and the launching of a small weekly newspaper, *La Démocratie de l'Ouest*, which later he published daily, himself taking to pieces and reassembling a printing press which he had bought cheaply in Paris. His career was now fairly started. He defended labor unions in court, won several libel actions in which his newspaper was defendant, was elected to the municipal council, and was sent as delegate to several national congresses of the then rising Socialist party. About this time an attempt was made to make political capital against him, out of an incident in which he was involved with a girl of St.-Nazaire. He was charged with and found guilty of improper conduct, and fined. He appealed to the local appeal court and the sentence was confirmed. Only after appeal to the supreme court in Paris, uninfluenced by local intrigues, was the verdict reversed and the sentence quashed.

Subsequently he was offered a post in Paris on the Radical newspaper *La Lanterne*, founded by the late Arthur Meyer, and he left Brittany forever. His career as advocate now ran parallel to his career as politician and journalist, for most of his cases were political cases. He defended strikers, so successfully that Clemenceau said of him at this time, "If I had stolen the towers of Notre-Dame I should not worry so long as Briand defended me." He collaborated with Jean Jaurès, the great Socialist tribune, on *l'Humanité*. He threw himself into the Dreyfus case. He was elected to the Chamber. He was, like Millerand and Viviani, expelled from the Socialist party. And seven years later, after figuring in two cabinets, he became Premier for the first time.

The most notorious act of his first premiership, one which was to gain him the bitter hostility of Jaurès and his early Socialist friends, which was, indeed, to be flung in his teeth when Jaurès and his contemporaries had long been in their graves, was the crushing of the national railway strike of 1910 by the simple expedient of declaring the railways to be of strategic necessity to France and placing them under military protection. If the strike had continued, the reservists among the railwaymen would have been called to the colors. As it was, the mere threat sufficed to end the strike. Briand was denounced as a traitor and renegade by the Socialist group in the Chamber, and when he coolly announced that if legal means of protecting the railway services had not been at his disposal he would not have hesitated to employ extra-legal means to ensure

the safety of France, cries of "Dictator!" assailed him from
all quarters. "Jaurès," he said afterwards, "was shouting so
much that I thought he would have a fit." He rode the
storm with unruffled serenity, left the tribune of the Chamber amid a forest of threatening hands, and returned quietly
to his apartment. There a number of alarmed friends,
politicians and newspaper editors found him placidly engaged in eating œufs sur le plat. His friends walked in
much excitement about the room, repeating the arguments
used in the Chamber, re-enacting a scene which they described as tragic. Briand said nothing, and continued to
eat his supper. A newspaper editor finally turned to him
in exasperation and exclaimed: "A question like this cannot be settled by eating two fried eggs."

The most celebrated of his other ministerial acts in pre-
war years was the settlement of the religious question, and
the framing of the law separating church and state.

§ 2

During the World War Briand was twice Premier. He
had opposed Joffre's original plan of resisting the Germans
south of Paris, and the result of his vigorous protest in
the Viviani Cabinet was the successful stand taken by
Joffre on the Marne. General Gallieni, the military gov-
ernor of Paris, whose action in creating a reserve army out
of the relics of the army of Charleroi and in sending that
army into battle in the commandeered red taxicabs of Paris,
became Briand's Minister of War in his first wartime Cabinet. He had had the first conception of the hopelessness
of the impasse in the West, and the need of breaking
through on an Eastern front. He had imagined the army

of Salonika, and had dragged British divisions for that army out of a reluctant and West-obsessed Kitchener.

In 1915, in both Great Britain and France, a campaign had started for the withdrawal of the Allied troops from Macedonia. It was supported by King Constantine of Greece, who for his own reasons offered to protect the embarkation of the troops at their base in Salonika. The base was held by a British force, while the actual fighting was done by a French army in Macedonia under General Sarrail.

A meeting of British and French representatives was summoned at Calais to discuss war policy in general, and the Near-Eastern theater of war in particular. The British government was represented by Asquith, Lloyd George, Balfour and Kitchener. France was represented by Briand and Ribot. The British came with the private determination to liquidate the costly adventure. Briand had privately decided that General Sarrail must be immediately reinforced, and that the British share of the reinforcements would amount to three divisions. Briand opened the meeting by reading the agenda. The first item on it stated briefly the necessity of sending fresh divisions to Salonika.

"The words had scarcely left my lips," narrated Briand later, "when Asquith rose. I can still see him standing there, his face pale and drawn, as he said, 'After mature deliberation, the Government of His Majesty the King has decided not only not to send fresh troops to Salonika but to recall those that are there now.'

"This was a terrible blow to me, and you can imagine my state of mind at that moment. I did not falter, however, or show by a single movement what an impression his words had made upon me. I had, as a matter of fact, what I thought was a good inspiration. I merely said, in my most indifferent voice, 'Let us proceed to the second item.'

"As I looked down at the agenda I became conscious of a certain agitation. The members of the British delegation looked at each other in astonishment. Before I could proceed, Lloyd George rose and said, 'Mr. Premier, have you nothing to say to us?'

"'Well, if you question me,' I replied, 'I will tell you, in the name of the Government of the Republic, what I have to say. We have organized an expedition in common. You were to hold the base at Salonika while our troops went forward. Those troops are now isolated—fifty thousand men who have fought gallantly to save the Serbs. My answer to your question is that those troops will go on fighting unaided to the last man. History will judge which of us is right.'

"There was a buzz of conversation. Balfour said, 'But we cannot end the discussion with those words. We must retire and deliberate again.' A recess was called until after lunch. Ribot said to me, 'Everything is ruined.' I replied, 'Wait! Nothing is ruined.'

"We met again after lunch and Asquith rose and reported the result of the conference that had taken place during the recess.

"'Mr. Premier,' he said, 'the Government of His Majesty the King, as a result of your highly effective pronouncement, has reconsidered its decision and has voted to send to Salonika the three divisions for which you ask.'

"At this, Lord Kitchener jumped from his seat, threw his portfolio on the table and left the room. Asquith turned to me and said, 'Won't you talk to him and try to make him understand?'

"I went out to look for Kitchener and found him on the pier. I tried to talk to him but he rebuffed me. I was insistent. 'This is absurd,' I said. 'You can't go off like this in wartime.'

"He began to argue with me, and finally I brought him back to the meeting. He picked up his portfolio and said resentfully, pointing at me, 'If we lose the war, it will be the fault of that long-haired lawyer.'

"Again I replied, 'History will decide who is right.' "

And in telling this story Briand was wont to recall that it was on the Eastern front that the enemy's front was first broken and defeated, and that after the battle Hindenburg wrote to the Kaiser, "There is only one thing for us to do now and that is to sign a treaty of peace."

§ 3

Although Briand had more than any other French politician been responsible for the organization of the successful defense of Verdun, he was invited to take no part in the peace negotiations and was ignored during the Paris Conference. Clemenceau reproached him with having acted as intermediary on the two occasions on which peace overtures were made to the Allies during the war. The first was undertaken by the Belgian Countess de la Mérode, who communicated to Briand in 1917, when he had been replaced by Ribot as Minister of Foreign Affairs, the substance of a conversation she had had with the German Governor-General in Brussels, Baron Lancken. The second was the more celebrated letter written by the Emperor

Charles to his brother-in-law Prince Sixte-Bourbon. Both peace efforts failed.

Briand had his revenge in 1919, when Clemenceau was candidate for the presidency of the Republic. Briand had already been chiefly responsible for Poincaré's election to the Elysée in 1912, as the successful candidate afterwards admitted in his memoirs. His popularity in the lobbies of the Chamber, his skill as a political strategist, his unique position as a man without a party, enabled him to rally enough votes in the National Assembly of 1919 to secure the defeat of Clemenceau and the election of the ill-fated Paul Deschanel. Two years later the new President rewarded his principal elector by calling on him to form a government.

Briand's return to power in 1921 was to inaugurate a long period during which either he was in office as Premier or Minister of Foreign Affairs, and sometimes both, or he seemed to be practically the only alternative to the actual holders of those offices. From 1925, after the fall of Herriot, he dominated the Chamber of Deputies, and from that year until his death in 1932 he was rarely out of the Quai d'Orsay. In all he was Premier no fewer than thirteen times. He directed the foreign policy of France for a longer period than has any minister since Talleyrand. Nevertheless, his first diplomatic efforts in the years immediately after the war were not particularly successful. He had little interest in financial questions and no head at all for figures, and both he and his colleague Paul Doumer, then Minister of Finance, had easily been outmaneuvered by Lloyd George at the Reparations Conference in Paris in January, 1921. Neither had he any particular flair for propaganda, and he failed to impress American public opinion favorably on his appearance in Washington at the head of the French delegation to the 1921 Naval Conference.

His first great success as a diplomatist was recorded at the Cannes Conference in January, 1922, when he secured an offer from Lloyd George to guarantee France against any future aggression by Germany. But Nationalist irritation at his too conciliatory policy towards Germany, the treachery of his Cabinet colleagues, and notably that of M. Louis Barthou, and finally the much-exploited incident of his unsuccessful golf contest with the British Prime Minister at Cannes, brought about his resignation. When he made his next entry on the European scene, the policy of the French Nationalists had been played for what it was worth by Poincaré. The Ruhr occupation had been carried out, and had proved futile from the standpoint of effective reparations. The defeat of the Nationalists at the 1924 elections and the end of the Ruhr occupation had cleared the stage for a new policy towards Germany, and Briand, a past-master in the art of conciliation, negotiation and compromise, had an opportunity worthy of his great natural talents.

§ 4

He was, in 1925, the year of Locarno, sixty-three years old. His appearance was sufficiently remarkable to excite comment. He could not have passed unrecognized in any town of France. Short, with shoulders so bowed that he seemed almost hunchbacked, with a long, untidy mane of graying hair, a noble brow, thick shaggy eyebrows, a good nose, a wide mouth partly concealed by a long straggling mustache, a heavy jaw, small hands and feet, he had in his later years the look of a tired circus lion. His eyes were almost closed; his mouth held wearily the end of a cheap cigarette; his hands, sensitive and eloquent, which he could use with such telling effect in the tribune of the Chamber, drooped immobile at his sides, he dragged himself wearily as if the weight of his leonine head were too heavy for the frail body and the small feet. His tread was cat-like and stealthy. He seemed lethargic: a slumbering intelligence, an indolent body, a cynical nature without passion or sentiment.

But appearances were never more deceptive than in the case of Briand. Physically he was indolent. He hated any exercise more violent than walking slowly through a friend's coverts with a gun, or holding the tiller of a small sailing boat, or appraising the crops or cattle on one of his tenant's farms at Cocherel in Normandy. He disliked the labor of writing, which had been so necessary and so painful an occupation of his law-student days in Paris. He rebelled against any long and continuous application to the study of any question. But he could listen intently. He read, on occasion, quickly and intelligently. He had a flair for grasping the essentials of a problem, however subtle. In the Quai d'Orsay he was well served by such experts in French diplomacy as Philippe Berthelot and Alexis Léger. In a political crisis, or on the eve of one of his more important speeches in the Chamber, he had a habit of eliminating the subject of his speech from the surface of his mind. At such a time he would entertain himself at luncheon—he never dined out—with the most trivial conversation. One day, in the middle of a parliamentary crisis, a secretary found him curled up on a sofa reading a magazine of women's fashions.

BRIAND

§ 5

But if externally he seemed indifferent to the all-engross-
ing topic of the hour, his speech, when it was finally delivered, showed that he had thoroughly mastered the subject
under discussion and that his sub-conscious mind had
throughout been active in preparation for the debate. On
days when success or victory depended upon a single speech,
Briand was accustomed to enter the Chamber alone. He
came in quietly, and crept with his cat-like and silent tread
to his seat in the middle of the front bench. There he
seemed to slumber. His eyes closed. One hand drooped
at his side, the other rested limply on the desk in front of
him. His shoulders seemed on such occasions even more
bowed than usual. His cheeks were the color of earth.
His manner was dejected, the bearing of a man defeated
by life. Around him the Chamber pulsed in noisy antici-
pation of the coming struggle. The debate began. The
journalists in the press tribune, the ambassadors in the
diplomatic boxes, leaned forward eagerly, counting heads,
wagering odds on the government's fall. Briand alone
seemed unconcerned.

At last, at a moment long foreseen, shrewdly calculated
by himself, his long slim forefinger made a sign to the
President. He left his place and climbed the stairs to the
tribune. Under the shaggy eyebrows the luminous eyes
looked down upon the enemy who crouched to strike. His
voice came at last, low, faltering, like an echo from some
deep cavern. It gathered force and energy. It held over-
tones as well as undertones. It vibrated like a harp. It
sang like a violin. It seemed like the voice of another
man who spoke with the lips of Briand, animating that

tired face, invigorating that weary body, galvanizing that slumbering intelligence into life and action. The effect was magnetic. The enemies of the man heard him spellbound, unwilling victims of his sorcery. His friends heard him in ecstasy. They were familiar with his magic, but it never lacked novelty. They were familiar with his ideas, with his policy, with his motives, but now they seemed suddenly convincing as never before: convincing, irresistible, inspired even.

The substance of his speeches was not remarkable. He scorned literary effects. His utterances read the next day in cold newspaper print rarely evoked enthusiasm. Yet he had a remarkable talent for presenting a case so that it seemed not only good but the best case possible. He spoke under what seemed the inspiration of a radiant common sense. He was tolerant, shrewd, witty, but above all human. He rarely attacked. Hardly once during his years out of office did he ever publicly criticize the acts of another government. His genius was seen in that rarest of the arts of the orator, the art of defense. He invariably employed upon his audiences, friendly or hostile, inside or outside parliament, the technique he had used with success as a young advocate pleading his earliest cases at the bar in St.-Nazaire and Nantes—the technique of conciliating the prosecution, and winning over the jury.

§ 6

But his real skill as an old parliamentary hand was seen at its best, perhaps, in the lobbies of the Chamber. No French politician in this century has enjoyed a greater popularity in the ante-chambers of power. It sufficed for Briand to walk in his gliding, stealthy, feline and pre-occupied way into the lobby for him to be surrounded by an eager group of deputies and journalists. Under the flattering warmth of their interest he expanded visibly. One hand characteristically in the pocket of his short, shabby coat, the other holding the eternal cigarette, the heavy jaw sunk on his chest, the eyes quizzical, the rumbling voice, musical in its lowest notes, uttering in his half-protesting manner epigram after epigram, comments picturesque, mordant and ironical on personalities and ideas. He loved these bantering conversations in the lobby, in which he would hear the gossip of the moment, get wind of the latest parliamentary intrigue, sense the coming storm, receive opinions which helped him to form his own. And whether the lobby was that of the Palais Bourbon in Paris or of the Council Chamber or Assembly Hall in Geneva, the Hôtel Carlton at Cannes or the Hôtel de Ville at Locarno, he carried with him to his death that familiar, democratic, informal habit of talking idly, philosophically, unhurriedly, with any group of friends, politicians or journalists who chanced to find him unoccupied, bored, and willing to be distracted.

Chapter XII

GENEVA AND LOCARNO

§ 1

LOCARNO found Briand at the zenith of his talents, his curiously combined powers of reflection and seduction. He went there as Vice-President and Minister of Foreign Affairs in the Painlevé Cabinet of 1925. His familiar, the grave, handsome, brilliant Philippe Berthelot, accompanied him. Three years earlier Berthelot had been forced to resign his post as permanent Secretary-General of the Quai d'Orsay on the ground that he had irregularly used the influence of the French government to refloat the foundering Bank of Indo-China, of which his brother, André Berthelot, was president. With the return of Briand to the Quai d'Orsay Philippe Berthelot was reappointed to his post and resumed all his old power at the Foreign Ministry.

The two men were friends of long standing. Briand had pronounced a funeral oration at the grave of Berthelot's father, the great chemist, who had died broken-hearted a few months after a beloved wife and associate. The son presented a remarkable contrast to Briand, physically and intellectually. He was orderly, precise, well-groomed, of great culture and many-sided in his interests, was a connoisseur and collector of Chinese art and modern French painting, had married a beautiful woman and encouraged her social ambitions. The chief was the antithesis of the lieutenant: disorderly, unpunctual, careless in dress, indifferent to art and literature, unsocial and a bachelor. He hated formal occasions, never wore dress clothes except at state banquets, and went to bed at nine o'clock every evening unless prevented by affairs of state. On the last enthusiastic night of the Locarno Conference, when the church bells were rung and an excited crowd clamored outside the Locarno town hall to be shown the famous Treaty (it was brought to a window and lights were thrown upon it, as if it were a sacred image or ikon), Briand was in bed and asleep less than two hours after the signature.

At Locarno Briand met the German Foreign Minister Stresemann for the first time. The friendship which afterwards formed between them was not spontaneous. The German came to the Locarno Conference stiff, uneasy and suspicious. He did not speak or understand French. Briand neither spoke nor understood German. Each watched the other warily, striving to guess the other's thoughts before the interpreter had translated his words. The real intimacy which sprang up between them later was created not at Locarno, but at Geneva. At Locarno, Briand's contacts were rather with Stresemann's colleague, Dr. Luther, the German Chancellor, a short, spectacled, round little man with a Jesuitical air. Luther spoke French fluently and with him Briand could dispense with the services of an interpreter. Briand invited Luther to lunch with him on several occasions at a little lakeside inn called the Albergho Elvezie, and here in a little vine-covered arbor in the inn-garden he broached for the first time to a German the conception of a future European reconciliation which had for years been forming in his mind. "You are a German," he said, "I am a Frenchman. On this ground alone we have many reasons for antagonism, for differences, even for disputes. But can I not remain a good Frenchman and still be a good European? Can you not be a good German and think at the same time of the superior interests of Europe? And on that ground can we not reach an understanding?"

When Briand went to London two months later for the formal ceremony of signing the Treaty he went as Premier, the Painlevé government having in the meantime been overthrown. There, in his speech, he referred to a letter he had received from an unknown Frenchwoman: "Allow a mother to felicitate you. At last I shall be able to look at my children without that terrible apprehension of war and to love them in security. . . ." He added: "The agreements of Locarno bring something new into the world, because they substitute a spirit of solidarity for a spirit of suspicion. It is by human solicitude that we must make war impossible. Here opposite me sit the delegates from Germany. That does not mean that I shall not remain a good Frenchman, or that they have not remained good Germans. But here we are all Europeans. By our signatures we affirm that we want peace. Our two races have for centuries clashed with each other on the battlefield. They have often left there, with their blood, the best of their forces. The agreements of Locarno will be valuable if they mean that those massacres will not begin again, and if as a result of them the foreheads of our women will never again be darkened by veils of mourning, our cities will not again be ravaged and our men mutilated. . . ."

§ 2

Later, in the French Chamber, when the Treaty came up
for ratification, Briand defended it in another of his rare
outbursts of emotion: "The wonderful thing in this country
in which so many families have lost their sons or brothers,
so many young men are mutilated, so many people have lost
all they had, is that the Pact of Locarno allows mothers
to look at their children with the hope that they will not
some day be torn to pieces on the battlefield. . . . Do you
think that I went without emotion to that rendezvous on
the side of the lake where I was to meet the German delegates? I went there and they came there, and we spoke together as Europeans. It is a new language that we shall all
have to learn. France does not belittle herself in taking a
part in discussions which prepare Europe for tomorrow.
Can you imagine France sitting aside in a corner draped in
her victory and looking at people belligerently? Impossible! Can you imagine such a France? Never! In signing these agreements, she has remained herself, the France
of yesterday and the France of tomorrow."

This was probably Briand's greatest effort in the Chamber. Even his war speeches in defense of Verdun and of
the Salonika expedition did not reach so high a level. But
the speech by which he will be remembered of posterity,
one uttered before a world audience and on a world stage,
was delivered at Geneva at the Assembly of 1926. It was the
occasion of the admission of Germany into the League, an
admission negotiated at Locarno in the previous year, and
indeed the very basis of the Rhineland Pact. Stresemann
and his colleagues had entered the Assembly, flushed,
nervous, stiff, fully conscious of the drama of the occasion.

Stresemann addressed the Assembly first, reading his speech in German. It was an able document, without recriminations or allusions to the responsibilities of the war. He made a solemn assurance of the pacific intentions of the German Republic, which he said had "the desire to collaborate with all nations on the basis of reciprocal trust."

Then Briand came to the tribune. All eyes were upon him as he crept painfully up the steps, one hand as ever in the pocket of his coat. He spoke, as was his custom, without notes. As upon all the great occasions in his life, he seemed to draw the substance of his speech from an inner source of inspiration. Like water pumped from a long disused well, the words at first came slowly. Gradually they increased in volume and speed, until in the end they gushed forth in a steady stream. His voice, low at first, laboring in its effort to convey ideas found with difficulty, grew in power and suppleness. He was listened to in a breathless silence. When at last he came to the great peroration, women in the diplomatic and the public galleries sobbed and many delegates betrayed emotion.

"Is it not a reassuring spectacle," he exclaimed, "to think that a few years after the most terrible of all wars, the same nations that fought so hard should meet in this Assembly and express their common desire to collaborate in the work of universal peace? Peace for Germany and for France. This means an end to all those sanguinary encounters which have tarnished the pages of all our past history. *It is ended, that long war between us. Ended, those long veils of mourning for the pains that will never be assuaged. Henceforth we will settle our differences by peaceful procedure. Away with the rifles, the machine-guns and the canon! Here come conciliation, arbitration and peace!* A country grows in history not only because of the heroism of its soldiers on the battlefield. It grows also when it appeals to justice and right to consecrate its interests. . . ."

He never reached those heights again. Three years later, when Stresemann was dead and the Socialist Hermann Mueller had replaced him at Geneva, Briand had returned to his old parliamentary debating technique of irony and innuendo. But Germany had changed in the interval. The tide of the Republic of Weimar was ebbing. The incoming tide of Hitlerism was soon to sweep victoriously up the shores of Germany.

§ 3

At Geneva in 1926, however, the Locarno spirit was still triumphant. Briand and Stresemann had acquired a certain degree of mutual confidence and respect at Locarno. At Geneva they were to become friends. On September 17, the two statesmen lunched together as Briand and Luther had done at Locarno, in a modest inn. The inn was in the village of Thoiry, in the Jura mountains, a short distance from Geneva. Their table was set in a dark and humble room on the first floor of the building, the walls of which still bear their signatures. After a luncheon which astonished Stresemann, who had not been prepossessed by the aspect of the village and its hostelry, the German drank several glasses of *eau de vie de Marc* and smoked several cigars. Briand, who was on a severe dietary régime, drank little wine and no liqueurs, but smoked innumerable cheap French cigarettes. During the conversation which followed the two ministers discussed an economic as well as a political understanding between France and Germany. Briand's friend and familiar Louis Loucheur, a steel industrialist who had frequently held the office of Minister of the Liberated Regions, had worked out a scheme for close economic co-operation between the heavy industries of both countries. It was proposed that they, with the collaboration of the Belgian steel industry, in which French capital was intimately and largely interested, should henceforth refrain from cut-throat competition and should agree upon a common schedule of prices and markets.

The Thoiry conversations aroused very great interest in many European countries, but nothing came of them. French industry at large was suspicious of the proposal. The political aspects of the scheme were even less alluring than the economic aspects. Many sections of the Chamber were afraid that France would be drawn too closely into the German orbit, that the interests of her allies would be sacrificed, that in particular Great Britain would view the combination with suspicion and alarm. The Loucheur plan was never realized. A feature of it was a proposal that Germany should issue reparations bonds against the security of her national railways, and that these bonds should be taken up by the banks in France, Great Britain and America. During the next three years Stresemann frequently reminded Briand that the Thoiry engagements had never been fulfilled. A certain coolness gradually sprang up between them. The warmth of the Thoiry period was never resumed, and when Briand and Stresemann met for the last time at Geneva in the autumn of 1929, in spite of the outward cordiality of their relations a note of disillusionment had crept into their mutual attitude. The wave of nationalism was rising higher in Germany. The concessions made by France had only excited Germany's appetite for further concessions. Behind Stresemann stood Hugenberg, and behind Hugenberg stood Hitler. The Locarno spirit had grown very fragile. There seemed less and less hope of any real co-operation between France and Germany. Ministers might be changed, but it was less easy to change the race memories of a people, its history, its mentality, its passions and its ambitions. Hitler, whose platform utterances were little more than a not very subtle evocation of Germany's past glories, was shortly to prove the truth of this. Stresemann, upon whose essentially Teutonic character, upon whose stability and strength with the nationalists in Germany, Briand's hopes had been based, was found to be a man of straw.

In 1928, nevertheless, Stresemann made a gallant gesture of friendship towards Briand in insisting, in spite of his doctors, on visiting Paris in person to sign the Briand-Kellogg Pact. This document owed its conception to a proposal made by Briand in a New Year message to the American people, given in the course of an interview with the Associated Press of America. Mr. Kellogg, then American Secretary of State, responded to the invitation, and a declaration was framed to be signed both by states members of the League and by non-members with the object of outlawing war. The Pact of Paris was signed in the Salon de l'Horloge at the Quai d'Orsay on August 27, 1928. Sixty-three states ultimately adhered to the Pact, which contained the following articles:

(1) The High Contracting Parties solemnly declare in the names of their respective peoples that they condemn recourse to war for the solution of international controversies, and renounce it as an instrument of national policy in their relations with one another.

(2) The High Contracting Parties agree that the settlement or solution of all disputes or conflicts of whatever nature or of whatever origin they may be, which may arise among them, shall never be sought except by pacific means.

The Briand-Kellogg Pact goes considerably farther in the abolition of war as an instrument of national policy than the Covenant of the League, for under it those signatories who are members of the League agree not to go to war even in cases where war is permissible under Article 12 of the Covenant. It still tacitly permits defensive wars, however. In 1930 the British government attempted to secure a revision of the League Covenant, bringing it into accord with the Pact of Paris, but the negotiations at Geneva were inconclusive, and there is still a notable gap in the Covenant. However, the subsequent Japanese aggression against Manchuria and the Italian conquest of Abyssinia made all talk of revision of the Covenant in a more comprehensive sense incongruous and unreal.

§ 4

In 1930 Briand made his last appearance at Geneva. He took the opportunity to launch his long-contemplated scheme for a European Union. He outlined his project at a luncheon offered by the French delegation to all the representatives of the states in the League, and a committee was appointed to examine the project Great Britain, however, looked at the proposal without enthusiasm. Soviet Russia, then outside the League, was frankly hostile; her inclusion in the Union, proposed by Briand and others, would have been opposed by a number of states; her exclusion from the scheme rendered the Union of illusory utility. Briand's speech in explanation of the scheme was not particularly successful. His arguments were presented without conviction. He seemed to have lost his early enthusiasm. It was clear that his powers were failing, physically and mentally. The death of Stresemann, the publication of Stresemann's correspondence and diaries, the revelation of what seemed to many Stresemann's duplicity towards Briand, and the revival of nationalist feeling in both Germany and France, had disillusioned and disappointed him. He suddenly appeared to his friends, his critics and his enemies as a prematurely tired old man, worn out by his long years on the European scene. He had few joys left him in life. His physicians had forbidden him wine, meat and cigarettes. His lips, that famous lower lip of his, sardonic, eloquent and mordant, hung dejectedly. His eyes were dull and half closed. He dozed in the Council and in the Assembly. When he presided over a committee he was forced to make a visible effort to follow the discussion. His friends realized, as he did, that his days were numbered.

In the summer of 1931 he rallied. He presided over the discussions between the British and the French governments at the Quai d'Orsay, and traveled with the British Foreign Secretary, Mr. Arthur Henderson, to visit Chancellor Brüning in Berlin. It was his first visit to Germany and his last. He was cheered at the station and in the streets, and some of the newspapers applauded his act of pious homage at the tomb of Stresemann. But the gesture had no political results. The days of the Republic of Weimar, like his own, were numbered. After his return to France he spent only a few more months in office. Towards the end of 1931 he retired from the Ministry of Foreign Affairs forever.

I went to see him during his last days at the Quai d'Orsay. He received me in his private apartments, simpler, shabbier, darker than the gorgeous state rooms below. He sat at a table covered with green Utrecht velvet. It was evening, and he had discarded his more formal attire for the fisherman's suit of blue overalls he wore sometimes at Cocherel. His hair had grown very gray and hung in thin and disorderly locks over his still leonine head. His cheeks were sunken. His eyes were without light. His voice alone preserved something of its magic. He spoke slowly, and as he spoke his slim and delicate hand caressed the texture of the velvet cloth.

§ 5

I never saw him again. Two months later he was dead. His body lay for a night on Talleyrand's bed in the little chamber next to the sitting-room in which I had last seen him. Then it was laid out in state on a catafalque in the handsome lobby of the ministry, to be blessed somewhat unexpectedly by the Cardinal Archbishop of Paris, in pious disregard of the state of impiety in which Briand had died. When the archbishop had left, a little old woman in heavy mourning slipped through the guards, fell on her knees before the bier and said solemnly: "God keep your soul. To the peacemakers, may God give His peace!" The remains of the dead Minister were given a state funeral the next day. His successor, André Tardieu, made the funeral oration. General Gouraud, the one-armed hero of Salonika and the Dardanelles, raised his sword in a spectacular salute to the man who had organized and inspired the Army of

POLITIS

the East. His peers and his contemporaries among diplomatists, Sir Austen Chamberlain, the old Spaniard Quiñones de Leon, the Greek Politis and the Czechoslovak Benes followed him to his temporary grave. With them walked the son of Stresemann. Later his body was taken to Cocherel, where it now lies, on a hillside overlooking the green banks of the Eure, and facing another hillside on which the great warrior Dugesclin delivered heroic combat against the English. A great block of Brittany granite covers the tomb. Émile, the old chauffeur-valet-companion of Briand, guards it as jealously as he guards the memory of his master and friend. The inscription on the stone is of a Greek simplicity. It might in justice have been amplified by Briand's often-repeated pledge to his countrymen and to the world: *"Tant que je serai là, il n'y aura pas la guerre.* As long as I am here, there shall be no war."

Chapter XIII

KNIGHT OF THE GARTER

§ 1

ONE of the strangest figures on the international stage at Geneva was Sir Austen Chamberlain. He entered on that scene reluctantly and with diffidence. When he left it, five years later, it was with an even greater reluctance. For during the years between 1924 and 1929, when Chamberlain was British Foreign Secretary, the League had progressed far beyond the experimental stage of the Protocol period. It had not only registered the end of the sanctions against Germany and the beginning of the era of reconciliation. It had welcomed the accords of Locarno. It had admitted Germany in a transport of optimism, emotion and idealism, which in retrospect may now seem of a touching innocence and naïveté. And it had provided an atmosphere of sympathetic and admiring encouragement for the subsequent efforts at European reconciliation of the great Locarno trio, Briand, Chamberlain and Stresemann.

Of the three it is possible that not even the diffidence with which the German approached the League was greater than that of the British statesman. Austen Chamberlain had the British Conservative's characteristic distrust of the evangelical ardor of democratic assemblies at home or abroad. He had, moreover, in spite of all his efforts to overcome it, the most insular Briton's distrust of foreigners.

He had read history patiently and avidly. He had spent a part of his youth in Paris; had made many enduring friendships in France; had studied French at the Sorbonne. But as he never succeeded all his life in speaking French without a strong British accent, so he never managed to rid himself of the instinctive British suspicion of the mainland of Europe and its inhabitants. He had not been born in the English Midlands for nothing.

Nor was his ancestry in favor of Geneva. He was the son of a man who had been a sturdy Birmingham republican, and had later become an even sturdier Birmingham monarchist. The subsequent years of Joseph Chamberlain were almost exclusively devoted to promoting the peace, prosperity and aggrandizement of the British Empire. If he had seen with alarm the rising naval power of Germany, and had at the beginning of the present century proposed an alliance with Germany, it was less with a view to securing the peace of Europe than to removing what threatened to be a dangerous obstacle to Britain's imperial interests.

Austen seemed no less imbued with that Victorian insularity than his celebrated father. Not even his closest friends and admirers suspected him of any special aptitude for diplomacy. His periods of office in Conservative or Coalition ministries had found him engaged in severely British or Imperial affairs. He had been a Civil Lord of the Admiralty from 1895 to 1900, a Chancellor of the Exchequer in the Balfour government of 1903 to 1906, Secretary of State for India in the Coalition government from 1915 to 1917, and Lord Privy Seal from 1921 to 1922. He had grown up in the shadow of a much-admired and much-loved father, and had absorbed from him that passion for the parliamentary scene which never left him. In 1890, before Austen's first entry into the House of Commons, he had already discovered for himself the hardships, disillusionments and vanity of a political career.

"It is a dog's life!" he commented one day to his father.

"You chose it for yourself!" retorted Joseph Chamberlain.

"Yes," admitted the son, "and if I had to choose again I'd make the same choice."

Two years later, Austen had been elected Member of Parliament for East Worcestershire. He sat on a back bench, a tall, thin young man, clean-shaven like his father in an era when beards, long mustachios and side-whiskers were still the rule rather than the exception, and like his father, wearing a monocle screwed firmly into his right eye. When his opportunity came he made his maiden speech. The subject, inevitably in that year, was Home Rule. The veteran Gladstone publicly felicitated Joseph Chamberlain on his son's first effort, describing it as "a speech that should bring joy to a father's heart." The stoical Joe is said to have shown emotion for the first and perhaps for the last time in public during his long parliamentary career.

§ 2

In 1924, when he went for the first time to the Foreign Office as successor to Ramsay MacDonald, Austen Chamberlain was sixty-one years old. He was tall, upright, stiff and spare, with a vigorous nervous carriage, a vivacity of movement in curious contrast to the studied precision of his speech, an alert eye which seemed as sharp and piercing as that of his father, an old-fashioned courtesy to his intimates and subordinates, and a cold, aggressive, uncompromising manner to his parliamentary critics. Liked,

DE VALERA

trusted and respected in that small circle of British families whose contacts with public life and administration have been close and intimate and privileged for three generations past, Austen was an enigma to the majority of his colleagues in the House of Commons and still more to the public at large. He was a man of undoubted integrity. In 1920, as Chancellor of the Exchequer, he had had the unpleasant duty of introducing a Budget which seemed unjustifiably onerous to a generation which had not yet experienced one of the budgets of his brother Neville. A member of the Opposition shouted:

"Two such budgets and England is ruined!"

"Twenty such budgets," retorted Austen grimly, "and England will have paid her debts."

But that kind of austere and self-righteous integrity, if it is admired, is not loved in England or in any other country. The phrase was in keeping with the known outward aspect of Austen's character. It only added another stone to that public edifice of reserve, hauteur, rigid conventionalism and impenetrability which Austen Chamberlain had so successfully built up during his long apprenticeship to office. Few suspected that behind the pale and polished mask, the smooth harsh features, the glittering monocle, there was a shy and sensitive man of great loyalty of mind, great kindness of heart, never oblivious even in the midst of affairs of state of his family responsibilities, his domestic felicity, his friendships and his rose garden. One summer day during his period as Foreign Secretary an old French woman, employed as cook by John Balderston, then a well-known American newspaper correspondent in London, was traveling in a third-class railway carriage to a town in Sussex. In the same compartment was a tall, well-dressed and gallant man with a monocle who talked to her pleasantly in French, helped her out of the train with her parcels, shook hands with her and wished her *"Bon voyage!"* When her employer, who recognized Sir Austen Chamberlain, asked her if she knew who her traveling companion had been, the old woman said she did not know. All she could say was that he was *"un monsieur très gentil, qui parle admirablement bien le français."*

§ 3

But this art of unbending in private life, the charm and even the grace of Chamberlain's conversation in relaxed moments, were unsuspected by most of his contemporaries. All that his prospective colleagues at Geneva knew was that a British Conservative of the old school had succeeded the Socialist MacDonald at the Foreign Office, and had jettisoned the Protocol and other embarrassing cargo accumulated during the brief and disastrous career of the first Labour government. The wave of optimism, of conciliation, of democracy which had carried the League on its crest during the Chequers conversations of the summer of 1924 and the handshaking, mutually felicitating League Assembly of September, had subsided. A period of reaction had, they felt, set in. And the unpromising figure of the new Foreign Secretary was to incarnate that new phase of British insularity in continental politics.

But in this foreign observers were agreeably surprised and at fault. The man who had served as model and prototype in the new Foreign Secretary's secret ambitions had been not Palmerston, not even Beaconsfield, but Talleyrand. By a curious paradox, the hero of the upright, rigid, unbending and austere Englishman was the corrupt, venal, scheming and supple Frenchman who had betrayed the monarchy, betrayed the revolution and betrayed Napoleon, but who, in all his treasons and deceits, had always adhered to some vague ideal of human tolerance and human happiness. He had restored France intact out of the wreck of the Empire. He had struggled to bring back to Europe, after war and revolution, the old *douceur de vivre*. From his early days in Paris, from his early readings in European history, Austen Chamberlain had formed, entirely in the tradition of Talleyrand, his own highly personal conception of diplomacy as the guardian of the necessary amenities of life, the custodian of the gracious conventions, the urbanities, the courtesies of international relations. Like Talleyrand and like Alexander, after the fall of Napoleon, he saw the peace of Europe, the old institutions, secure in the hands of a Holy Alliance of the Great Powers. He had a Bismarckian if not, indeed, an eighteenth-century attitude towards the problems of Europe. He did not worry about the little nations. He once quoted to me a Bismarckism which he often cited in private: "When the eagles stop quarreling the sparrows are silent."

§ 4

He came, then, to the Continent of Europe after a lifetime of secret aspirations and intellectual preparations for the rôle of diplomatist. He had heard Joseph Chamberlain's private version of the origins of the Entente Cordiale, the rejected offer to Germany, the Moroccan crisis, and the diplomacy of Edward vii. He had witnessed, as a Cabinet colleague, the impotence and the failure of Lord Curzon as Foreign Secretary. He had witnessed, as a member of the Opposition, the pretensions, the vanities and the follies of Ramsay MacDonald in the same office. His opportunity had come when he was at the zenith of his own intellectual powers, to create a new standard in British diplomacy, to achieve the one conspicuous success of a political career which had been commendable but not yet in any way remarkable.

He was aided, like Talleyrand, by the collaboration of two other men eager to play a great rôle in the pacification of Europe: Briand and Stresemann. The friendship which sprang up between Briand and Chamberlain is even more remarkable than that which began after Locarno between Briand and Stresemann. Stresemann, it is true, was a German and therefore a traditional enemy of the Frenchman. But he was, like Briand, the son of an innkeeper who was also a brewer. He was a man of an equal simplicity of habit: convivial, a great trencherman, a robust drinker. At Locarno he sat day after day drinking beer with the German journalists in the shadow of the cool arches of a tavern. Moreover, he was a continental. He understood the century-old problems, preoccupations and passions of the peoples of the mainland, bloodthirsty and yet satiated, weary of war yet warlike, jealous, apprehensive, vain and proud. There was more in common between Briand and himself than there was between either of them and the aloof, Conservative British minister, the righteous delegate of a world empire, the proud descendant of middle-class manufacturers and their like who had defied kings, limited the power of the hereditary nobility, and governed with a parliament whose sovereign rights and privileges had not been challenged since the reign of Charles I, who lost his life in trying to curb the insolence of his commoners.

§ 5

The friendship between Chamberlain and Briand sprang from the mutual attraction of opposites. No two men were more dissimilar in appearance, speech, habits, traditions and thought. Briand was lazy, careless, negligent in dress, informal in speech, acquired knowledge by intuition, by divination or by instinct. Chamberlain was industrious, careful, precise and even elegant in dress, precise and almost pedantic in speech, and had acquired his knowledge by long study and application. Briand knew all sorts and conditions of men, understood them all, and loved them all. Chamberlain knew only one sort of man—his own—understood him imperfectly, and gave him loyalty if he deserved it, support if he needed it, and affection only in rare circumstances. Outside his own family and his immediate circle of friends, one felt that he loved abstractions rather than human beings. He had an exalted notion of his duty, of his country, of his sovereign, of his father, of his wife and his children, and of his party leader. But he did not love mankind at large. Nor did he love mankind in little. He was content to do his duty, to follow the dictates of his conscience, to observe the principles of his religion, and to support the doctrines of his party. In short, he was a very perfect Englishman, of a type now become rare. But a perfect Englishman is not precisely the type to enter upon terms of close affection and mutual understanding with a good Frenchman, and Briand was as good a type of Frenchman as the next man. He was a rare Frenchman, one in a hundred thousand, but he was French for all that. And his Breton ancestors had for hundreds of years past contested with British sailors the supremacy of the narrow seas.

Yet the miracle happened. The two men met, charmed each other and were conquered. It could not have been possible but for one lucky chance—the chance that Chamberlain liked the French, admired French culture, spoke the language and understood it. For the personality of Briand was almost entirely verbal. It was inarticulate in his appearance, even in his shaggy leonine head, his long drooping lower lip, his small eloquent hands. These features of his, or some of them, prepossessed people against him who had never heard him talk, or who could not understand his speech. But to one who understood, the cynical voice, the deep, musical notes, the lazy, good-humored philosophy of his comments on life, on politics, on the most commonplace, everyday events, were a fascinating, rich and inexhaustible source of pleasure and instruction. Chamberlain admired in Briand the logic, the rationalism, the wit, the tolerance, the passion for the soil and for liberty that is France. Briand admired in Chamberlain the reserve, the independence, the solidity, the stubborn courage, the sporting sense, the integrity that is England. Each liked the other for not insisting upon his own country's monopoly of these virtues, for a certain modesty and simplicity inherent in both men, and for their mutual recognition of their respective countries' national defects, passions and prejudices—the imponderables of which the most adroit statesman is at times the victim.

§ 6

Yet both men were at first mutually suspicious. Their early diplomatic contacts were hardly less auspicious than the correspondence of Curzon and Poincaré. Chamberlain was at the outset hostile to the project of the Rhineland

Pact, originally offered in a speech delivered by Stresemann at Stuttgart in the autumn of 1923, and revived by him at the beginning of 1925 on the counsel of Lord d'Abernon, then British Ambassador to Germany. The new British Foreign Secretary had other plans—a pact of mutual defense between Great Britain, France and Belgium. He replied unfavorably to Stresemann's offer of a Rhineland Pact and dismissed it almost contemptuously as "unwise and premature." But Herriot, before his downfall in April, 1925, had welcomed the offer. Briand, who succeeded him at the Quai d'Orsay, was equally favorable to the plan. And a curious combination of circumstances in England—the hostility of the majority of Chamberlain's Cabinet colleagues to his own plan, the resentment of the Labour and Liberal opposition at the destruction of the Protocol, and the threat of an angry debate in the Commons—caused the Foreign Secretary to refer publicly, and almost diffidently, to the proposition made by Stresemann. It was Lloyd George, ironically enough, who revealed to the Conservatives and to the House in general the real significance of the offer they had received. "But this is of the highest importance!" the former Prime Minister exclaimed in surprise. "This is the first time we hear of this proposal. Do I understand that Germany is willing freely to recognize her western frontiers, and that she no longer demands the revision of these frontiers?"

Nevertheless, neither Chamberlain nor his colleagues held the same views as the French government regarding the reply to be made to Stresemann. Briand drafted a Note and submitted it to the British government with the suggestion that a single reply should be made to Germany in the name of all the former Allies. Chamberlain rejected the draft in terms which Curzon himself could not have bettered, for frigidity and arrogance. He amended the draft line by line and almost word by word, and declared that only as so amended could his government agree to the despatch of a joint Note. The Quai d'Orsay was indignant. Hints of the unfriendly character of the British reply had already appeared in the French press. But Briand calmed his subordinates and reassured the newspapers. To Chamberlain's surprise he accepted the British suggestions in their entirety. And the British refusal to accept any engagements concerning Germany's eastern frontiers was declared agreeable to the French. In this first skirmish between the two ministers Briand had shown the greater subtlety. When later he met Chamberlain he employed all his arts of seduction to good effect. And he himself realized that behind the stiff exterior, the formal phrases, the rigidly prescribed code of conduct of the British statesman there was concealed a good deal of common sense, good humor, and generosity of thought and heart.

Much subsequently depended at Locarno upon this humor, tolerance and good sense of the British delegate. Stresemann and Luther were stiff, ill at ease, suspicious and nervous, as German diplomatists frequently are when the eyes of the world are upon them. Chamberlain's courtesy and Briand's simplicity disarmed them. Over the Rhineland Pact itself, the pledge to respect the existing frontiers of France, Belgium, and Germany, whose security was further guaranteed by Great Britain and Italy, there was little trouble. The real work on this part of the Treaty had already been done, largely upon Chamberlain's insistence, to do him justice, in the Foreign Offices of London, Paris, Berlin and Rome. But difficulties arose over the eastern frontiers of Germany. Poland and Czechoslovakia, both Allies of France, wished an equal guarantee to be given to their common borders with Germany. The Germans refused to pledge any indefinite recognition of a territorial *status quo* which implied the abandoning of the interests of the Germans in Polish Silesia and in Czechoslovak Bohemia.

Great Britain had from the outset refused to shoulder any further responsibility for ultimate intervention in European affairs by the extension of the Rhineland guarantee to the eastern frontiers of Germany. The French Nationalists, already suspicious of Briand's policy of conciliation towards Germany hardly a year after the end of the Ruhr occupation, protested violently that under the proposed Locarno Treaty France was abandoning her eastern allies to their fate. The Polish Foreign Minister, Count Skrzynski, protested, pleaded, threatened by turns. He was a tall, nervous, aristocratic figure, the eccentricities of whose private life were the talk of the chancelleries of Europe, and who unaccountably inspired such an aversion in Briand that that tolerant man evaded him on all possible occasions. (Skrzynski was shortly afterwards killed in an automobile accident.) At one time the Poles threatened to walk out of the Conference. Chamberlain persuaded them to stay. In the end a series of arbitration treaties between Germany and Poland and Germany and Czechoslovakia were concluded, by which those countries agreed not to have recourse to force in the settlement of disputes and to refer all frontier or minority questions arising between them to arbitration. These arbitration treaties were attached as Annexes to the Rhineland Pact, and like the French treaties of alliance with Poland and Czechoslovakia also confirmed and ratified at Locarno, were mentioned in the Protocol to the general Treaty.

§ 7

In the meanwhile a golden sun shone down on Locarno out of a cloudless sky. The month was October, but the water of Lake Maggiore was as warm as the Atlantic in July. The ripe grapes hung in purple clusters on the white dusty hillsides outside the town, and the little market square was crowded every morning with peasants carrying great hood-shaped baskets of wicker, piled high with the fruits of the vine. Mingled with the Italian accents of the Ticinese were the guttural sounds of German, the fluid notes of French, the accents of almost every nation in Europe, for every nation, represented at the Conference or not, had sent its journalists to describe this historic day of reconciliation between the old rivals on the Rhine. The monocle of Chamberlain gleamed in the sun among the red cushions of an astonishing red Rolls Royce, a car with long silver horns like trumpets, glittering and demoniacal, made to the order of some Indian maharajah and now fallen to the humbler estate of a Swiss hire service. Riding at anchor in the little harbor lay the Italian lake steamer *Fleur d'Oranger*. It belonged to one of the many Italian companies in which Briand's friend Loucheur, that man of many enterprises, had a financial interest, and on Mrs. Chamberlain's birthday Briand and Loucheur gallantly invited all the chief delegates to an excursion on the lake.

The boat was happily named. The party was like a wedding party. There, in that convivial atmosphere, the last doubts of Stresemann and Luther, Skrzynski and Benes, disappeared. The Belgian Foreign Minister Vandervelde, a

Socialist lawyer with a dark imperial, eye-glassed, deaf, wearing a hat from the Boulevard St. Michel of Mürger's *Scènes de la Vie de Bohème*, leaned happily against the rail of the gilt and white steamer. Loucheur, an astonishing man with round red cheeks, very round black eyes like buttons, a round nose, and a black mustache which ended in round curls, pledged Mrs. Chamberlain's health in champagne. Briand told anecdote after anecdote which Luther translated to Stresemann. There was an air of enchantment about the scene—the blue lake, the mountains, the radiant sky, the soft Italian voices of fishermen on the Isola dei Pescatori, and above all the hot October sun. The Germans, shaven-headed, red-cheeked, thick-necked, some of them like Stresemann with dueling scars on their cheeks, drank in the sunlight and the lake airs greedily. They were like men emerging from a long nightmare of fear and dread.

§ 8

The Locarno idyll lasted several days longer. Mussolini came up from Rome, hastily and spectacularly. He took a special train to Milan, drove a racing car from Milan to Stresa, and a speedboat from Stresa to Locarno. On the following day the Treaty was signed in the town hall. It was seven o'clock in the evening, and the soft night of the lakeside in autumn had descended. A great crowd of townspeople and peasants had gathered outside the hall. When the news of the signature was learned the church bells were rung, there were cheers from the crowd, and a cry to be shown the miraculous document. It was brought to a window and held up under the eyes of the people. There was a strange exaltation in the atmosphere that night, as if something new had been born in this small town, so tranquil and remote from the European conflict. Women prayed. Some women wept. The little mayor of Locarno, black-hatted and wearing a large silk lavallière cravat like an old-fashioned painter, beamed from the steps of the town hall. His town had suddenly gained worldwide celebrity and he had suddenly become an international figure only a very little lower in stature than the great heroes of the occasion.

The next day the triumphant statesmen returned to their respective countries: Stresemann and Luther to be alternately cheered as liberators and cursed as traitors; Briand also to receive both cheers and curses, but with the cheers for the time predominating; and Chamberlain to be greeted at Victoria like a victorious general returning from the wars, the Prime Minister and his colleagues of the Cabinet on the platform, and with them a representative of the King: felicitations, cheers, and star and the ribbon of the Order of the Garter.

Chapter XIV

CHAMBERLAIN AT GENEVA

§ 1

IT was thus aureoled as the Man of Locarno that Sir Austen Chamberlain made his second appearance at a League of Nations Assembly. Delegates to the previous Assembly in 1925, on the eve of Locarno, had not been particularly impressed by the new British Foreign Secretary. He had rejected the Protocol drafted in the previous year. He seemed cold, unresponsive, aloof, typically British in his sense of reality. With him Great Britain seemed to have returned to the indifferent if not actually hostile attitude of the days of the Lloyd George Coalition. He typified the isolationism of British foreign policy, its detachment, its selfishness: a national egoism summed up by Palmerston in the declaration: "England has neither eternal friendships nor eternal enmities: her interests alone are immutable."

But between September, 1925, and September, 1926, had occurred the miracle of Locarno. The Germans were to be admitted to the League. Briand and Chamberlain were the two sponsors at this moving ceremony of initiation. Chamberlain now appeared in a new light to the ministers of the little nations assembling in Geneva. They were a critical audience. They were conscious of their lack of power, collectively or individually. But they were also conscious that they had it in their hands to confer not power but prestige—that instrument awarded in compensation to democracies. In 1925 they had given Chamberlain merely the respect due to his country. In 1926 they gave him the respect due to himself. He had ceased to be the bearer of an honorable and at one time prodigious name, encased in a frigid mask, and adorned with the historic monocle of his father. He had become a statesman in his own right, a man of skill, suppleness, humor and integrity, a worthy foil to the matchless Briand.

In contrast with the careless Briand and the coarse Stresemann, plebeians both, sons of innkeepers, politicians of a jovial, tub-thumping, demagogic order, Chamberlain seemed to come from another world: a world coldly and effortlessly patrician, a man born to rule. Foreigners approached him in diffidence, awed by his dignity, his correctitude, his glassy stare. They went away charmed by his courtesy, his ease, his good nature, his simplicity of heart. Some of them, it is true, sneered at his English distrust of first principles. Some of them saw nothing but a conventional politeness in his manner, took his stiffness for coldness, his reserve for indifference. The Germans never quite got over their first instinctive suspicion of him. Stresemann found himself unable to relax in Chamberlain's company as he was finally able to relax in that of Briand. Nor could he ever forget Chamberlain's disdainful rejection of his first offer of a Rhineland Pact. Although superficially there was more in common between Chamberlain and the average German diplomatist than there was between him and any Frenchman, the nervous, hypersensitive Stresemann could not fail to sense Chamberlain's Gallic preference.

§ 2

Yet if Geneva conceded skill, integrity and statesman-ship to Sir Austen Chamberlain, it never awarded him the tribute of popularity. The blunt, industrious little Benes was popular. The elegant, ironic Italian Scialoja was popular. The Socialist Henderson, plain-speaking "Uncle Arthur," achieved popularity in a later day. Even Lord Robert Cecil, the aristocratic Cecil, the "vulture chasing butterflies" of the Comtesse de Noailles' picturesque metaphor, was liked no less than esteemed by his colleagues on the League of Nations. But Chamberlain, respected, even admired as he was, never attained any general affection. In the Assembly he concealed his real character as successfully as in the House of Commons. His manner was didactic, uncompromising. His formal and invariable habit of referring to "His Majesty's Government," when Briand said simply, "France," or even more simply "I," when Stresemann said "Germany" or the "Reich," intimidated and irritated other delegates. The men who manufactured world opinion, the correspondents of newspapers and news agencies from Tokio to Buenos Aires, looked down from their galleries upon the thin, carefully groomed figure, the sleek head, the shining eyeglass of the British statesman and formed of him, consciously and subconsciously, an impression too near to the traditional caricature of the Englishman to be either just or flattering. He was, in many foreign eyes, the embodiment of English diplomacy since Pitt: proud, egoistic, commercial, perfidious Albion. Foreigners were apt to apply to him the picturesque words once used by Anatole France of Lloyd George: "He is a clever fellow. He reads his Bible and sings his psalms, but he serves his country and himself."

He was no orator. The tricks of the demagogue came to him uneasily, or were totally disdained. The art of appealing to, of sensing the spirit and mood of, a cosmopolitan assembly he had never possessed, and perhaps it was this talent in Briand which so attracted him. He did not understand other men as Briand did. Yet he respected them. He realized that they were different, that their interests were not the same as his own, that they were accountable to critical parliaments, or even more critical dictators, that they represented peoples restless and uneasy, haunted by the fear of insecurity. Individually he could charm them, win them by his courtesy, his frankness, his inherent simplicity of character. But collectively he intimidated them. He saw them not as men but as states; as a coalition of foreigners. He addressed them not as a man, but as the spokesman of an hereditary monarchy, a country with a long tradition of power and of parliamentary government. Successful as had been his own recent departure from tradition, he incarnated, nevertheless, the tradition of Britain's magnificent isolation. Even with the laurels of Locarno fresh upon his brow, with the award of the Nobel Peace Prize still recent in men's memories, he could not remove from the minds of his hearers that spectacular obsession. He was the typical Englishman familiar to Europeans since the beginning of the nineteenth century, since the romantic era in literature, Wordsworth and Byron and George Sand, the Grand Tour and the eclipse of Napoleon.

Although he failed to impress himself upon the League Assembly at large as anything more than an automaton speaking with the voice of the Foreign Office and of Down-

ing Street, in the more intimate, informal atmosphere of the
Council and the Commissions Sir Austen Chamberlain
achieved a considerable personal success. He was affable,
even-tempered, persuasive and an optimist. He was an
admirable foil to the cynicism of Briand, to the nerves and
sensitiveness of Stresemann. He discarded his monocle for
a pair of horn-rimmed spectacles, which had the advantage
of making him suddenly appear at once older and more
human. He revealed a certain whimsical sense of humor,
a humor characteristically English, for all his occasional
French turns of phrase and borrowed Gallicisms. He could
not prevent himself from occasional retorts of a parliamentary vigor and bluntness, retorts which fell crushingly and
brutally upon the ears of foreign statesmen accustomed
to a more delicate and rapier-like touch, to the art of the
innuendo rather than that of refutation or rebuff. But even
when he had all unwittingly wounded the vanity or the
susceptibility of a colleague, his subsequent manner was so
open and candid, his smile so engaging and his words so
free from malice that his adversary had perforce to overlook
the slight and attribute merely one more injury to the thick
skin, the egoism, the imperturbable self-complacency and
self-righteousness of the British nation at large.

His success as mediator or as arbiter was more due to his
scrupulous sense of honor and his impartiality than to any
special skill in negotiation. He was above all intrigue; he
never betrayed a confidence; and if he never forgot his
own country's premier interests, he had a friendly and a
tolerant eye for those of other countries. Also his word was
accepted as his bond. In the summer of 1926 when he was
touring the Mediterranean on Sir Warden Chilcott's yacht
Dolphin he had a long private conversation with Mussolini,

who boarded the yacht in harbor at Leghorn. Mussolini reminded him of Italy's long-standing claims to a rectification of the frontier of Italian Cyrenaica and the British protectorate of Egypt. Chamberlain asked him not to press the matter at that moment, and promised him that at the first convenient opportunity he would give Italy satisfaction on that score. Mussolini expressed himself as content to wait. "Your word is good enough for me," he told Chamberlain. Subsequently Great Britain kept the pledge made in her behalf by the Foreign Secretary.

§ 3

Less productive of results was the interview at Geneva during the following year between Chamberlain and Litvinoff, the Soviet Commissar for Foreign Affairs. Both men had come to Geneva to attend the meeting of the Preparatory Commission for the Disarmament Conference. Their governments had broken off diplomatic relations a year earlier as a result of the police raid on the office of Arcos in London, ordered by the Conservative Home Secretary, Joynson Hicks. They met as strangers in the restricted and intimate atmosphere of a commission meeting in a small, glass-walled chamber normally used at that time for sessions of the Council. The eyes of Geneva and of the world were upon them. The gossip of Geneva centered in them. Would they meet privately to discuss Anglo-Soviet relations? Which would make the advance—the English Conservative or the Russian Bolshevik? For several days they affected to ignore each other's presence in the Commission. For several days their respective delegations issued frigid denials of any intention on the part of either statesman to attempt to meet the other.

The meeting of the Commission drew towards its end. The departures of the British and the Soviet delegates were announced. Litvinoff's train left on a Saturday. Chamberlain's on the following Monday. On Friday the gulf between the two Foreign Ministers and their countries seemed as wide as ever. The early optimism of those diplomats who had hoped that an embarrassing and even dangerous quarrel between two governments might be honorably ended at Geneva gave way to pessimism. The fear of those governments interested in prolonging the breach gave way to exultation. On the night before Litvinoff was due to leave Geneva there was still no sign of any intention on the one hand of soliciting a meeting or on the other of granting it. Then, at midnight, the situation suddenly changed.

Indiscreet if well-intentioned gossip had been responsible for a report that the British minister was secretly anxious to meet Litvinoff. The authority for the statement was stated to be Chamberlain's private secretary, Mr. (now Sir) Walford Selby, the present British Minister in Vienna. As a result of this indiscretion, Litvinoff was induced by the writer to state that he would be willing to make a formal request to be received by Sir Austen if he were privately assured that the request would be granted. In the meantime Chamberlain's secretary, informed of the course taken by the negotiations for a meeting between the two, very properly denied that he had ever made or authorized such a statement of the British minister's feelings. Litvinoff shrugged his shoulders in cynical disillusionment. There matters might have rested if the writer had not, in desperation, communicated to Austen Chamberlain the whole story of the incident, and suggested that if Litvinoff were satisfied of the response that might be made to his request, he might even now be willing to renew it officially.

The answer came to me that night. It took the form of a cryptic telephoned message from the Foreign Secretary that if reasonable request were made to him, courtesy would dictate an appropriate reply. Armed with this hint, I walked across the Pont de Mont Blanc and woke up the Soviet delegation. Litvinoff and his wife had already gone to bed. They came into the sitting-room of their suite in pajamas, and we discussed the situation.

Ultimately, if reluctantly, Litvinoff agreed to make the experiment. I took up the telephone, called the Hotel Beau-Rivage, asked for the secretary of the British delegation and handed the receiver to Madame Litvinoff. In her calm, unhurried English voice the niece of Sir Sidney Low inquired if Sir Austen Chamberlain would receive Mr. Litvinoff on the following morning. Sir Austen had retired for the night, but early on the following morning the reply was received that Sir Austen would be glad to receive Mr. Litvinoff at three o'clock on the following afternoon. The time fixed for the appointment obliged the Soviet Commissar to cancel his reservations on the morning train to Berlin. He did so reluctantly.

§ 4

The interview took place, and on his return from it Litvinoff said with a grimace that it was not worth postponing his departure for. Chamberlain had received him with courtesy but without cordiality. There had been the usual accusations concerning the close relationship between the Soviet government and the activities of the Communist International. The usual Russian retort had been given that although the Conservative party in England might be responsible for the Conservative government, the Conservative government was not responsible for the activities of the Conservative party. The two men parted without either having proposed any solution of the existing quarrel between their governments. Litvinoff shared the regret expressed by Chamberlain in his subsequent reply to a question in the House of Commons that the ineffectual meeting had taken place.

But later in the day he had cause to change his attitude. Briand, on whom he called at the Hôtel des Bergues, to make his formal leavetaking, pointedly felicitated him on his gesture. The Foreign Ministers of Poland and other states on the borders of Russia were even more lavish in their compliments. The mere fact that Chamberlain had received the Soviet diplomat was sufficient to create around the bland, non-committal figure of Litvinoff a sudden aura of prestige and importance. On his arrival in Berlin, on the way to Moscow, the German government, always sensitive to any fresh veering of the European wind, was effusive in its attentions. Nevertheless the meeting, whatever influence it may have had on the Soviet's relations with other powers, had no effect on Anglo-Soviet relations. It was not the Conservative government which renewed diplomatic activities with Soviet Russia, but the Labour government of 1929; not Chamberlain who was responsible for ending the feud, but his successor, Arthur Henderson.

Chamberlain's private, and characteristic, reaction to the Bolshevik Foreign Minister was expressed in his own words to me some days later: "Do you think it was pleasant for me to shake the hand of the representative of men who killed the cousin of my sovereign?"

Chapter. XV

THE LIBERATOR: GUSTAVE STRESEMANN

§ 1

FEW hotels in Switzerland are more Teutonic in their interior decoration than the Hôtel Métropole in Geneva. Lobby, dining-room, bar, staircase, bedrooms, *salons*—all are reminiscent of the unfortunate era in hotel architecture which dominated Central Europe in the eighteen eighties. From 1926 to 1933 the Hôtel Métropole was the headquarters of German diplomacy at the League of Nations. It provided the background for the tragi-comedy of the Council of 1926, the triumph of Stresemann at the subsequent Assembly, the jubilant return of Stresemann from his conversations with Briand at Thoiry, the blunders of Chancellor Hermann Mueller at the Assembly of 1928, and the last act of the drama of Stresemann himself.

From this heavy, somber and pretentious building the man who had been acclaimed as the successor to Bismarck emerged, yellow-faced, shrunken in his massive garments, a corpse reanimated for a supreme gesture of life, to make his valedictory speech before a silent and apprehensive Assembly. To it the dying man returned, unable to walk without halting for breath the few yards which separate the hotel from the Salle de la Réformation. When he left the scene of his diplomatic victories again it was to take the train for Berlin, a man already twice condemned, knowing even before death overtook him that his life work had been

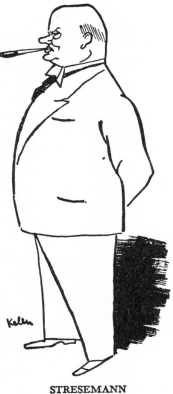

STRESEMANN

rejected, that his party had abandoned him, and that before many months the whole structure of Franco-German reconciliation he had painfully built up would lie in ruins.

Stresemann's first appearance on the international scene was in 1924, when as German Foreign Minister he was invited to join Mr. Ramsay MacDonald and M. Edouard Herriot in the Dawes Plan conversations in London. Neither at that time nor subsequently was his physical aspect prepossessing. He looked like one of the grosser types of Teuton: square and solidly built, bull-necked, bullet-headed, a red face closely shaven, a fleshy nose, heavy sensual lips, a cruel mouth and small eyes set close together and very light in color. His voice was astonishingly high-pitched and shrill for so powerful a man. His movements were clumsy and nervous. His eyes were restless and suspicious. His small hands, covered with red hairs, were never at ease. Yet once he had overcome his first feelings of mistrust and gained self-assurance he was capable of an unsuspected charm. His laugh was of a boyish spontaneity and candor. His tastes and habits were simple: cigars, brandy, plain if abundant dishes. He wore those vast, ill-cut, flamboyant suits so much affected by German business men. And at heart, like many Germans of a severe and practical and unromantic appearance, he was sentimental and romantic. He had a weakness for Goethe and for Napoleon. His first political act had brought him, as a university student, into conflict with the Imperial police. He had laid a prohibited wreath of laurels on the graves of the victims of the German Revolution of 1848. His first love affair had been unfortunate. His prospects had been considered insufficiently promising by the parents of the young girl with whom he was secretly betrothed.

The girl withdrew her promise. After twenty-five years of married life to the vivacious, intelligent and beautiful Kaethe Stresemann he still felt the pangs of that adolescent betrayal. No statesman in Europe concealed a more anxious, fearful and sensitive heart behind a more arrogant, brutal and intimidating exterior.

§ 2

In 1924, at the beginning of his five years of office as Germany's Foreign Minister, he was forty-six years old. He had been born on May 10, 1878, the youngest son of the keeper of a beershop in the Koepenikerstrasse in Berlin. He had, in whimsical or in practical mood, taken as the subject for his doctoral thesis the economic uses of old beer bottles. His first appointment was that of secretary to an association of chocolate manufacturers in Saxony, and all his subsequent political life was to be founded on the growing identity between politics and the interests of German industry. At twenty-nine he entered the Reichstag as its youngest deputy. Thereafter his progress was rapid. He was an able orator, in the florid German manner. He spoke with ease and assurance. His voice, although shrill and even falsetto to non-German ears, was capable of subtle inflections and modulations, and was an admirable vehicle of emotion and sentiment. He was persuasive, eloquent and convincing. In private negotiations, in party discussions, he was even more eloquent.

During the war he was one of the most earnest and uncompromising of the advocates of a military peace for Germany, a peace with annexations and compensations. Until October 1, 1918, he confessed afterwards, he had thought Germany invincible. He had supported the policy of submarine warfare, naïvely trusting in the assurances of Tirpitz and the other leaders of the navy that Germany possessed enough submarines to carry it to a successful issue. To the end he believed Capelle's disdainful remark that the military value of American intervention was nil. Even after the collapse of 1918 he remained an unrepentant monarchist, and it was not until 1922 that he learned from Von Helfferich that when the decision to begin unrestricted submarine warfare was made Germany possessed only an inadequate number of U-boats, and that the High Command had been over-optimistic regarding the possibilities of building a large submarine fleet. Disillusioned by this tardy revelation of wartime inefficiency in high places, Stresemann thereupon decided to give his entire adhesion to the Republic. Even then almost his first act on taking office in August, 1923, was to authorize the Crown Prince to leave his exile in Wieringen and to reside in Germany.

Stresemann became the head of the German government at the height of the occupation of the Ruhr. For the first time his own party, the Populists, entered into coalition with the Social Democrats, a combination which was destined to govern Germany almost uninterruptedly until Stresemann's death. A few months later, braving calumny, insults and the menace of assassination, Stresemann took the courageous step of abandoning resistance in the Ruhr in a desperate attempt to save the mark from complete collapse. He faced a furious Reichstag and a press which threatened him with a trial for treason before the High Court. He climbed the steps to the tribune of the Reichstag slowly and painfully, like a man climbing the steps to the scaffold. He had taken his decision alone, against the vote of his party, in the teeth of the opposition of his colleagues and of the other parties. His government of the Grand Coalition had been denounced in bitter mockery as the government of the Grand Capitulation. And in truth, as Stresemann admitted to the Reichstag, Germany had surrendered without conditions. Nothing less would have satisfied Poincaré, or arrested Germany's course to ruin.

The new Chancellor's defense was listened to in a silence even more contemptuous than the cries of hatred and indignation which had greeted him before he began to speak. Only a few half-hearted cheers from the Left greeted him when he had finished. Nevertheless, he had just made the greatest of his political speeches, and had for the first time outlined the policy which was to set him apart from, and above, all his contemporaries in Germany; his famous exhortation to Germans to renounce party passions and personal ambitions and to set their faces for the first time on the ideal of the state; an exhortation which curiously anticipates, although in nobler fashion, the subsequent state-exaltation of Hitler and his followers.

A few years afterwards, when Stresemann had achieved his brief-lived popularity and even his period of adulation, he said, in a moment of retrospect: "The greatest courage that a man can manifest is perhaps the courage to withstand unpopularity; to know that he is right, that he could not have acted otherwise, to find himself suddenly alone, hated, insulted, calumnied; to ask himself how he will resist an entire nation in error, how he can prove that he alone was in the right. . . . No more terrible ordeal than this has fate in store for any man."

§ 3

Stresemann's historic opportunity came in the autumn of 1925, exactly two years after his surrender to Poincaré over the Ruhr. The prelude to Locarno had not been free from difficulties, foreseen and unforeseen. Austen Chamberlain, as has been said, at first rejected the offer of a Rhineland Pact as imprudent and premature. It was in part the enthusiasm of Lloyd George and the British Liberals, in part the unhesitating acceptance of Herriot and later of Briand, that transformed the British attitude into one of modified approval. The real negotiator of the Pact was neither Chamberlain, Briand nor Stresemann, but Lord D'Abernon, whose influence in Germany during the early post-war years was so great that he was sometimes described as the de facto German Chancellor. The Pact was only possible, however, because it had found in Stresemann a romantic German who loved the memory of Napoleon, and for the sake of that great figure was even prepared to love France.

To love England was more difficult. Between England and Germany, in Stresemann's eyes, lay the pre-war naval and commercial rivalry, the declaration of war in August, 1914, the overthrow of the Hohenzollerns, and lastly, Chamberlain's unfortunate and contemptuous words regarding his own Rhineland offer. But France was less the historic enemy of Germany than a neighbor with whom she had too often unhappily been embroiled, the fellow victim of British arrogance and British perfidy. With the defeat of Poincaré at the 1924 elections the greatest obstacle to Franco-German understanding had been removed. A new generation of politicians was in power in Paris. The Quai d'Orsay was directed by a man of picturesque personality, Bohemian habit and rare imagination, a man, like Stresemann, of lower middle-class if not actually working-class origin, a romantic like Stresemann himself.

Before his arrival at Locarno, Stresemann had taken care to inform himself very precisely as to the character, idiosyncrasies and habits of Briand. He listened avidly to the anecdotes concerning Briand recounted to him by French and German diplomats and journalists. His curiosity was aroused in advance. He prepared himself to meet one of the most original minds of the age, a statesman of distinction, a personality of robust courage and independence. In this he was not disappointed. He found a man cut out of different cloth from the traditional type of statesman-bureaucrat familiar in Germany, where even under the Republic the social and professional hierarchy had not greatly changed, where statesmen could never be mistaken for anything but statesmen, and soldiers, privy counselors, clergymen, diplomats, doctors and professors were required rigidly to conform to a pattern already made for them. He found in Briand a man of careless dress, of informal speech, of cynical candor, of warm humanity, of ripe experience; a man whose long familiarity and frequent disillusionment with men of all classes and conditions in particular had, nevertheless, not caused him to despair of mankind in general. He was impressed by Briand. He succumbed to the spell which the old sorcerer knew how to exercise when the occasion demanded. He was seduced by Briand's wit, his humanity, his charm, and above all his sincere evocation of a world to be born anew out of the ruins of the world of 1914-18.

As for Briand, he had been agreeably surprised by the character of this anything but prepossessing Teuton. He had not been favorably impressed by his first sight of Stresemann: stiff, fleshy, brutal in aspect as he was. But he rapidly revised his opinion after their first encounter. "When I sat down for the first time opposite Stresemann at Locarno," he related afterwards, "we began to discuss the text of the Pact on the various points which had not yet been revised. We were working in an entirely practical and objective manner. The necessary exchanges of views proceeded easily, and we were drawing near a rapid end to our labors. Suddenly the colleague of Stresemann [Chancellor Luther] thought it his duty to sound the sentimental note, which hitherto we had been very careful to avoid.

"He began, in his most precise French, to describe to us the state of Germany. He spoke with telling phrases, evidently prepared in advance, of the injustice of which his country was the victim, and the terrible sufferings of the German people. I felt that the discussion was about to leave the realm of the practical and be dangerously side-tracked towards old sentimental grievances. I saw the shadow of discontent steal over the countenance of Chamberlain, and his long face grow even longer than was its custom. I realized that if this sort of thing continued I should myself be forced to take up the theme of my own country's sufferings. So I put my hand on the shoulder of the speaker and said to him, 'Do not go on, or you will make us all weep!' The other man naturally grew red with anger and gave me an unfriendly look. But I watched the expression of Stresemann. I saw a gleam of mirth in his blue eyes. Then, as he caught my glance, he burst out laughing, and this settled everything. It was then that I realized he was a man."

§ 4

Both Stresemann and Briand had insisted on the purely inaugural character of the Locarno Treaty. On the night when the Pact was initialed the French minister had said: "A new era must begin with Locarno, otherwise we shall have labored in vain." And in London, during the ceremony of signature, the German carried this note a step farther and made the boldest speech yet made in favor of the new Europe. "What I would desire to see in this treaty," he said, "is not a juridical edifice, but the moral basis of a great evolution. In it statesmen and nations proclaim their will to march along the road of understanding and peace. The forms of international collaboration therein inscribed would have no reality if they did not disclose the desire to create new conditions of life in Europe."

But unexpected difficulties were raised in the execution of the Pact. Its primordial condition had been the immediate admission of Germany into the League of Nations. At the League Council held in March, 1926, three months after the formal signature of the Treaty, several states refused their consent to a seat for Germany being created on the Council unless they were similarly provided with seats. Stresemann and the other German delegates, come to Geneva in the expectation of a unanimous invitation to join the League and its Council, were forced to cool their heels impatiently at the Hôtel Métropole, and to return to Berlin disillusioned and empty-handed. It was Stresemann's first experience of the bureaucratic machinery of Geneva, and he returned from it in disgust. "If we had all been gathered at one table," he said indignantly, "that is, Briand, Chamberlain and I, with those who had raised difficulties, Poland, Brazil and Spain, we should have arranged everything in a single afternoon. As it was, the Geneva people took weeks and settled nothing at all."

A few weeks before this farcical journey to Geneva he had given Mussolini a taste of the irony he could display on occasion. The opportunity had arisen out of the incidents between men of German race and Italian functionaries in the South Tyrol. The German press had begun a campaign against the Duce's acts of repression against the Tyrolean Germans. Mussolini had retorted with a speech of characteristic insolence. When the speech was reported to Stresemann he went pale with anger. The great veins on his neck swelled up, his eyes grew bloodshot, and his hands trembled. But the answer he subsequently made in the Reichstag revealed nothing of this carefully controlled emotion. He replied to Mussolini's speech with quotation after quotation from the Duce's own utterances, and finally he concluded with the sardonic interrogation: "Is the present course of Italian evolution an epoch in the world's history, as the head of the Italian government states, or is it merely a picturesque episode in the history of Italy? The future alone will tell."

§ 5

Six months after the fiasco of the League Council of March a compromise had been reached over the seats demanded by the three recalcitrant states, and the admission of Germany could be formally celebrated. It was the greatest day in the history of the League. Geneva seemed to be en fête. The sun shone brilliantly on the lake, on the gray and green façades of the houses, on the great glistening leaves of the plane trees in the little squares and on the Quai Wilson. The streets were filled with large and shining cars, many of which for the first time flew the pennon of the German Republic from their radiator caps. The Salle de la Réformation was crowded from floor to ceiling with delegates, journalists, photographers and visitors. Mrs. Woodrow Wilson, the widow of the Founder of the League, sat in her accustomed place in the front row of the gallery. Near her sat the pretty Frau Stresemann.

In a tense silence the voting took place on Germany's request for admission. The President of the Assembly, the Jugoslav Foreign Minister Nintchich, announced the result in his precise, clipped French. There was a polite clapping of hands from the floor, and a more robust cheer from the galleries. Then one of the doors behind the presidential tribune opened and the members of the German delegation entered. First the tall figure of Von Schubert, permanent Under-Secretary of the Wilhelmstrasse, beak-nosed, bald-headed, red-faced and round-shouldered. Then the German jurist Dr. Gauss, who had drafted the Treaty of Locarno with the British representative Sir Cecil Hurst and the French lawyer Fromageot. Last came Stresemann himself, broad-shouldered and rigid, his great neck sunk in a stiff white collar, his round cheeks almost purple, his little eyes shining with emotion, his robust body encased in a tightly fitting black morning-coat.

Without further formalities, the President invited Stresemann to address the Assembly. In spite of the warmth of his reception, the German leader seemed confused and embarrassed in the tribune. His first words were uttered in a shrill and almost defiant tone. But as he progressed with his speech the familiar words of his manuscript reassured him. The words themselves were friendly, conciliatory, earnest and even noble in inspiration. He spoke of the lessons of the war, the duty of the new generation of mankind, the moral revolution accomplished in 1918, the needs of international co-operation. He urged the necessity of reconciling national duties with international duties. In some passages of his speech he seemed to be echoing the words of Smuts:

"Of far greater importance than the material factors is the spiritual life of the nations. From one end of the earth to the other thought is in lively ferment. Some nations defend the principle of absolute national independence, and refuse any form of international structure, unwilling to sacrifice national realities to the sentiment of humanity. I am with those who believe, however, that no country which belongs to the League of Nations has in any way renounced its own identity. The divine Architect has not created mankind as a uniform edifice. He has created the peoples of different blood, of different language, and has given them to dwell in countries of dissimilar climates. But He cannot have conceived a universe in which men subvert their finest inventions to the service of war, and in which they no sooner create a common civilization than they destroy it. He serves humanity best who, solidly rooted in his own nationality, develops to the highest degree the spiritual forces with which nature has endowed him, and reaching across the frontiers of his own country contributes something to all men. That is what all the great men of history have done, in all countries. It is upon the spiritual plane that nations are one with mankind, but they can equally unite upon the political plane if they have a clear understanding of their common evolution and the will to serve it."

§ 6

Stresemann had spoken in German. His voice was not altogether disagreeable to non-German ears, in spite of its shrillness, and many of the delegates were obliged to wait for the translation before they could understand the speech. But the quality of the speech itself, the earnestness of the voice, the universality of the language uttered by Stresemann, made an immediate and considerable impression upon the Assembly. Nevertheless the real success of the day was not Stresemann's but Briand's. There could have been but one reply to so frank and friendly an appeal from one of the belligerents of 1914-18. And there could have been but one man to deliver it. In a silence heavy with emotion Briand left his place at the end of the French delegation's row of desks in the Assembly hall and crept noiselessly up the stairs to the tribune. His voice seemed at first to come from a great distance, so faint and weary it was with exhaustion. As it gained strength, familiar chords could be heard in it. Then the deep notes were struck. It was the great "Away with the guns!" speech, already referred to in this work, the greatest speech made by Briand at the League, the greatest, perhaps, of his entire career. The strange, harsh undertones of the voice were heard to their most telling effect. Three times, in his great apostrophe to war, the orator thundered the words, "It is finished!" and such was the power of his voice and of his almost apocalyptic vision that his audience trembled as if the heavens had indeed opened and the dove of peace had descended to reign upon this earth forever.

When the speaker left the tribune Stresemann alone did not join the rush of effusive delegates to felicitate Briand. Instead, he sat silently at his desk, sunk, as it seemed, in meditation. But his greeting to Briand after this reply was frank and enthusiastic. He had lost nothing of his admiration of the Frenchman. On the contrary, it was soon to be redoubled. But he had just experienced his first encounter with world opinion as incarnated in the League Assembly, and still suffered from the inevitable reaction. His high forehead, so pale in contrast to the tanned red cheeks, was beaded with perspiration. The veins stood out on his neck and his hands. He breathed with difficulty in the crowded and overheated Assembly hall. Outside, in the sunshine of the lake-shore, he felt more at ease. But he was never, either in 1926 or in subsequent years of attendance at League Assemblies, to enjoy the degree of self-confidence that other statesmen displayed in Geneva. Physically he felt constrained in the hot and close atmosphere of the Salle de la Réformation. His own protest was ultimately to secure the transfer of the Assembly to the Geneva Electoral Building, but that he was not destined to witness in the flesh.

§ 7

His discomfort in the League of Nations atmosphere was even more spiritual than physical. Like most Germans, he was nervous and embarrassed in a large assembly. Like most Germans, he could never forget for a moment that he was German. Briand, even the insular Chamberlain, could talk affably and without any secret obsession of national prestige to Germans, Americans, Czechs, Austrians, Greeks and Italians. Stresemann was not only conscious of his origins but was aware of that vast unseen audience of sixty-five million Germans waiting to reproach him with the slightest infidelity to the national cause. Every speech he delivered at Geneva, therefore, must be written. He must have documentary proof of his words and acts to flourish in the face of those critical, censorious, bitter and merciless judges in Germany.

His real pleasure in Geneva, his only moment of relaxation, was in the company of journalists, at midnight, in the narrow, smoky café Bavaria, an old-fashioned German *Bierhalle* with one door fronting the lake and another door opening on a back street. There, when Briand had long since retired to bed, and the leaders of other delegations, if they were not also asleep, were engaged in more formal distractions, Stresemann sat at a little table and drank beer. Around him pressed men of all nations and conditions, his colleague Von Schubert; the tall, lean, melancholy figure of the German Socialist, Rudolf Breitscheid; the little, dark, witty Alsatian Socialist, Grumbach; German, Austrian, Hungarian, French and British newspaper correspondents, members of the League Secretariat, delegates returning to their hotels in dress clothes from some function; the celebrated Hungarian caricaturists Derso and Kelen, whose drawings of Stresemann still hang on the walls of the Bavaria, and even the stolid citizens of Geneva, no longer impressed by celebrities, but sensible nevertheless of the jovial and unpretentious manners of the German Foreign Minister.

Chapter XVI

PRELUDE TO HITLER

§ 1

ONE night during this notable Assembly of 1926 Stresemann returned to the Hôtel Métropole laboring under manifest excitement. He looked exhilarated, although physically he was near collapse. Some hours later, when his amazing constitution had recovered, he left the bed to which his doctor and his colleagues had consigned him, and made his way to the Bavaria, stalking through the crowded, noisy and smoke-filled rooms of the café like a youth eager for pleasure. It was the night after the conversations at Thoiry.

Evading the vigilance of the newspaper correspondents, Briand and Stresemann had been driven quietly to the mountain inn in the Jura which will ever afterwards be associated with their memory. They had lunched together, alone save for an interpreter. The meal was long, the dishes plentiful, and of a delicacy rare enough in so small and humble a place—*saucission de Lyon*; baked mountain trout; partridges; *morilles*, a kind of mushroom, cooked in cream; and roast duck with orange sauce. Afterwards they had talked, long and confidentially. The theme of their conversation was the creation of a real and permanent understanding between France and Germany. Locarno had been but a prelude. It had opened up the way towards a reconciliation. The real treaty of peace had yet to be concluded. France was anxious to liquidate the outstanding account for the reconstruction of her devastated areas. The economic co-operation of France and Germany was necessary. The franc was falling. French currency must be stabilized, and with German assistance. Germany wished to see the Rhineland freed of the Allied troops of occupation, and thus to regain her full sovereignty and prestige in the eyes of the world. She was also interested in the recovery of the Saar.

In the end the two ministers agreed on a common policy. In order to render France the immediate financial assistance necessary if the franc was to be buttressed, Germany would mobilize the credit of her state railways, held as security for the repayment of reparations. She would issue railway bonds to the capital value of 1500 million gold marks, of which France's share (52 per cent.) would realize 780 millions. In return for this concession, the French government would agree to a premature evacuation of the Rhineland. Finally, and with some diffidence, Stresemann raised the question of the Saar. "No material sacrifice will be too great for us," he told Briand, "if by it we can restore the liberty of the Saar." He would not surrender a single village of the Saar to a foreign Power, even in return for concessions elsewhere, or for facilities in the repurchase of the Saar coal mines. But he offered outright a sum of 300 million gold marks in return for the restoration of the Saar territory, the coal mines included, to Germany.

No binding agreement was made between the two men. No documents or signatures were exchanged. They had merely outlined ideas which they held in common, and reached agreement on a policy which they mutually promised to pursue. Both men knew that their ministerial colleagues might oppose the policy. Both men knew that they were equally liable to be overthrown by their respective parliaments, to be denounced by the newspapers of their respective countries, to be betrayed by their respective bureaucracies. But each had confidence in the courage, the imagination and the goodwill of the other. Briand, in particular, based on the support of Stresemann the hopes of European collaboration now vaguely taking shape in his mind. He was among the many Frenchmen in 1926 (Poincaré was another) who feared above all things the economic and financial domination of the United States. "If we do not combine together," said Briand to Stresemann at Thoiry, "we shall be swallowed up by international capitalism. Look at the growing importance of the great vested interests, the industrial cartels. They will soon dictate to us the policy we shall follow. We politicians must not allow the direction of affairs to be taken out of our hands." And when Stresemann had drunk the last of his glasses of *vieux marc de bourgogne* and Briand had smoked the last cigarette, his final words to his German companion as they shook hands were: "It is lucky that we are in agreement. Otherwise . . . the American bankers would have taken the last shirt from our backs."

§ 2

This was in September, 1926. Less than two months later the franc collapsed. The Briand-Caillaux ministry was overthrown. M. Herriot's one-day Cabinet saw the franc quoted at 260 to the pound sterling, and angry crowds threatened the deputies inside the locked gates of the Chamber. Poincaré, the old enemy of Germany, returned to power, and it seemed as if the last great act of his political career was to render any Franco-German reconciliation impossible, for by stabilizing the franc he destroyed the principal concession which Germany could offer in exchange for the exacuation of the Rhineland—the mobilization of the first series of reparation bonds, discussed by Briand and Stresemann at Thoiry.

But even during the two months which elapsed between the inn-table conversations in September and the return of Poincaré to power, Stresemann had experienced a certain disillusionment. He had returned to Berlin from Geneva and in haste had summoned a Cabinet committee, meetings of financial experts, bankers and treasury officials to work out in detail the proposed issue of bonds. To the same end Briand had promised to send a high French official to Berlin in the following month. October passed and the official had not arrived. Stresemann's anxious inquiries through intermediaries in Paris produced only evasive replies. But in Germany Stresemann's popularity was at its zenith. He had first been awarded the Nobel Peace Prize. He composed himself to have faith in this destiny (like his hero, Napoleon, he slept soundly at nights) and in Briand.

The year 1927 opened without bringing any further news of the Thoiry proposals. The American market was definitely hostile to any bond issue so long as France had not ratified the American war debt agreement. The attitude of the French nation towards Germany seemed to have undergone another of its frequent changes of heart. At the sessions of the League Council in March and June, at the Assembly in September, Briand urged Stresemann to have patience. All his political life he had waited and the waiting game had brought him in the end to power. But patience was the only political quality which Stresemann lacked. He was restive, suspicious, too highly strung for such tactics. Moreover in any waiting game with time he played at a disadvantage, for he was a sick man. Even more than in the case of Briand, who was fifteen years older, his days were numbered. Time, in Germany, seemed to favor the partisans of revenge rather than those of reconciliation, and so in the end it proved.

Meanwhile the months passed, and as the value of the German concession had declined as a result of the stabilization of the franc, so the value of France's supreme card in the Rhineland gage of security declined as the year of the ultimate evacuation prescribed by the Versailles Treaty drew steadily nearer. In the summer of 1928 Stresemann, although visibly in failing health, went to Paris to sign the Briand-Kellogg Pact in the name of Germany. He was the first German Cabinet minister to visit Paris since 1870, and apart from a hostile demonstration by French royalist youths at the railway station, was cordially received. He had an hour's conversation with Poincaré, and found him, to his surprise, not hostile to a premature evacuation of the Rhineland if Germany showed herself in good faith regarding reparations payments. And when Poincaré reproached him with having abandoned the Thoiry proposals, impetuously, in surprise and indignation, he poured into the French Premier's attentive ear the whole story of the conversations, of his disillusionment, of his hopes and of his patience. But before Poincaré could reply, his own physician had intervened with a peremptory order that the conversation must cease. He never saw Poincaré again, and the discussion was never resumed. Stresemann left Paris the next day for Berlin under the melancholy eyes of Briand, who realized that the physical effort of the journey had overtaxed his friend's failing powers.

He was too weak to attend the League Assembly in the following month of September. The German Chancellor, Hermann Mueller, a Socialist, round, suspicious, unimaginative and secretly hostile to France, led the German delegation in his stead, and his clumsy references to the "two-faced international policy" of certain states, by inference France, brought a sharp admonition from Briand. Stresemann recovered sufficiently to attend the December meeting of the Council, which was held at his request in the more clement atmosphere of Lugano, Geneva having been prohibited him by his doctors.

He went reluctantly, sensing in advance the futility of his journey, and already completely disillusioned in regard to the League. "The whole organization," he exclaimed on the eve of his departure, "is nothing but a mass of deception! What is it we are told, that the little nations and the great enjoy equality in the League? The votes of the little nations count for nothing beside the vote of a single Great Power. That is how the votes are counted. And what does it amount to, the League's achievements? Briand always declares that it prevented a war in the Balkans. But if he and Chamberlain had sat down together at the same table and had drafted a stern note to the two quarreling states, they would have prevented war just as well, without needing to bring in the delegates of fifty other states as audience. Locarno was accomplished without the League of Nations. And the League was not even present at that American preachifying in Paris, the Kellogg Pact. It postpones all the important questions, all the difficult questions, to the Greek Kalends. Disarmament?—

the League has not advanced it a step. On the subject of economic peace, the customs union, it produces nothing but solemn resolutions. It is true that it has built up a powerful organization. But all the Budget is swallowed up by the bureaucrats. The result is *nil*. They have not even protected the rights of minorities. They promised the nations a paradise and they gave them torrents of paper. One of these days I would like to bang my fists on the table."

§ 3

The day came sooner than he expected. At Lugano all his discontent, his irritation, his impatience at the delays in realizing his dream of Germany's liberation suddenly exploded on the head of an unfortunate Pole. The victim was the pale, blond, suave Polish Foreign Minister, August Zaleski, who had innocently raised the delicate subject of the German minorities in Polish Silesia after having given what seemed to Stresemann to be an undertaking not to do so. Stresemann expressed his resentment at Zaleski's speech by banging the table. The gesture restored the German minister's prestige in his own country, which loves such physical demonstrations of strength, and fortunately did no great damage, since the speech which followed it was based, as Briand was able to point out, on a misunderstanding.

He made one other gesture of indignation. It occurred during the Hague Conference in 1929, in which the German delegates played the part of interested spectators in a drama in which the chief actors were the late Viscount (then Mr. Philip) Snowden on the one hand, and Briand and his colleague Henry Chéron on the other. M. Chéron was a Norman, stout, bearded, affable and honest, the most honest, perhaps, but also the most incompetent French Minister of Finance in history. He loved the sound of his own voice. He loved to make a speech full of impressive figures. He made a speech at one of the first meetings at The Hague in which the milliards danced to his own delight. Snowden, who equally loved figures and understood them better than his French colleague, described M. Chéron's arguments as grotesque and ridiculous. The words aroused no protest at the time. The interpreter, if he privately thought them unconventional, prudently glossed them over in his translation. At luncheon that day M. Chéron, whose equanimity was unruffled by any suspicion of so brutal an attack, was basking in the happy consciousness of a notable speech notably well delivered, when his colleague, Loucheur, Briand's Minister of Public Works and intimate, maliciously asked him what he thought of Snowden's reply.

"Not bad at all," said Chéron tranquilly. "Very favorable to our point of view."

"If you believe that you will believe anything!" retorted Loucheur bluntly.

Whereupon he explained to the disillusioned little Norman lawyer the actual words used by Snowden. M. Chéron was bewildered and indignant. Members of other delegations added fuel to the flames. And soon the unhappy Chéron found himself reluctantly the center of an incident which threatened to make him as ridiculous as the British Chancellor's vigorous adjectives had suggested. He was induced to make a formal protest against the undiplomatic language used by Snowden. The little Yorkshire minister's first instinct was to stand by his words and refuse to apologize or withdraw. "Cockahoop!" he chirped, in the dialect of his county when asked by a British newspaper correspondent if he had any statement to make in comment on the French protest. "Tell them in England that the British delegation feels cockahoop!"

But the next morning wiser and more generous feelings had prevailed. The Chancellor rose at the conference table and said that he had at no time wished to cast any reflections on the personal character of the French Minister of Finance. The portly M. Chéron, much touched, came round the table and shook hands effusively with his colleague. "At one moment I thought he was going to kiss me!" said Snowden afterwards. The incident ended in mutual expressions of goodwill. But for a moment it threatened to bring the conference to a premature and disastrous end.

§ 4

Three men saw in it an ill omen: Arthur Henderson, Briand and Stresemann. To the last-named it was the first of a series of calamities. He had come to The Hague with the double objective of securing agreement to the Young Plan, which placed Germany's reparations debt henceforth on a commercial instead of a political footing, and of negotiating the withdrawal of the Allied troops from the Rhineland. Of the two the latter goal was naturally of greater importance in his eyes. His health was failing rapidly. He wished to go to his grave with the acclamation of "Liberator!" ringing in his dying ears. More than ever he played with time a losing instead of a winning hand. The disputes between France and Great Britain, and later between Great Britain and Italy, over the division of the spoils to be wrung from Germany disgusted and exasperated him. He felt that the fate of Europe was being jeopardized for the sake of a few millions sterling. It may be that in his heart he knew even then that the millions were paper millions, that they would never be forthcoming. All the more secret reason for his exasperation, his indignation, his despair. He had gambled everything on the promised evacuation of the Rhineland. And now it was endangered by a dispute between the ex-Allies over the revision of the Spa percentages. Henderson, the chairman of the political commission at The Hague, told him tranquilly to have patience. Briand shrugged his shoulders, made a vague gesture with his eloquent hands, but evaded any direct response. Nothing could be decided regarding the date of the evacuation until the financial commission of the conference had reached agreement.

The deadlock lasted a week, two weeks. In the end Stresemann could wait no more. He wrote a letter to Briand, a letter full of bitterness, full of the reproaches unuttered since the beginning of the silence which had fallen over the proposals of Thoiry. In it he declared that he would hand in his resignation as Foreign Minister of the Reich if the withdrawal from the Rhineland were not settled at The Hague. Stresemann's letter produced the result that might have been foreseen. The leaders of the six delegations met at the Binnenhof once more, and the German minister addressed them. It was agreed to make one last attempt to reach a settlement. All parties were now in more conciliatory mood, and with the aid of the Belgian Premier, M. Jaspar, as mediator a compromise was found which gave the inexorable British Chancellor over 80 per cent. of his demands, and left the French share practically intact.

The settlement was a miracle of manipulation. Some of the benefits accruing to Great Britain under the new proposals would doubtless have proved illusory, even if they had been paid. But in the end the entire settlement proved the sheerest illusion. It was swept away in the Hoover moratorium, the financial crash of 1929 and 1930, and any political advantages that might have been gained by Europe as a result of the Rhineland evacuation and the Franco-German reconciliation based thereon were lost by the death of Stresemann and the rise of Hitler.

§ 5

For Stresemann did not long survive the victory of his efforts to free the Rhine. He went from The Hague to Geneva for the 1929 Assembly of the League. He appeared at the tribune of the Assembly like a man under sentence of death. His robust frame had collapsed, his eyes were two tragic holes in a livid face, his clothes fell in folds over the shrunken limbs. He began in a faltering voice to read from a manuscript, as was his custom in Geneva. He spoke without emotion of The Hague, of the Saar, of the question of minorities. Then, in a gesture of dissatisfaction and weariness, he thrust the manuscript aside and spoke directly to the Assembly. He mentioned Briand's project of the European Union. He uttered for the first time publicly the questions which had long been troubling him privately concerning the mission of the League. He warned the Assembly that if the League did not show itself energetic and audacious enough, it was doomed to extinction. The nations would return to the old methods of direct diplomacy. He expressed the doubts which many people entertained as to the League's progress, its real share in the degree of international co-operation already attained, the strength of its roots in the affection and confidence of the nations.

Finally he approached a subject which was of particular importance to Germany and to Europe in general: the political education of youth. The real reason for the unrest of the world, he urged, was to be found in the absence of any idealism, any readiness for self-sacrifice. "We would willingly believe, and we are glad to believe, that heroism is undying, that men will always be found willing to die for a great ideal. Nevertheless a warning must be uttered to those who still live in the memory of military heroism shown during past centuries by the youth of all nations. The technique of modern warfare will in future leave less and less room for individual heroism. . . . It seems to me that in the vast field still open to the victories of mankind over nature there are great enough opportunities for heroism, and even for the laying down of lives for a great idea. It is in that field, in the passionate researches of man into the secrets of his own relations with the universe, that men should seek to serve the cause of humanity."

It was Stresemann's last speech at Geneva, his last utterance to the world. He returned to Germany to find that instead of the acclamation of Liberator he was received with the epithet of Traitor. His own party, his immediate colleagues, were the first to denounce him. The Nationalists of Hugenberg had redoubled their attacks. The National Socialists of Hitler were preparing for the conquest of that generation of youth whose power Stresemann had so clearly seen. He rose from his bed once more to confute the adversaries in his own party who demanded the rejection of the Young Plan, and thereby threatened the entire structure of The Hague settlement, with its liberation of the Rhine from Allied occupation. He succeeded in silencing, if not in convincing them. He returned to his home to die. When the delegations returned to The Hague in the following month of January to record their agreement and to sign the charter of the International Bank of Settlements, Stresemann's seat was occupied by another. And within seven years all the principal characters in the drama of The Hague—Briand, Snowden, Henderson, Stresemann, Chéron, Loucheur—were to be united in the common fate.

§ 6

In spite of the undoubted sincerity of the feelings of friendship and admiration he had for Briand, Stresemann left memories in France not entirely free from bitterness and disillusionment. After his death his correspondence was published. A letter written to the Crown Prince after Locarno seemed to show a certain duplicity of character. It was written probably in the hope of conciliating the parties of the right, on which the Crown Prince had a certain influence: it was cited by the French Nationalists to support their own charge that Briand had all along been the dupe of Germany. But Briand himself uttered no word of reproach or of criticism against the memory of his colleague. He had warned Stresemann, on the day after the conversation of Thoiry, against building too great hopes on so uncertain and fluid a thing as public opinion in France and Germany. Hearing that the German minister, in great excitement, had revealed to a large crowd of newspaper men at Geneva a good deal of the substance of their inn-table discussion, Briand had adjured him to show more moderation. "Do not get so excited, my dear Stresemann!

Politics is not a cinema." His own profound mistake in dealing with Stresemann had been to credit him with the ironic philosophy, the sense of history, the passion for logic, which he himself possessed to a profound degree, qualities not uncommon in France, and almost totally unknown in Germany. Himself almost deficient in vanity, he had failed to become aware of the vanity of Stresemann. Equally he had not realized the dominant note played by emotion, sentiment, prestige and romanticism in the formation of German character and German history.

But if he had failed thus to appreciate all the difficulties surrounding Stresemann, he knew from the beginning that their political fate was the same. They would each know popularity and hatred, the effusiveness and the treachery of false friends, the exaltation of success and celebrity, and the silence and oblivion of the tomb. In France at least an attempt is being made, after years of neglect, to do honor to the memory of Briand. A statue to the greatest of parliamentary figures of this century and the greatest of French foreign ministers since Talleyrand has been unveiled outside the Foreign Ministry on the Quai d'Orsay. But in Nazi Germany, Stresemann's tomb is despised and neglected, and courageous would be the German who now proposed in public to celebrate the memory of the man who died at the moment he had secured the withdrawal of the last foreign soldier from German soil.

Chapter XVII

THE MARTYR: ARTHUR HENDERSON

§ 1

THE year 1929, which was the last year of prosperity before the world economic collapse, was also the last year in which the illusion of world peace persisted. Its summer had seen agreement reached after many disputes at The Hague, had recorded a promise that the last British soldier on the Rhine should be "at home by Christmas," and the last Frenchman withdrawn not many months later, and the political debt of Germany to the Allied governments, which had hung like a millstone around the neck of Europe since 1919, transformed by the Young Plan into a commercial debt which optimists believed would not unduly incommode Germany in the years to come. One of the major artisans in this important work of conciliation and of construction was the Socialist Foreign Secretary of Great Britain, the Right Honourable Arthur Henderson, M.P., who arrived at Geneva from The Hague with his Prime Minister's telegram of felicitations in his pocket, a telegram phrased more frigidly than the effusive message which had rewarded Snowden's bellicose attitude at that conference, but, nevertheless, one which must have cost Mr. MacDonald some degree of embarrassment.

Henderson took his duties as Foreign Secretary with the earnestness, patience and conscientiousness with which he did everything. He had not been Mr. MacDonald's own choice for that office. When it was made clear to him that his own party, in addition to the duties of Leader of the House of Commons, would scarcely permit him to double the posts of Prime Minister and Foreign Secretary, as he had done in 1924, Mr. MacDonald had decided to offer the post to Mr. J. H. Thomas, his closest intimate among the senior members of the Labour party and Trade Union coalition which had triumphed at the elections of 1929. But the parliamentary Labour party, and with it some of Mr. Thomas's own colleagues on the General Council of the Trade Union Congress, objected to the choice. It was represented to the prospective Prime Minister that the second most important office in a Socialist government fell by right to the man who after Mr. MacDonald himself was the natural leader of the Labour party, its secretary, organizer and most influential personality, the calm, stolid, Wesleyan Methodist Arthur Henderson. And Henderson himself supported these representations by one of his rare acts of self-assertion. He intimated to Mr. MacDonald in his bluntest north-country fashion that he intended to go to the Foreign Office. And for once Mr. MacDonald sacrificed his own personal inclinations and yielded to the inevitable.

§ 2

There was a silent feud of long standing between the two men. In the early years of their association in the Labour party there might have been active rivalry, if Henderson had not been aware of his own limitations as parliamentary leader, and not been equally aware of the platform graces, the good looks, the silver voice which were

MacDonald's greatest asset, and would undoubtedly prove equally valuable to the rising Labour party. In 1924, when the first Labour government had been defeated largely owing to the blunders of Mr. MacDonald, and the greatly depleted rank and file of the parliamentary Labour group clamored for a new leader, it was Henderson's vigorous refusal of the office, and his equally vigorous support of the defeated ex-Premier, which secured Mr. MacDonald's re-election to the leadership. Nevertheless, the knowledge of his old colleague's loyalty and self-abnegation did nothing to increase Mr. MacDonald's opinion of Henderson. On the contrary, it seemed to embitter his feelings towards him, to sharpen the tone of disdainful condescension in which he invariably spoke of the secretary of the Labour party to his familiars. When the former iron-molder of Newcastle-on-Tyne entered the gloomy portals of the building in which Palmerston, Salisbury, Sir Edward Grey, Lord Curzon, and Ramsay MacDonald himself had directed British foreign policy, it was to encounter a steady stream of criticism, disparagement and, what was far more galling to the new Foreign Secretary, of contemptuous indifference from No. 10 Downing Street.

A man with less courage, or less public spirit than Arthur Henderson might have succumbed under the strain. A man of less shrewdness might have been outmaneuvered. But the iron-molder had not only a strong streak of native obstinacy, but also an equal streak of shrewdness. When General Dawes was appointed American Ambassador to the Court of St. James, the House of Commons was not sitting. The Prime Minister was at Lossiemouth. The King was at Windsor. While still on the high seas the new ambassador received an urgent message from Mr. Mac-

Donald inviting him to visit him at Lossiemouth immediately after his arrival. The slight to the Foreign Secretary was as obvious as the desire of the Prime Minister to keep the conversations with America in his own hands. But the Foreign Office had a card up its sleeve. If the Foreign Secretary might be ignored, the King could not. The new ambassador had not yet presented his credentials. Before General Dawes left for Lossiemouth, therefore, Mr. Henderson had the satisfaction of escorting him to Windsor for presentation to the King. His visit to Lossiemouth was accordingly delayed by a day.

At The Hague, Henderson suffered the spectacle of the embarrassing and potentially perilous pugnacity of his colleague Philip Snowden with the same long-suffering equanimity which he had long displayed towards the scarcely concealed dislike of the Prime Minister. His own share in the negotiations was confined to the political side: the evacuation of the Rhineland. On the financial side he had no authority, except as a Cabinet colleague of the Chancellor of the Exchequer, sharing with him the collective responsibility of the British government for the policy to be followed at The Hague. Even if he had wished to express an opinion at certain stages of the financial negotiations, his belligerent colleague left him little opportunity of doing so. There was little community of feeling or of policy between the Treasury and the Foreign Office sections of the British delegation. The Treasury had an old bone to pick with France, as indeed with each of the former Allies, and it cordially endorsed its temporary chief's animadversions against France and Italy. At the height of the crisis, when Snowden's refusal to accept the share of German reparations allocated to Great Britain

HENDERSON

under the Young Plan seemed to other delegations to be inspired by the secret desire to wreck the Plan entirely, and no way seemed open out of the deadlock produced by such intransigence, Henderson sat gloomily day after day in his sitting-room in the hotel at Scheveningen, while farther along the same corridor his little Yorkshire colleague looked happily and belligerently out of another sitting-room at the North Sea, whose waters were no grayer and more steadfast than his own eyes.

It seemed to be written in Arthur Henderson's destiny that he should be repeatedly ignored and neglected by his colleagues. He had been "left on the doormat" by Lloyd George in 1917, on his return from Russia, to which country he had gone with Sir George Buchanan's recall in his pocket, and with it the letters of his own appointment as British Ambassador Extraordinary in Petrograd. He had been relegated to the Home Office, a post of only secondary importance in the first Labour government in 1924. He had only secured a portfolio in the second Labour government proportionate to his seniority and services by the blunt intimation that he would refuse any other office. He had been consistently ignored by Mr. MacDonald since he went to the Foreign Office. He was ignored by his colleague Snowden at The Hague. And in 1933, towards the end of his career, when he labored courageously and vainly in Geneva as President of the Disarmament Conference, his former chief and colleague MacDonald was to negotiate the return of Germany to that Conference in open and contemptuous disregard of the courtesy due to its president.

§ 3

Nevertheless, in Geneva, in the autumn of 1929, his skies seemed for once favorable. The Hague Conference had ended happily, despite his forebodings. If he was ill-appreciated by two of his Cabinet colleagues, he had the affection and the respect of the majority of them. And by the statesmen of the Continent of Europe he was liked and esteemed. Briand referred to him as "L'Oncle Arthur." Stresemann had faith in his honesty. The foreign ministers of the little nations saw in him a typical representative of England, blunt, rugged, honest, unimaginative and courageous. At Geneva he moved in an atmosphere familiar to him, an atmosphere of almost religious fervor, recalling that of the Nonconformist chapels and assemblies in which he had been reared.

As much as Ramsay MacDonald distrusted and disliked Geneva, Arthur Henderson liked it, and for much the same reasons: the dull, comfortable hotels, the white boats on the lake, the simplicity of a small town with a carnival air in summer, the old ladies, the lack of social pretense, the democratic character of the League and its conversations in committee rooms and hotel lobbies. In his Victorian sitting-room at the Hôtel Beau-Rivage, surrounded by anti-macassars and potted palms and lace curtains, and with glimpses of the blue lake to be had through the windows, Arthur Henderson looked and felt as one of Queen Victoria's ministers might have looked and felt, representing in a foreign capital the might, the wisdom and the disinterestedness of England. He received the deferential visits of the statesmen of the little states without any airs of condescension, talked to them simply and bluntly, gave them advice which was at times astonishingly subtle and astonishingly shrewd, and never left them under the slightest misapprehension as to the attitude of Great Britain as far as they were concerned. The result was that whereas MacDonald's greater suppleness in negotiations, greater charm in conversation, produced only mistrust, dislike and often sarcasm, the blunt, inelegant iron-molder from Newcastle won for himself respect and at last genuine affection.

His successful years at Geneva were 1929 and 1930. His first visit to that town as a British minister, in 1924, when he was Home Secretary in the first Labour government, had been overshadowed by the presence of Mr. MacDonald, and its memory clouded by the subsequent collapse of the Protocol. But now, five years later, he had emerged triumphantly from a difficult negotiation at The Hague. He represented a government which seemed assured of several years in office. Great Britain had abandoned its first attitude of indifference, and its second attitude of conditional patronage, for a policy of vigorous partisanship of the League. On all the League committees, on the Council, in the Assembly itself, hitherto the spiritual domain of the little nations, the British government, with Henderson as its spokesman, employed for the first time a policy of vigorous and generous initiative.

Yet the most lasting memory of this plain and blunt iron-molder's activities at Geneva is of the tragic years from 1932 to his death. He had left Geneva as His Majesty's principal Secretary of State for Foreign Affairs. He returned to it a man without office in England, without a seat in Parliament, broken in health, disillusioned by the collapse of the second Labour government, the secession of MacDonald, Thomas and Snowden, and the overwhelming victory of the National Coalition, and hurt more than anything else perhaps by his own defeat at the polls, followed in rapid succession by the crushing defeats of his two sons—a cataclysm made possible only by the bitter election broadcasts of his erstwhile colleague Philip Snowden. He returned to Geneva clinging to one hope which he had salved from the wreckage of his party and his own political career in England—the hope of achieving some general limitation of armaments, if not actual disarmament, as the result of the conference finally convened by the League in February, 1932. For that reason, if for no other, he had obstinately insisted, in spite of British government pressure, on his right to retain the office of President of the Disarmament Conference to which he had been nominated by the League Council in his last year in Downing Street.

§ 4

The Disarmament Conference was assembled in order to give meaning to Article 8 of the League Covenant, in which "the Members of the League recognize that the maintenance of peace requires the reduction of national armament to the lowest point consistent with national safety and the enforcement by common action of international obligations." So far as those members of the League who were also signatories of the Treaty of Versailles were concerned, the Conference was also to fulfil that implied pledge in the preamble to Part V of the Treaty, which dealt with the military, naval and air disarmament of Germany, a preamble from which Germany had long extracted the utmost propaganda value, and which read: "*In order to render possible the initiation of general limitation of the armaments of all nations, Germany under-*

takes strictly to observe the military, naval and air clauses which follow."

The Conference opened in February, 1932, at the Bâtiment Electoral, a building in which the elections of the canton of Geneva are held, and which from 1930 onwards had been the scene of the Assembly of the League of Nations and the International Labor Conference, pending the completion of the new Palace of Nations in the Parc Ariana. For the first few days of the Disarmament Conference its President, looking down on a rare assembly of the world's statesmen from the height of his tribune, might well have shared the illusions which beset President Wilson on his arrival in Europe in 1919. The same glittering array of morning coats, the same high promises, the same fair speeches, the same earnest atmosphere of idealism and co-operation. The veteran Henderson knew a temporary reinvigoration. He looked in better health and better spirits. He was very changed from the depressed, beaten man he had been on the night of the victory of the National government, and very different from the thin, yellow-eyed, ashen-cheeked man who was to pace the lobbies of the new Disarmament building in 1934 and 1935, desperately clinging to a vain hope of agreement, grimly haunting the foreign offices of Europe so long as a chance remained of a disarmament convention which would banish or arrest the specter of war.

During the three years of his presidency he was to see all his hopes destroyed. He was to witness the secret and finally the public rearmament of Germany, her first and second withdrawal from the Disarmament Conference, and the collapse in rapid succession of the British Disarmament plan and the Four-Power Pact. Twice he was to be publicly slighted by his former Prime Minister and colleague. The first occasion was that of the much-advertised negotiations by which Mr. MacDonald brought back Germany to the Disarmament Conference in triumph. The second was that of the sudden production of the MacDonald plan for the limitation of armaments, a plan which, as its reputed author somewhat naïvely announced to a stupefied conference, had the unique advantage of containing figures; an advantage which did not, however, prevent its rejection along with many other plans without figures. On neither occasion was the President of the Conference either consulted or informed concerning the intentions of the British government, although he finally secured a public pledge from Sir John Simon that in any future informal meetings between the Great Powers on disarmament questions the President would be invited to attend as an observer.

Towards the end of the Conference the gravity of its President's condition was patent to all. Once he fainted in a meeting of the Standing Committee. His health seemed to reflect the growing seriousness of the international situation. Blow after blow fell, and left his hopes of an agreement in ruins, but after each onslaught he raised his head gallantly above the débris of his ambitions and refused to give up the battle. When the German government suddenly decided to withdraw from the Conference for the second time, he drafted a telegram of reply to Baron von Neurath regretting that "this grave decision should be taken by your government for reasons which I am unable to accept as valid."

Protests arose from some of the delegates who felt that they should have been consulted before the reply was drafted. General Tanojos, the representative of Hungary, then one of the disarmed nations, objected to its terms. The President abruptly silenced him with the words: "You are aware of the facts." M. Dovgaleski, the then Soviet Ambassador in Paris, declared that his government could not accept the reply proposed by Mr. Henderson, because it contained certain references to the negotiations with Germany which had taken place outside the Conference. Soviet Russia would agree to the telegram being signed by Mr. Henderson, but not to its being sent in the name of the Conference.

Henderson was now thoroughly angry, and showed it. He said bluntly that the conversations and negotiations had been authorized by the General Commission during the previous summer, when he had adjourned the proceedings for three months to permit of them, and that at that time the Soviet government had made no objection. Count Raczynski, the Polish delegate, supported the objection of M. Dovgaleski and was snubbed with the retort that Poland had also been a member of the committee which authorized the conversations. The Turkish delegate, Husnu Bey, was about to add his own protest to the others when the President impatiently struck the table with his presidential gavel. "If there are no further objections the telegram will be sent forthwith." There was a general murmur of astonishment, and some embarrassed laughter, but no further opposition. Henderson then rose and dismissed the meeting with the words: "The General Commission stands adjourned until 26th October. I hope that all Governments will return their delegates to Geneva with instructions to conclude a Convention as soon as possible."

§ 5

In this characteristic fashion "Uncle Arthur" treated the departure of Germany. He refused to be drawn from the straight and narrow path he had marked out for himself by constraint, intimidation or coercion. With or without Germany he was determined to go on with the negotiation of a disarmament convention. When the General Commission reassembled he said publicly: "I am heartened that no single Power has yet expressed its opinion that the Conference should come to an end. In fact, many Powers are desirous that we should continue our work without intermission." Yet the next day, paradoxically enough, he adjourned the General Commission until December 4. But to all the delegates it was evident that the Disarmament Conference without Germany was like *Hamlet* without the Prince of Denmark. Mussolini announced that henceforth the Italian representatives would be present as "observers" only. The Japanese participation had already become purely formal. The Stavisky scandal broke out in France, the Daladier government was overthrown, and its successor, the Doumergue Cabinet, decided to be represented at Geneva only by a permanent official of the Quai d'Orsay, M. Massigli. Another blow was struck at the conference by the sudden decision of Mr. Norman Davis, Mr. Roosevelt's ambassador-at-large, to return to America. And soon after Hungary followed Italy in deciding to maintain her representative at Geneva in the quality of observer only.

Still Henderson refused to give up the battle. When the Conference had been reduced to a mere shadow of its former self, he might be seen pacing the empty lobbies of the disarmament building like a captain pacing the bridge of an all but abandoned ship. His once sturdy frame had fallen away. His clothes hung upon him loosely. His face was ashen. His always deep-sunk eyes were sunken even more deeply in their sockets. He made one last assertion of his dignity and his will to dominate the calamity which seemed imminent. He threatened to resign if the governments did not take a more active interest in the proceedings and send ministers instead of permanent officials to represent them at Geneva. There was a sudden flurry of excitement in response. An apparently rejuvenated Henderson again gazed down in satisfaction at a distinguished gathering, which included Sir John Simon and Mr. Anthony Eden as representatives of Great Britain. M. Barthou, the new French Foreign Minister, the Soviet Commissar Maxim Litvinoff, M. Titulescu of Roumania, Colonel Beck of Poland, M. Politis of Greece and Dr. Benes of Czechoslovakia. At the last moment, and unexpectedly, Mr. Norman Davis returned from Washington to add wisdom, sound sense and quiet humor to the proceedings.

§ 6

But it was the last flicker of life in a dying patient. M. Barthou and Sir John Simon exchanged diplomatic amenities, in the course of which the French Foreign Minister, a glittering ornament of the Académie Française, caused some astonishment and embarrassment by referring to the British Foreign Secretary as his "almost friend." M. Litvinoff made a long rhetorical appeal for total disarmament. Committees were created to examine the questions of traffic in arms, air disarmament, security and guarantees of execution—committees which are still in existence. But gradually the principal delegates departed again. Sir John Simon left Mr. Eden, the future Foreign Secretary, in charge of British interests. M. Barthou left for Paris, and Paris for Marseilles, where he died with King Alexander of Jugoslavia under the assassin's pistol. Mr. Davis made a speech expressing America's alarm at the return to the pre-war policy of the alignment of powers in alliances and counter-alliances, and also departed from Geneva. Finally, the President of the Disarmament Conference followed them.

He returned to Geneva no more. After his election as member for Clay Cross in 1933 he took his seat in the House of Commons. He made an occasional intervention in the debates in the House. And then his appearances at Westminster became more and more rare. His health failed steadily, hastened in its decline by the doom of his hopes of disarmament. The knowledge that the defeat his party had suffered in 1931 was only temporary, that Labour would probably recover all and more than its losses at the next elections, seemed powerless to aid him at this last and gravest time of crisis.

As he approached his end, he, who all his life had been a man of party, its creator and its servant, seemed to have put party interests behind him. He had a larger view of the world, and the destruction of his hopes for the world he was leaving far overshadowed any disillusionments or belated satisfactions he might feel regarding the destinies of the British Labour party. In his last days the insular iron-molder of the North, the sturdiest and least imaginative of Britons, long separated by barriers of language and caste and class and culture from other nations and races, had become truly an internationalist, a very worthy citizen of the world. And the world, undisarmed and rapidly rearming although it was, mourned him without reserve on that October day in 1935 when death claimed him at last.

Chapter XVIII

THE REVOLUTIONARY: LITVINOFF

§ 1

MAXIM LITVINOFF is, with Lloyd George, one of the few survivors of one of the most spectacular conferences of the post-war era, and one unique in the sinister fate which rapidly overtook many of its leading characters. Of the statesmen and diplomats assembled at Genoa in the spring of 1922 no fewer than four died at the hands of assassins: the Bulgarian Premier, Stambulisky; the Russian Ambassador, Forowsky; the German Foreign Minister, Rathenau; the French Foreign Minister, Barthou. One committed suicide—the Soviet Ambassador to Japan, Joffe. One was to spend long years in exile—the former Soviet Ambassador to Paris and London, Christian Rakowsky. Four were to die prematurely, two of them at least disillusioned and broken-hearted—the Russians Tchicherin and Krassin; the German Ambassador, Maltzahn; the Italian ex-Premier, Facta. Of all the various delegates at Genoa, Litvinoff's career is unique in that it has shown since 1922 an almost uninterrupted series of successes.

The present Soviet Commissar for Foreign Affairs made his first appearance in Geneva in 1927, as leader of the Soviet delegation to the Preparatory Committee for the Disarmament Conference. He was then deputy People's Commissar for Foreign Affairs. He had not yet succeeded the late George Tchicherin as the head of the Moscow Foreign Office. He had made four previous incursions into Western European diplomacy. The first, of brief duration, was his period as Soviet Russia's first Ambassador to England, an embassy which ended after the murder of Captain Cromie in Petrograd in the arrest of Trotsky's Ambassador and his removal to Brixton Prison. The second was his successful negotiation with Sir James O'Grady in Stockholm of the exchange of British and Russian prisoners of war. The third was as member of the Soviet delegation to the Genoa Conference in 1922. The fourth was as chairman of the Soviet delegation to the now generally forgotten conference held at The Hague later in the same year. But until 1927 he was an unfamiliar figure in Western Europe. At Genoa he had been chiefly engaged in the negotiations with Germany which resulted in the signature of the Rapallo Treaty. Subsequently he had been a frequent visitor to Berlin. No foreign observer knew Republican Germany better. None better understands the motives, the secret difficulties, the psychology of Hitler's Third Reich.

§ 2

Maxim Maximovitch Litvinoff was born in Russia, at Bielostock, in 1876. His parents were Jews. His ancestral name, as the anti-Soviet press loves to recall, was not Litvinoff. Like that of many other Russian revolutionists, his name was almost literally a *nom de guerre*, and like theirs was taken from Russian literature. His self-chosen homonym was a famous character of Turgenieff. He was educated at a Russian *gymnasie* or secondary school. He did his military service in the army of the Tsar. In 1898, at the age of twenty-two, he joined the Social Democratic party, was frequently denounced to the police, and in 1901 was imprisoned in Kiev for running a secret printing press. Two years later he escaped. When the Social Democratic party split in 1903 he followed Lenin into the Bolshevik camp. He helped to create, in St. Petersburg, the famous Bolshevik newspaper *Novaya Zhizn* (*New Life*) under Lenin's editorship. In 1907 he was again denounced to the police, and left Russia to find refuge in England.

During the next ten years he lived in London, earning a modest living as a ledger clerk in a London bookselling firm, and during the war giving lessons in Russian to, among others, Mr. Rex Leeper of the British Foreign Office. He wrote regularly for the *Novaya Zhizn* and for the other Bolshevik party organ, *Pravda*, was a member of the executive committee of the party, and a delegate to several international socialist congresses, at Stuttgart, Brussels and other places. In March, 1918, Trotsky, the first People's Commissar for Foreign Affairs of Bolshevik Russia, appointed him Ambassador to the Court of St. James. The official Russian embassy at Chesham House had refused to acknowledge the Revolution of October. Litvinoff established his modest embassy in two rooms in Victoria Street. A few months later, after the murder of the British naval attaché in Petrograd, the police raided Litvinoff's offices and arrested the Ambassador.

On his release and deportation to Russia he was fêted as the first victim of the capitalist world's rancor against the new Soviet state. He was appointed a member of the Collegium of Foreign Affairs, and Assistant Commissar under Tchicherin at the Moscow Foreign Office. Later he was elected to the central executive committee of the Soviet Union. At Genoa, where he appeared in April, 1922, as member of a brilliant and picturesque delegation which included the ex-aristocrat Tchicherin, the ex-engineer of the Siemens-Schuckert electrical firm, Nicolai Krassin, the ex-Doctor of Medicine of Montpellier University, Christian Rakowsky, the ex-inmate of Siberian jails and future Ambassador to Japan, Joffe, the Polish philosopher and future victim of assassination, Vorowsky, and the rich, Rabelaisian, stout, black-whiskered Georgian, Mdivani, known familiarly to his colleagues as the Oil King, Litvinoff remained in the background. But he was far from remaining inactive. He spoke German fluently, and was in daily contact with Walther Rathenau, the ill-fated German Foreign Minister, shortly to be murdered by German nationalists, and with Dr. Maltzahn, then the chief permanent official of the Wilhelmstrasse, also destined to die prematurely. Visitors to the Russian delegation's headquarters at the Hôtel de Genes and at Santa Marguerita found him modest, unassuming and reserved, if given to occasional excursions in sardonic humor.

On the day of the signature of the Rapallo Treaty, Rathenau was in despair, and Litvinoff was in raptures. The German Minister had signed the treaty more as an act of defiance and disillusionment than as a deliberate act of policy, undertaken after long reflection. The draft of the treaty had been discussed for months past, and the Germans had repeatedly postponed the day of signature. To the last Rathenau had counted on a gesture of conciliation or a promise of British support from Lloyd George, which would have enabled him to dispense with a collaboration he secretly felt to be both humiliating and dangerous. But the British Prime Minister had remained deaf to all his appeals. France was represented by Louis Barthou—another of the singular Genoa series of statesmen foredoomed to assassination. In Paris M. Poincaré reigned at the Quai d'Orsay, and despatched telegrams almost every hour to his lieutenant in Genoa warning him to remain intransigent to either German or Russian demands. The Ruhr occupation was already threatened. Nervously, unhappily, in desperation, the German Foreign Minister turned to the only quarter which offered friendship and support, his fellow outcasts, the hated, feared and unregenerate representatives of the Soviets.

It was a fatal decision for Germany. Soviet Russia, if, as it proved, she gained nothing by the Rapallo Treaty, had at least nothing to lose. But the treaty, and especially the circumstances of secrecy in which it was signed, gave the French delegate the pretext he sought for denouncing the bad faith of Germany, gave the British Prime Minister an opportunity of casting the responsibility for the failure of the Conference on other shoulders and provided M. Poincaré with yet another justification for the march into the Ruhr. Disastrous to Germany, the treaty also proved Rathenau's death-warrant. He was assassinated a few months later, and his murderers, although known, were never brought to trial. It was the first of the many criminal weaknesses of the German republic by which Hitler was later to profit.

§ 3

In 1927, when Litvinoff came to Geneva as the chief representative of the Soviet Union on the preparatory committee for the Disarmament Conference—the first time the U.S.S.R. had received or had accepted an invitation to attend a meeting organized by the League of Nations—he created a world sensation by proposing the total abolition

LITVINOFF

of all armies, navies and air forces, all armaments, fortresses, war bases, munition factories, war offices and general staffs. The speech in which this policy of the U.S.S.R. was solemnly outlined was regarded by the French, British and other delegates at Geneva as an attempt to bring the proceedings under ridicule. But a few days later, when it was seen that the proposals had been made in all seriousness and had attracted a considerable amount of attention and sympathy in America and other countries, the Preparatory Committee began to show Litvinoff more respect. The incident of his unexpected meeting with Sir Austen Chamberlain, described in an earlier chapter, also added to his new prestige.

The laurels carried off by the Soviet delegation from this first appearance at Geneva were enhanced, moreover, by the wit and culture of Litvinoff's colleague, Anatoly Lunacharsky, the Soviet Commissar for Education. Lunacharsky had lived in his days of exile in France, spoke French perfectly, and could cite Descartes, Pascal, Montaigne and Voltaire with the most scholarly members of the French delegation. In his first speech at the meetings of the Preparatory Committee he rallied the French delegate Paul-Boncour on the illogic of the proposals of the country which had produced Descartes. Paul-Boncour replied in kind, but less effectively, and the members of the Committee regarded the spectacled and mild-mannered Lunacharsky with a new respect. But the greatest impression created by the Soviet delegation at Geneva in 1927 was due less to Litvinoff and Lunacharsky than to their talented wives. Madame Litvinoff was the former Ivy Low, a niece of the late Sir Sidney Low, affable, witty and attractive. She had married her husband during his last year of exile in London, had accompanied him to Russia, and had become the center of a little cultural colony in Moscow. Madame Lunacharsky was an actress for the cinema, well known in Berlin and Moscow, young, beautiful and elegant.

In Geneva, where the wives of visiting statesmen are usually plain and dowdy, and of an unpromising age, the youth and beauty of Madame Lunacharsky attracted attention. She wore, like Madame Litvinoff, furs which, banal and inexpensive and imperative in the bleak Russian winters, are rare enough to be worn only by the very rich in Western Europe. Unlike Madame Litvinoff, she wore rings with large amethysts and turquoises, stones which are also comparatively commonplace and inexpensive in Russia, but which in the eyes of European delegates, journalists and League secretaries gleamed with the insolence and the rarity of a maharajah's emeralds. Newspapers, already bored by the subject of disarmament, found the jewels of the Bolshevik's wife a more exciting topic. For some reason difficult to explain except on the ground that Russia is a semi-Oriental country, jewels have always been associated with the wives of high Russian personages, whether they be Tsars, grand dukes or commissars. The semi-precious stones in the rings of the cinema star became diamonds and emeralds. Several stenographers in the Soviet delegation whose necks were adorned with cheap strings of artificial pearls were credited with real pearl necklaces. In Geneva the glitter of the Soviet proposals for total disarmament was outshone by the gleam of Bolshevik furs and stones. But in the world outside, paradoxically enough, the mendacious and exaggerated reports of the Soviet ladies' luxury served to attract attention to the political activities of their respective husbands.

§ 4

In 1930, when Tchicherin's increasing ill-health made his retirement inevitable, Litvinoff succeeded him as principal Commissar for Foreign Affairs. Thereafter the foreign policy of the Soviet Union, which under Tchicherin's direction had reflected the somewhat timorous, petulant and suspicious character of Tchicherin himself, assumed an unexpected boldness and initiative. In 1932 Litvinoff brought before the Disarmament Conference his celebrated formula for the Definition of the Aggressor. In the following year, at the World Economic Conference in London, not only were they induced to adhere to his formula, but Roumania and the other states on Russia's western borders, hitherto suspicious of and even hostile to the Soviet Union, concluded pacts of non-aggression with their powerful neighbor. A few months later occurred the arrests and trial of the British engineers in Russia. It was the occasion of a celebrated verbal duel between Litvinoff and Sir Esmund Ovey, the British Ambassador in Moscow. When Sir Esmund, who had previously been British Minister to Mexico, heatedly demanded the release of the prisoners, Litvinoff retorted blandly: "You appear to think that you are still dealing with Mexicans!"

In 1934 the U.S.S.R., at Litvinoff's instigation, entered the League of Nations and acquired a seat on the Council and one of the permanent under-secretaryships. In the same year the long hostility of Czechoslovakia was overcome, and influenced partly by Russia's new orientation in European affairs, and her desire to ally herself to the Western democracies, partly by the threat of Hitler's Third Reich on her own borders, Czechoslovakia concluded a defensive treaty with the Soviet Union similar to that already in existence between the Soviet Union and France. But a diplomatic act of even greater importance than Russia's admission into the League was the negotiation in the same year by Litvinoff and President Roosevelt, with the assistance of Mr. William C. Bullitt, the present United States Ambassador to France, of America's recognition of the U.S.S.R.

Litvinoff has now become one of the elder statesmen of Geneva. He has already presided over sessions of the League Council. He will sooner or later be elected as President of the League Assembly. Inevitably he has become the spokesman of a group of states in Europe directly menaced by Nazi Germany or fundamentally opposed to the Nazi creed of racial inequality and German racial unity. Two years ago he enunciated the doctrine of "Peace Indivisible," a slogan which has since been adopted by France. And although his country has formidably rearmed since 1927, when he first proposed the total abolition of arms, he still periodically utters a plea for complete disarmament. "The Soviet Government," he said in Geneva in the summer of 1936, "has always considered, and continues to consider, total disarmament to be the maximum guarantee of peace. . . . I wish to believe that humanity will not have to go through yet another Armageddon before all the peoples come to this conclusion."

§ 5

The modest ledger clerk of the Hampstead garden suburb, the harassed revolutionary, the sometime inmate of the jails of Kiev and Brixton, has long since become familiar with the capitals of Europe and of the United States as the minister and envoy of a first-class power, the greatest Asiatic state, and the third greatest in the world. Much of the prestige of his name is due, perhaps, to the unique stability of the government of which he is a member, to the great military and aerial power, the potentially enormous economic power, of the Union of Socialist Soviet Republics for whose foreign policy he is responsible. But primarily his diplomatic successes are his own. He was not born to a career of diplomacy. He has had to overcome a good many natural disadvantages. He has never succeeded in speaking English or French without a strong and not very attractive accent.

His appearance is not prepossessing. He is short, stout, bald, with shrewd eyes behind thick spectacles. He has never acquired the verbal agility, the grace and the disarming smile which made his former colleague Rakowsky so brilliant and so popular an ambassador in Paris. His manner is at times abrupt and sarcastic to the point of insolence. His speech is direct, uncompromising and occasionally brutal. But his mind is keen and logical. He has proved himself of unshakable loyalty to his party, to his colleagues and to his word, once given. He is utterly without vanity. His success has not changed him. At Genoa, when he and his fellow-delegates were invited to an official reception, and the Bolsheviks found themselves obliged to put on the despised evening dress of the bourgeoisie (Moscow had at that time practically no diplomatic corps, and no formal evening functions), Litvinoff came into the Soviet delegation headquarters one day carrying a large brown-paper parcel full of stiff shirts and collars, and distributed them among his colleagues with a humorous grimace of disgust. Fourteen years later he represented his government at the funeral of George v, and subsequently had a long private audience of Edward viii. His impressions of that sovereign were indiscreetly published afterwards in a Russian newspaper. "I found him to be," said Litvinoff, "just the average English mediocrity who only reads one newspaper."

Chapter XIX

THE DICTATORS: PILSUDSKI AND
VOLDEMARAS

§ 1

THE sudden recrudescence of the long dispute between Poland and Lithuania in the autumn of 1927 brought two rival European dictators to the December Council of the League: Augustinas Voldemaras, the President-Dictator of Lithuania, and Josef Pilsudski, the creator and permanent dictator of modern Poland. The two men presented types in startling contrast. Voldemaras was small and dark, with a bullet head and hair which stood upright on it in stiff, black bristles. His face was a mottled red in color. His eyes were suspicious and bloodshot. He wore ill-cut black clothes and looked like a peasant at a funeral. He had seized power in Lithuania, had suspended constitutional liberties, and threatened incessantly to march on the ancient Lithuanian capital of Vilna, which the Poles had held despite all protests since General Zeligowski's *coup de main* in 1920.

Incongruous as was his appearance, unbridled his language, the career of Voldemaras had been of unexpectedly brilliant promise. He had graduated in classics and in philosophy, and had been a professor in Tsarist days at the University of St. Petersburg. He formed the first cabinet in an independent Lithuania in 1918, and in 1919 he led the Lithuanian delegation to the Peace Conference in Paris.

In 1920 he attended the first Assembly of the League of
Nations and solemnly shook hands with Paderewski in sign
of Polish-Lithuanian amity. A month later the Polish
general Zeligowski seized Vilna and the recovery of that
captured capital henceforth became the dominant passion
of the little Lithuanian's life. In 1922 he was appointed
Professor of History at the University of Kovno, and his
lectures were of so provocative and political a nature that
inevitably they created around him a students' nationalist
movement hostile to Poland. Four years later he was
elected to Parliament, and in the same year became Prime
Minister and Minister of Foreign Affairs, with dictatorial
powers. In his acts and speeches he anticipated the manner
of Hitler. He was a highly successful orator of the hysterical school. He enjoyed great popularity among students
and young workmen. His bellicose threats against Germany, which was disturbed by the oppression of the Germans in Memel, and against Poland, apprehensive of an attempt to recover Vilna, seemed likely in 1927 to lead to
an Eastern European war.

Voldemaras violently disliked the Socialists and Communists in his own country, and repressed their political
activities with ruthlessness. He made many enemies in
Lithuania as elsewhere. On a May evening in 1929, as he
and some friends were leaving their car to enter the doors
of the state theater in Kovno, seven shots were fired at him
from ambush. One of his companions was killed, and three
others wounded. Voldemaras was unhurt. In his feud
with Poland Voldemaras turned eagerly to Soviet Russia
as a powerful protector, and listened patiently, if with ill-
concealed resentment, to the counsels of caution which
Litvinoff gave him at Geneva. At the table of the League

Council, however, he threw restraint to the winds. He attacked the Poles in language so violent, and in a voice so shrill with anger, that the sympathy of the Council members went by a natural act of revulsion to the calm, elegant, polished Polish Foreign Minister Zaleski, who sat aloof and unmoved during the tirades of his adversary.

In the middle of this debate the news came that Pilsudski himself was on his way to Geneva, and the interest in the little Lithuanian dictator waned. Voldemaras was after all but a professor of history turned politician, in a League overflowing with other professors of history turned politicians. Pilsudski was a soldier, one of the few great martial figures of this century, and pacifist, orderly Geneva has always shown an almost feminine curiosity in the personalities of soldiers.

§ 2

Pilsudski arrived at Geneva quietly one morning: an unassuming old man of medium height, in a dark gray civilian suit and a felt hat. He had never been seen in Poland without uniform, even in his days of political retirement between 1920 and 1925. The world had imagined him in his marshal's cloak of greenish gray. Only when he removed the felt hat and one saw the high temples, bleak and square and chiseled as in granite, the fierce blue eye, the grizzled, drooping mustache, did the real Pilsudski become visible. He looked then like an old wolf of the Russian forests. The amiable Zaleski, trotting nervously behind him, had suddenly lost the look of faintly disdainful calm with which he faced the accusations of Voldemaras across the Council table. The old marshal had some quality in his gaze, in the squareness of that granite head, in the fierce Viking droop of the mustache, which made his lieutenants and ministers not only look like children but feel like children. He governed Poland with the aid of a group of young officers whom the wits of the opposition (those of them who were not in prison) contemptuously described as "the colonels." Colonel Joseph Beck, who succeeded Zaleski as Foreign Minister, and still occupies that office, was among them. The marshal's technique of dictatorship was based on two principles. One, borrowed from the Imperial House of Austria, was "Divide to Govern," which he applied with complete success. The other was "Govern by Others." He had neither title nor office as dictator. He was neither President of the Republic nor President of the Council of Ministers. In some years he was Minister of War. In others he was simply Inspector-General of the Army. But he, and he alone, chose President, Premier and Cabinet. The system worked so successfully, from the standpoint of the dictator, that since his death his successor as Inspector-General of the Army, Marshal Rydz-Smigly, has not only attempted to succeed to the political as well as to the military rôle of the great marshal, but has actually been invested with his rôle by President Moscicki, the nominal head of the Polish Republic.

Pilsudski began his political career as a revolutionary student in Russian Poland. He was a member of the celebrated anarchist and nihilist organization Bojowka, an association of terrorists which was nicknamed "le Club des Assassins" by its Social Democratic rivals. In his youth he showed extraordinary audacity, courage and resource. Among his early revolutionary exploits had been the hold-up and robbery of a Tsarist government train loaded with bullion. Many times condemned to imprisonment, and having as often escaped from Russian prisons, he had spent

PILSUDSKI

the years which immediately preceded the World War in German or in Austrian Poland. Soon after the outbreak of war the Tsar announced his intention of bestowing autonomy upon Poland, but Pilsudski's long experience of Russia, and an instinctive Russophobia which was to influence his policy until his death, inspired him to reject any policy of collaboration between the Poles and Russia. Instead he threw in his lot with Germany, organized a Polish legion and fought against Russia on the eastern front until 1917. Then, characteristically, he rebelled against Prussian arrogance and Prussian ambitions, and was arrested and imprisoned in the military fortress of Magdeburg.

At the Armistice he was released from prison, resumed command of his legion and immediately proclaimed the independence of the new Polish state. But his association with Germany during the war had made him suspect to the Allies. Poland was represented at the Peace Conference by Paderewski and Roman Dmowski, both hostile to Pilsudski. Like Foch in France, the Polish marshal was elbowed out of the post-war political discussions by the politicians. In 1920, however, when the ambition of the new state led it into the foolish expedition into the Ukraine, and Trotsky's Red Army retaliated by marching to the gates of Warsaw, Pilsudski vindicated himself as soldier and statesman by successfully organizing the defense of Poland and ejecting the Bolsheviks. Since then his prestige had been almost legendary. He had dismissed the quarreling *Sejm* by words and acts of a more than Cromwellian brusqueness. He had emerged from self-sought obscurity to overthrow his enemies, and he returned to it, in appearance at least, to watch over the security of the republic he had founded.

§ 3

In Geneva the old revolutionary, the former train-bandit, the warrior who had fought with Hindenburg at Tannenburg, reminded one of a wolf in a sheepfold. He had never visited Switzerland. He knew practically nothing of Western Europe and of the post-war world of political conferences. In the Hôtel des Bergues, dressed like a tourist, sitting at table with men in black coats and striped gray trousers, he looked strangely out of place. But it was his hosts, and not he, who seemed embarrassed at this incongruous encounter.

Briand gave a small luncheon-party in Pilsudski's honor in his private rooms on the floor below that occupied by the marshal. To it were invited the Polish Foreign Minister Zaleski; the British Foreign Secretary, Sir Austen Chamberlain; the Italian delegate Scialoja; and the German Foreign Minister, Gustav Stresemann. Stresemann had never met Pilsudski before, and having for long based a hope on Pilsudski's great authority for a satisfactory solution of the Polish Corridor problem, came to the party preoccupied by this secret anxiety, nervous, eager and ill at ease. To his surprise Pilsudski greeted him cordially in German, shook him warmly by the hand, threw himself back luxuriously in an armchair, crossed his legs and drew him immediately into conversation.

"Do you know Major Von P——?" he asked abruptly. "He is the man who arrested me and took me to Magdeburg."

Stresemann, taken aback by this embarrassing opening, and anxious to avoid all controversial subjects except the one which secretly occupied his mind, replied evasively.

But Pilsudski was now plunged in a full tide of reminiscence.

"He was a very good officer, full of talent, full of talent. . . . What has become of him?"

"I have not the slightest idea," said Stresemann, now thoroughly irritated.

The Polish marshal closed his eyes in happy retrospect. "It was a glorious army, the old army of Germany," he said, with emphasis, rolling his r's in German. "I have always had a great deal of respect for the German army."

The conversation between the Polish dictator and the German Foreign Minister had been followed by the other guests with curiosity and some anxiety. Stresemann's embarrassment was obvious to all. Briand, who did not understand a word of German, and feared the worst, walked nervously up and down the room with a half-smoked cigarette between his nicotine-stained fingers. Sir Austen Chamberlain, who knew German slightly, but had not understood the drift of the conversation, looked more and more solemn. The witty and cosmopolitan Scialoja alone followed the dialogue with a smile of ironic detachment.

Pilsudski, lost in his memories, wished to return to the exciting topic of his prison experiences. "When I was at Magdeburg . . ." he began. But then he looked up and saw the look of constraint and displeasure on the face of Stresemann. He laughed, a strange laugh that was more like a snarl, and said suddenly, "Do not think that I blame the Germans, Herr Minister. I always remember that they might have had me shot, and that in another country I should certainly not have escaped shooting." Stresemann looked relieved, and joined in the laughter.

But neither then nor thereafter did he broach the subject

of the Polish Corridor with Pilsudski. To Briand, who rallied him on his diffidence, he objected that he could not very well ask a man he met for the first time to surrender a portion of Polish territory. It was left to an adversary of Stresemann—the Nazi Chancellor Hitler—to conclude the first political understanding between Poland and Germany. But in the ten-year pact which Pilsudski's Ambassador signed in Berlin in January, 1933, the surrender was made not by Pilsudski but by Hitler. The pact amounted to a virtual renunciation by the Nazi dictator of all German efforts to regain the Corridor.

How far it affected Poland's existing alliance with France was not known to anybody but the Polish marshal himself, and the fate of that alliance is to this day uncertain, in spite of the cordial visit to Paris in September, 1936, by Pilsudski's successor, Rydz-Smigly, and his reassurances to the French Cabinet and General Staff. Pilsudski himself told the Soviet Ambassador in Warsaw that Poland would never be a party to a German attack on France or Russia. But his lifelong aversion to Russia, Tsarist or Bolshevik, and his professional admiration for the old German Army, indicate fairly conclusively the secret directives of his foreign policy, a policy which to this day is still powerful in Poland, and causes much secret anxiety to France and Czechoslovakia.

§ 4

Pilsudski's encounter with Voldemaras in Geneva took place on December 10, 1927. Voldemaras had invoked the assistance of the League on the ground that the occupation of Vilna constituted a danger to peace under Article 2 of the Covenant. The League Council had appointed the Dutch Foreign Minister, Jonkheer Beelaerts van Blokland, as *rapporteur* on the dispute between Poland and Lithuania, and the Council met in secret, with Voldemaras and Pilsudski as the only non-members present, to hear the Dutchman's report. Beelaerts van Blokland was reading a long draft resolution which he hoped might terminate the state of war existing between the two countries since Zeligowski's *coup de main* in 1920 when the Polish dictator suddenly interrupted him.

"I want to know," exclaimed Pilsudski, "whether we are going to have peace or war. If it is peace I shall telegraph to Warsaw for a Te Deum to be sung in all the churches and for the ringing of all the bells!"

The moment was dramatic. All eyes were turned to the table at which the red-faced, black-haired little Lithuanian professor sat, stiff and awkward in his black clothes. Voldemaras had at first some difficulty in speaking. Finally, he stammered, "Lithuania wants peace."

Both parties thereupon signed a declaration by which Pilsudski agreed to recognize the inviolability of Lithuanian territory, and Voldemaras agreed to end the virtual hostilities existing between the two countries. But the fate of Vilna remained undecided, the Poles refusing to recognize it as part of Lithuania, and the Lithuanians refusing to renounce their claim to it. The gesture, therefore, bore no fruit. In the following year, it is true, a frontier agreement was signed by the Lithuanian dictator and the Polish Foreign Minister Zaleski, remedying some of the more obvious disabilities of Lithuanian peasants with land on both sides of the disputed frontier. But no formal relations were resumed between the two governments, and the state of war, or rather of suspended hostilities, continues between them to this day.

§ 5

Paradoxically enough, Pilsudski was himself a Lithuanian, like the great Polish poet Mickiewicz. He was born near Vilna, on his family's estate at Zulow. He had inherited from his parents the pride, the capriciousness and also the characteristic physical appearance of the small Lithuanian noble. In 1900, when he was tried by a Russian court for revolutionary activities, he was asked by the judge why he, the scion of an old, noble and wealthy family, wished to overthrow the government and the established order. His answer was typical of the whole romantic generation to which Pilsudski belonged. "When the kings of Muscovy stood upon the bent necks of the boyars to mount their horses, my forefathers were already freemen. How, then, can you expect me not to fight for freemen today?"

For a Lithuanian, and a former revolutionary in Heine's "war of liberation of humanity," his part in the annexation of Vilna is still difficult to explain. Zeligowski seized the city in October, 1920, in flagrant violation not only of the Treaty of Suwalki signed by Poland and Lithuania two days earlier, but also of the Covenant of the newly created League of Nations. The Polish government promptly disowned Zeligowski's action as that of a rebel, but it made no attempt to surrender the captured city. The Conference of Ambassadors, on which France enjoyed a majority (thanks to her alliance with Belgium and her casting vote as chairman), in 1923 confirmed Poland in her possession of Vilna, and the League of Nations approved the decision. In the same year Pilsudski himself, in a moment of almost Mussolinian candor, publicly assumed responsibility for Zeligowski's act. In a speech at Vilna, on August 24, 1923, he said:

"It is so. I tore up the Suwalki Treaty, and afterwards I issued a false *communiqué* by the General Staff. Thus I prepared for General Zeligowski's campaign. It was done by myself. It was my order that led to the result."

In the previous year, on Pilsudski's temporary retirement from politics, he had made a secret confession of his responsibility for the Vilna *coup* to a few diplomats. The incident is described by the then Italian Minister in Warsaw, Francesco Tommasini, in his book, *La Risurrezione della Polonia* (Milan, 1925).

"On December 6, 1922" (wrote Signor Tommasini), "Pilsudski, when taking leave of the Diplomatic Corps, invited my colleagues the Ministers for South America, France, England and myself, to the Belvedere, being desirous of seeing us again. We were invited to go from the lower floor, where the official ceremony was held, to his private apartments on the upper floor, where he himself speedily arrived. In the meantime he had changed his marshal's uniform for the dress of a Polish legionary, and said: 'I wished to receive you in the dress in which you found me when you visited me for the first time, and I desire to talk to you in a friendly manner.'

"At first the conversation turned on Lloyd George's anti-Polish attitude in the summer of 1920, and in this connection Pilsudski, in his picturesque words, a little vague but charming, tendered a patriotic apology for his 'children' (*i.e.*, his legionaries). Subsequently, on rising, he stated that he had to report a certain confidential matter, begging us to promise to keep the secret, and strongly emphasizing the strictly impersonal character of his report, asked us to pass into his bedroom. When we were seated round the table, he stood in the middle of the room and said:

" 'Gentlemen, one day I had to tell you that General Zeligowski was disobedient to my orders and occupied Vilna. Now, when I have become a simple citizen, I feel it my duty to correct that statement and to relieve Zeligowski from all responsibility. *He acted according to my orders,* and also, having a loyal soldier's conscience, he could never have ventured on a formal act of rebellion. I had [he added ironically] a great deal of trouble before I could persuade him to dispense with my giving him instructions in writing to rebel.'

"While we showed great interest in this revelation, we did not conceal from him that it had not astonished us. I do not think that I shall be guilty of indiscretion in reporting that episode, because Pilsudski himself has already reported it in a public speech."

§ 6

The visit to Geneva in connection with the Lithuanian dispute was Pilsudski's first and last. He made no further political excursion from his own country. His rare journeys abroad were henceforth confined to recuperative trips to the Carpathians or the Adriatic. In Warsaw he stirred little from his house except to walk a few hundred yards each morning to his bleak office in the Inspectorate-General of the Army.

His last important intervention in foreign policy was to authorize the signature of the ten-year pact, already referred to, between his country and Germany, an act which signified at once Poland's self-liberation from the tutelage of France, and her desire to assure herself of peace on her western frontiers for some years to come. His last important conversation with foreign statesmen was that held in April, 1934, with the French Foreign Minister, Louis Barthou, who had hastened to Warsaw to endeavor to patch up the badly damaged Franco-Polish alliance. When Barthou told him that the era of French concessions to Germany had ended, the old marshal broke into harsh laughter. "You will yield again!" he predicted. Events have since proved him justified.

In his later years Pilsudski became hardly less accessible to visitors even than Stalin. Many members of the diplomatic corps in Warsaw, including the British Ambassador, had never met him. The British Consul-General, on the other hand, was an old friend, and saw the marshal fairly frequently. At home with his wife and daughter he played patience and drank innumerable glasses of weak tea, either from old habit or to allay the pangs of the internal malady which eventually caused his death.

He had always been more feared than loved, and it is probable that even by his closest intimates, the young men who planned the policies of Poland over their vodka in the Europaiske Hotel, his end was greeted with more than philosophic resignation. He belonged to the heroic phase of Polish history, and in classic as in modern times it has been found too grimly true that heroes have no place in politics.

Chapter XX

DIPLOMATISTS OF THE DECLINE

§ 1

THE years 1920 to 1925 had witnessed the slow rise to world prestige and influence of the League of Nations. The years 1926 and 1930 saw the League's apotheosis as an organization for the promotion and maintenance of peace. In 1931 began the period of decline. In February of that year, with the Japanese invasion of Manchuria, was forged the first link in that fatal chain of cause and consequence which, after demonstrating the League's impotence to punish the aggressor against China, saw it unable or unwilling to check the violation of the Treaty of Versailles and the Treaty of Locarno perpetrated by Hitler in the re-militarization of the Rhineland, and finally resulted in the tragic failure to prevent the Italian invasion and conquest of Abyssinia.

The statesmen of the League's period of grandeur had vanished from the stage. Death had claimed Briand and Stresemann, and was soon to claim Henderson. Sir Austen Chamberlain was to survive Briand by seven years, but during that time he was not a member of the British government. New figures entered the Geneva scene: Paul-Boncour, Daladier, Barthou and Laval for France; Sir John Simon, Sir Samuel Hoare and Mr. Anthony Eden for Great Britain; Mr. Norman Davis for the United States; Baron von Neurath, Herr Nadolny and Dr. Goebbels for

Germany; Litvinoff, Potemkin and Dovgaleski for the U.S.S.R.; Baron Aloisi for Italy; Mr. Matsuoka for Japan; a pleiad of brilliant and inscrutable Chinese ministers— Quo, Yen, Lu and Wellington Koo—and a strangely assorted duo pleading for Ethiopia; the French professor of international law, Gaston Jèze, who was to be howled down in his lecture-room at the Sorbonne by a mob of French royalist students for his defense of the victim of aggression; and the Emperor Haile Selassie's minister in Paris, black Wolde Mariam Jesus.

§ 2

Joseph Paul-Boncour had been largely obscured at Geneva during Briand's years of activity on the League. At Briand's death his ambition was, as it remains, to walk in Briand's shoes and wear Briand's mantle. He was, in many respects, infinitely more gifted than his predecessor. He had physical beauty—a small head like a cameo, set on shoulders too broad for his height; thick, silvery hair flowing back in a fine wave from a wide forehead; small hands and feet; a magnificent voice, and great culture. He looked like a French Ramsay MacDonald, a MacDonald in miniature. He had also a great reputation as an advocate in the French Court of Appeal. His resemblance to Robespierre, real or fancied, was notorious, as was the vanity he showed in the resemblance—a bust of the great Conventionnel stands on the mantelpiece in his cabinet. Before the war he was a Radical. After the war he became a Socialist. When the French Socialist party consistently refused to join a bourgeois government except in the conditions realized by the victory of the Popular Front in the elections of May, 1936, and Boncour found his ministerial ambitions constantly defeated, he resigned from the party and entered a Radical government as Minister of Foreign Affairs. Subsequently he was invited to form his own government, but retained with the premiership the direction of the Quai d'Orsay. He was a conspicuous failure in both offices. Vanity and self-esteem are the last faults to be forgiven a French politician by his contemporaries. They will pardon venality, duplicity, mendacity, and worse vices, but not such failings as vanity and stupidity.

Paul-Boncour had had his successes at Geneva. He was one of the authors of the Protocol which so aroused the enthusiasm of the 1924 Assembly, and the author of the famous triple slogan—"Disarmament, Arbitration, Security." In 1926 he made a speech on disarmament and security before the Assembly which was greeted with acclamation, and moved the Canadian President Dandurand to such admiration that he decided to dispense with a verbal translation. But in the following year Boncour's subserviency to French military interests at the Preparatory Commission drew from his fellow Socialist, Louis Brouckère, the tall, stern, Assyrian-bearded editor of the *Peuple* of Brussels, the rebuke that "it was astonishing to find a Socialist as spokesman of the French General Staff." And since the collapse of the Disarmament Conference the modern Robespierre has fallen upon an involuntary oblivion.

§ 3

Louis Barthou had made a brilliant and unexpected return to the political scene in France, as Minister for Foreign Affairs in the Doumergue Cabinet formed after the Stavisky riots in February, 1934. He was a minister in the pre-war tradition, cultured, erudite and witty; a member

PAUL-BONCOUR

of the French Academy; a charming conversationalist, an epicure, a collector of rare editions and engravings, a writer of distinction. He had all the tenacity and courage of Poincaré, and a good deal of his obstinate and incurable nationalism; but was not deficient, like Poincaré, in the gifts of humor and imagination. After ten years of exclusion from any major government post he suddenly found himself at the Quai d'Orsay in the room but lately vacated by Briand.

After the sulky good looks and rather deliberate eloquence of Paul-Boncour at Geneva, the nonchalance, the brilliant common sense and livening gaiety of the septuagenarian Barthou were like a breath of fresh air in Council and Assembly. Barthou came to Geneva with something of the late Philippe Berthelot's disdain for the "fumisterie" of the League of Nations. But he wasted no time in futile criticism. He declared roundly that Germany was rearming, and that France would not agree to any measure which prejudiced her security. He spoke in the Poincaré tradition, and left none in any doubt as to his meaning. He told the journalists in Geneva, and placed no embargo on quotation, that he "did not trust the word of any German when it came to the policy of the Reich towards France. The French alone could accurately assess the German at his real value, and there would never be disarmament unless France was absolutely secure against invasion." Nevertheless he showed himself adaptable and supple enough in the negotiations which preceded the Saar plebiscite, cordially accepted the regulations proposed by the Italian Baron Aloisi, and concurred without rancor in the result of the elections—an overwhelming majority for

Hitler—as achieved by the "free vote" for which he had publicly pressed.

With a few vigorous words Barthou succeeded in retrieving French foreign policy in particular, and possibly Europe in general, from the illusions and futilities of 1933, when Mr. Ramsay MacDonald satisfied himself that a proposal to limit the French and German armies in Europe to 200,000 men each would save the cause of disarmament from disaster, and that a subsequent proposal for a Four Power Directory, including Great Britain, France, Germany and Italy would create a new era of conciliation in Europe.

§ 4

For the years 1932 and 1933 witnessed Mr. MacDonald's return to European diplomacy in a major rôle. We have seen him in Geneva in 1924, glorified and then abased by the Protocol and his own defeat. At the Assembly of 1929 he returned to Geneva as Prime Minister of the second Labour government, but played little part in the proceedings of the Assembly. His only noteworthy utterance was made at a luncheon of the International Association of Journalists accredited to the League of Nations, at which, half jocularly, half seriously, he warned France and its Premier, who sat at the same table, against the notorious French habit of capriciousness. Briand, to whom the salient points of the speech were translated by his friend Loucheur, growled in disgust, "That doesn't encourage me to go on." In 1932, Mr. MacDonald, now Premier in the National Coalition government, revived his old acquaintance with M. Herriot at the Lausanne Reparation Conference, which effectually buried the long-deceased corpse of German reparations. And in December of the same year Mr. MacDonald and M. Herriot arrived in Geneva with the purpose of bringing Germany back to the Disarmament Conference, which the German delegation had left some months earlier. Baron von Neurath, newly appointed Foreign Minister in the Von Schleicher government, equally arrived in Geneva. Sir John Simon, then Foreign Secretary, accompanied Mr. MacDonald, and Paul-Boncour, the French Foreign Minister, supported M. Herriot.

Von Neurath had no difficulty in convincing the British delegates of Germany's right to equality in the matter of armaments. He told them with the bluntness of a former German cavalry officer that unless Germany were given the right to equip herself at least with "token weapons" of the tanks, heavy artillery and military airplanes prohibited to her under the Versailles Treaty, she would not only refuse to return to the Disarmament Conference, but would also proceed to rearm in these categories in defiance of the Treaty. Not only Mr. MacDonald and Sir John Simon, but also Mr. Norman Davis, President Roosevelt's ambassador-at-large, recognized the justice of this demand. They seem to have believed Baron von Neurath, however, when he told them that it was the moral issue, the question of equity and prestige, which concerned Germany most anxiously. M. Herriot for once did not share Mr. MacDonald's optimism. He said privately and publicly that the German demand for equality of rights was merely a veiled demand for the right to rearm.

After a week of negotiations, of luncheons and dinners, from which the President of the Disarmament Conference was, upon the British government's insistence, excluded, a formula was found upon which Germany agreed to return to the Conference. On the night of December 11, 1932, in the British Prime Minister's sitting-room at the Hôtel Beau-Rivage, a document since known as the Declaration of Geneva was signed by Baron von Neurath, Paul-Boncour, Baron Aloisi, Ramsay MacDonald and Sir John Simon. It declared notably that "one of the principles which should guide the Conference on Disarmament should be to grant to Germany, and to other Powers disarmed by Treaty, equality of rights in a system which would provide security for all nations."

Two months later the Von Schleicher government had been succeeded by Hitler. The German delegate to the resumed disarmament discussions was not Baron von Neurath but Herr Nadolny, an uncompromising German diplomat who was later appointed German Ambassador in Moscow. The British delegate was Mr. Anthony Eden. The French plan for disarmament had been rejected by Germany, and a new crisis had arisen in Geneva. One morning in March, 1933, the British Premier arrived in Geneva almost without warning. The same day, in some complacency, he announced to the General Commission of the Conference the outlines of the British draft plan, details of which were later issued to the delegates. The plan was received with incredulity and enthusiasm. It was Mr. MacDonald's third day of triumph in Geneva (the first had been that of the launching of the Protocol, the second that of the Declaration of Geneva). But twenty-four hours later the British ministers were on their way to Rome, and the excitement provoked by the MacDonald disarmament plan was forgotten in the storm of protest excited by the signature of the Four Power Pact in Rome. In each case the British Premier had received the representatives of the world's press after the event and had modestly accepted in advance the world's felicitations on a great achievement. In each case the achievement proved worthless, and almost its existence was forgotten within a few months, and none more so than the ambitious World Economic Conference which followed.

The new French Prime Minister, M. Édouard Daladier, had accepted the proposal for the Four Power Pact without enthusiasm. "For what purpose?" he had asked bluntly when he was informed that Mussolini was bent on an understanding between the four Western European Powers. Nevertheless, under pressure from Mr. MacDonald and Sir John Simon, he agreed to join the Pact, as his predecessors Herriot and Boncour had agreed to sign the Declaration of Geneva. Afterwards he recanted. But the Pact was ultimately destroyed not by the reservations attached by France to her signature but by the spirited opposition of Benes, the Czechoslovak Foreign Minister, and the Little Entente.

§ 5

Under Mr. MacDonald, Sir John Simon had played but a secondary rôle in European affairs. But in the more remote and more complicated field of Far Eastern politics the Foreign Secretary was given a free hand.

The Manchurian crisis provided the League with its first real trial on a matter of world importance. It had been successful in minor issues like the prevention of the Greco-Bulgarian war. It had equally failed on minor issues, like the Italian bombardment of the Greek island of Corfu. The Japanese aggression against Manchuria focused the attention of the world on the League in a degree of anxiety never before witnessed. The facts of the case to be judged were admirably simple. On the night of September 18-19, 1931, an explosion took place on the South Manchurian railway near Mukden. The damage to the railway, if any, did not prevent the punctual arrival of the south-bound train from Chanchun, and, according to the report of the Lytton Commission, "was not in itself sufficient to justify military action. The military operations of the Japanese troops during this night cannot be regarded as measures of legitimate self-defense." Nevertheless the Japanese had made their plans as if they had had foreknowledge of the pretended attack. They advanced into Manchuria and seized the Three Eastern Provinces of China, subsequently establishing them as an independent state under the name of Manchukuo and under the nominal rule of the deposed Chinese Emperor Henry Pu.

The Nanking government immediately protested to the League. A Commission of Inquiry, consisting of a French general, an American major-general, a German doctor, an Italian count and a British peer, the Earl of Lytton, and presided over by the last-named, was sent to Manchuria. The Commission was not appointed until nearly four months after the explosion, and twelve months had elapsed before it reached Tokio. Its report was signed at Peiping on September 4, 1932, and was not published until October 1. The commissioners unanimously found Japan guilty of having perpetrated an unprovoked aggression against China, and although they did not acquit China entirely of faults against Japan, and suggested that some modifications should be made in the régime which existed in Manchuria prior to the aggression, they declared that any attempt by the Japanese to maintain Manchukuo as a so-called independent state would be unsatisfactory. They added that the Japanese régime in Manchuria was "opposed to the interests of China. It disregards the wishes of the people of Manchuria, and it is at least questionable whether it would ultimately serve the permanent interests of Japan."

§ 6

A Special Assembly of the League was called to consider the Lytton Report, and both China and Japan sent immense delegations to Geneva to defend their respective causes. The Japanese were headed by Mr. Matsuoka, a rich Japanese industrialist of the Christian faith, who installed himself and his followers in the Hôtel Métropole, and with the aid of a corps of interpreters, press attachés and secretaries, settled down in methodical Japanese style, modeled upon the best American publicity methods, to the conquest of world opinion. Mr. Matsuoka spoke English haltingly but with feeling. He was a man of considerable charm in private life, and given to more display of sentiment than is usual in the Japanese. On nights of crisis in Geneva, when it became increasingly plain that the Committee of Nineteen appointed by the Assembly to consider the Lytton Report would deliver a verdict against Japan, a small pathetic figure in a brown kimono would emerge from Mr. Matsuoka's private sitting-room into the lounge of the Hôtel Métropole bearing a bottle of French cognac. As a diplomat he could be relied upon for originality, at least in his improvisations in the Assembly, which frequently startled the delegates, and not least his Japanese colleagues. The most celebrated of his outbursts was uttered in the Assembly on a day in December, when he suddenly abandoned his written speech and loudly demanded:

"Suppose that public opinion were so absolutely against Japan as some people try to make out, are you sure that so-called public opinion will persist for ever and never change? Humanity crucified Jesus of Nazareth two thousand years ago. And today? Can any of you assure me that the so-called world opinion can make no mistake? We Japanese feel that we are now put on trial. Some of the people in Europe and America may wish even to crucify Japan in the twentieth century. Gentlemen, Japan stands ready to be crucified. But we do believe that in a very few years world opinion will be changed and that we also shall be understood by the world as Jesus of Nazareth was."

The Chinese delegation was more circumspect in its conduct and its utterances. Its four leaders, the diplomats Quo, Yen, Lu and Koo, dispensed much dignified hospitality at their headquarters on the Quai Wilson, and to all inquiries replied patiently that they had faith in the Covenant and in the members of the League of Nations. The members of the League justified their faith to the extent of endorsing the recommendations of the Committee of Nineteen, and of solemnly condemning the act of aggression committed by Japan. But although the President of the Swiss Republic, Dr. Motta, boldly mentioned the word "sanctions" in a plain hint that the time might soon arrive for the application of Article 16, no members of the League were found ready to undertake sanctions against the aggressor. Japan not only refused to evacuate its puppet republic of Manchukuo, but advanced into the province of Jehol. When the Assembly passed its resolution, accepting the recommendations of the Committee of Nineteen, based on those of the Lytton Report, Mr. Matsuoka and his followers walked sadly out of the Assembly, and two months later the Japanese government gave formal notice of its withdrawal from the Council and Assembly of the League.

On February 27, 1933, three days after the vote of the Assembly, Sir John Simon announced in the House of Commons that the British government had decided to declare an embargo on the export of arms to Japan, pending international agreement, but it rendered this sanction farcical by the intimation that the embargo would apply equally to arms for China. The other states took no action at all. And a fortnight later the futile British embargo was raised.

§ 7

Sir John Simon was much criticized in Geneva and elsewhere for his part in the Manchurian controversy. Although he had, like the other representatives of the Great Powers, shown a natural irritation at the repeated maneuvers of Mr. Matsuoka to gain time and evade the inevitable, he had given other delegates the impression that his own sympathies were with Japan. He had pointed out very judicially that the Lytton Report did not condemn Japan alone. "It is admirable and impartial . . . a memorable document . . . but if its recommendations are examined closely it will be found that the investigators discovered evils and delinquencies on both sides." And at a luncheon of British, American and French newspaper correspondents in Geneva on the day after he was reported to have promised official British support to China against the Japanese aggressor, he astonished his hosts by proffering the excuse that nothing could be done "because what is China after all but a geographical expression." The phrase was reported in a French newspaper, and although the usual official denials were issued, the report gained ground that the British Foreign Secretary was pro-Japanese in his sympathies.

Sir John Simon was hardly less unfortunate than Mr. MacDonald in the reactions he provoked from both delegates and journalists in Geneva. More genial and less affected in manner although he was, he succeeded in creating little sympathy among foreigners. His calm, judicial manner irritated, his occasional note of condescension infuriated them. His agility in debate, his skill in advocacy (demonstrated when he succeeded in winning over the League Council to the British side in the Anglo-Persian oil dispute) confounded them. Yet there is no suspicion in Geneva of lawyers as such. Half the delegates to the League meetings are men who have risen to political eminence through their practice of law. But the peculiarly Anglo-Saxon combination of forensic ability and religious piety is invariably suspect in countries where the majority of successful politicians are either open agnostics like Briand, Viviani and Loucheur, or are but perfunctory partisans of a church long since deprived of influence in state affairs.

In this matter Lord Cecil is the exception which but proves the rule. He succeeded in breaking down that natural continental mistrust of theological lawyers by the sheer earnestness and patience of his zeal for the League. Sir John's failure to acquire personal prestige at Geneva is probably due to his own equivocal political position. Nominally a Liberal, he has always appeared at the League as the spokesman of a government largely Conservative in composition and in sympathies. He is not a Conservative, yet he is not as Liberal as the Conservative Lord Cecil, or even as the late Sir Austen Chamberlain. The League has

learned to tolerate and even to understand Radicals, Socialists, Communists, Fascists and even Nazis, but the peculiarly British brand of Liberal-Conservative or Conservative-
Liberal, or National Liberal, it has not yet digested.

Chapter XXI

ABYSSINIAN CRISIS

§ 1

EACH of the two great international storms which have shaken Geneva during the past few years has cost a British Foreign Secretary his post. Sir John Simon had not gained prestige, either in England or abroad, for his handling of the Manchurian crisis. The second withdrawal of Germany from the Disarmament Conference, which this time was accompanied by her resignation from the League, was soon followed by his transfer from the Foreign Office to the Home Office. His successor, Sir Samuel Hoare, was even more unfortunate. His brief career as Foreign Secretary came to a sensational end early in the crisis over Abyssinia.

Yet his début at Geneva had been admirable and even brilliant. At the Assembly of September, 1935, when Mussolini was adding to the already considerable profits of the Suez Canal Company with every fresh division sent to Massowa, Sir Samuel made a generous and courageous speech in the Assembly in which after pledging British support of the League and its ideals as the most effective way of ensuring peace, and reaffirming the need for the collective maintenance of the Covenant in its entirety, and collective resistance to all acts of unprovoked aggression, he suggested for the first time that Great Britain would be ready to enter any scheme for pooling the material resources of the world and offering economic advantages in undeveloped territories to nations without colonial outlets of their own.

Within three months of this auspicious beginning the new Foreign Secretary had been disavowed and discredited by his government, and his political career seemed temporarily wrecked.

Sir Samuel Hoare came to the Foreign Office fresh from a period of successful administration of Indian affairs. He was intelligent, sensitive, imaginative and tolerant, one of the most popular men in the House of Commons, and one of the few British politicians since the death of Edwin Montagu who had won the respect and confidence of Indians from Gandhi downwards. But if he seemed to have made some progress towards an understanding of the Oriental mind in his contacts with Indians, he showed little sign of it in his subsequent negotiations with the thinly veneered Oriental who was Premier and Foreign Minister of France during part of the critical years 1935 and 1936.

§ 2

M. Pierre Laval was born at Auvergnat, which is to say that he is a native of the Yorkshire of France, the province of Auvergne having something of the Yorkshire richness of dialect, originality, shrewdness and caution. He comes from a region singularly prolific in evidences of the early invasions of Gaul by the Phoenicians and the Romans. In his brown skin, his dark eyes, his negroid nose and lips, there are suggestions of the mixed racial origin to be seen in many inhabitants of the mountainous Auvergnat country. In M. Laval's case the somber pigmentation of skin and eyes is heightened by his habit of wearing an old-fashioned white cravat.

His political career has been as curiously varied as his ancestry. In 1914 his sympathies were with the extreme Left. He was a young lawyer, a revolutionary Socialist, and the mayor of the industrial Parisian suburb of Aubervilliers. In the secret dossiers of the Ministry of the Interior at the beginning of the war he was listed as a man whose activities must be closely scrutinized. During the war he remained in close association with the small group of French pacifists, syndicalists and Socialists who acclaimed the Russian Revolution of Lenin and Trotsky and formed the first nucleus of the French Communist party. In 1919 Laval entered the Senate as an independent Socialist with Communist leanings. His orientation towards a more conservative platform in politics was slow. He took no active part in national controversies. He concerned himself largely with problems of municipal administration, housing and social reform.

By 1930 he had begun cautiously to emerge as a politician of the Left Center. He appeared at Geneva in September of that year, but aroused little interest. His opportunity arrived after the French elections of 1932, when neither the Left nor the Right had a preponderant influence in the Chamber of Deputies, and the field was open to independent leaders adroit enough in political maneuvering to collect among groups and parties the elements of a government majority. By this time Pierre Laval's chief supporters were men of the Right. The Right wing in France has always been the natural refuge for deserters or apostates from the extreme Left. Former Socialists like Millerand, Gustave Hervé, Viviani; former Communists

LAVAL

like Pierre Laval and Jacques Doriot; even, to take an extreme case, the Royalist propagandist and philosopher
Charles Maurras, once a revolutionary of almost anarchist
views, have equally been acclaimed in their age of maturity
by various parties of the ultra-Conservative wing. Laval's
political development bears a remarkable resemblance to
that of Mussolini. It is not astonishing, therefore, that he
should have been the French Foreign Minister who first
ventured, after the reluctance of Poincaré, the hostility of
Herriot, the hesitations of Briand, the delays of Tardieu,
the haggling of Barthou, to make the journey to Rome and
discuss a settlement of the long outstanding Franco-Italian
problems with the Fascist dictator in person.

The late Louis Barthou, M. Laval's immediate predecessor at the Quai d'Orsay, was invited to visit Rome in the
summer of 1934, at the end of the series of diplomatic
journeys he was planning to Poland, Czechoslovakia, Roumania and Jugoslavia. The minister was pressed to accept
the invitation by M. de Chambrun, then French Ambassador to Italy, but Barthou prudently declined on the ground
that diplomatic preparation for the interview with Mussolini had not yet been made. Conversations thereupon began between the Foreign Offices of the two countries,
through their respective Ambassadors in Rome and Paris.
The old and thorny question of naval parity was by tacit
consent waived, and the attention of the negotiators was
concentrated on the status of the Italian colonists in the
French protectorate of Tunisia and the delimitation of the
frontier between Italian Libya and the French Soudan.
In October, 1934, Barthou was assassinated in Marseilles
with Alexander, King of Jugoslavia, and the fruit of these

Franco-Italian negotiations was plucked by his successor, Pierre Laval.

Laval went to Rome three months later, in January, 1935, and on behalf of his government signed a pact of friendship with Italy which pledged Franco-Italian support for the independence of Austria, promised Italy's respect of the French mandate over Syria and protectorate over Tunisia, ceded to Italy the small French island of Doumetraich in the Red Sea, readjusted in Italy's favor the frontier between Libya and Tunisia, and finally promised French recognition of Italy's economic interests in the hinterland of the Italian colony of Eritrea. The hinterland in question is, of course, Abyssinia, and this clause in the Rome Agreement between France and Italy has always been cited by Italians and by others as tacitly promising French support in advance to any Italian enterprise undertaken in that hinterland in defense of Italy's economic interests. At the Stresa Conference, a few months later, Mussolini is said again to have given a hint to the French Premier of his preoccupations with Abyssinia, and to have received a reply which the Italians interpreted as giving them *carte blanche* for their activities in East Africa.

§ 3

Whether these commitments of M. Pierre Laval were known to Sir Samuel Hoare or not—and the natural presumption is that they were—the British Foreign Secretary seemed not to have been unduly influenced by them when he went to Paris in December of the same year to discuss the Italo-Abyssinian crisis with the French Premier. In the meantime the invasion of Ethiopia had begun. The army of Mussolini crossed the border from Eritrea on

October 3. Adowa was captured on October 7. On October 10, a specially convened Assembly of the League condemned Italy as an aggressor; fifty states assenting to the resolution; Siam, Austria and Hungary alone dissenting. The arms embargo on Abyssinia was raised, but since the Italians were soon in possession of the Djibouti-Addis Ababa railway, and Djibouti is practically the only port through which sea-borne arms may enter Abyssinia, the raising of the embargo (imposed to stop slave-raiding and arms smuggling in the years before the Italian dispute) proved futile.

On November 18, by which time the Italians had captured Makale, the first League sanctions—financial and economic—came into force. But it was already realized that they would be ineffectual in arresting the war. The Italian government had accumulated adequate reserves of food supplies, metal, munitions, and oil fuel. Even if the ultimate sanction could be applied, with the United States, the largest oil producer in the world, out of the League, it was doubtful if it would prove deterrent to Mussolini. The conquest of Ethiopia and its destruction as an independent state would already have been accomplished. Diplomatically, politically, perhaps even ethically, there seemed to the British government, as there now seem to many others, adequate reasons for pressing a compromise on both Mussolini and the Emperor of Abyssinia before the irrevocable had occurred.

No member of the British Cabinet, certainly not Sir Samuel Hoare, foresaw the storm of opprobrium and protest which his action would provoke. His gesture for peace was not even a personal gesture. His plan was not his own but that of the permanent staff of the Foreign Office. A high official of that department had been engaged for weeks past in conference with M. Massigli of the Quai d'Orsay in an effort to discover a solution of the problem acceptable to Italy and the Negus, to Great Britain, France and the League. If Sir Samuel was, as afterwards proved, the scapegoat of the drama, it was an innocent and naïve victim of government terror of public opinion who left Downing Street for Paris on the morning of Saturday, December 7, 1935.

On the evening of the following day Sir Samuel Hoare and M. Pierre Laval issued a cautiously worded but nevertheless highly significant communiqué outlining the results of their conversations. The next day, December 9, the world's press in general, led by the French newspapers in M. Laval's confidence, hailed the agreement as historic, and hinted that Mussolini had already given his consent to the terms of the proposed solution. The Italian press alone suggested, with more accuracy, that however favorable to Italy, the compromise would be rejected by the Duce. The celebrated communiqué was thus phrased:

"Animated by the same spirit of conciliation and animated by the close friendship between England and France, we in the course of our long conversations of today and yesterday sought the formulae for a friendly settlement of the Italo-Ethiopian dispute. There can be no question at present of publishing these formulae. The British Government has not yet been informed of them, and once its agreement has been received it will be necessary to submit them to the governments concerned and to the decision of the League of Nations. We have worked together with an equal anxiety to reach a peaceful and honorable solution as rapidly as possible. We are both satisfied with the results which have been obtained."

§ 4

Five days after the issue of this statement, on December 13, the details of the Hoare-Laval agreement were published. The settlement proposed was outlined under the general headings of "Exchange of Territories" and "Zones for Economic Expansion and Settlement." The negotiators suggested that the region of Adowa should be ceded to Italy, together with the Danakil province and considerable portions of the Ogaden and neighboring provinces. Abyssinia would be required to permit further the economic exploitation of large tracts of Abyssinia by Italy, and in return for these generous concessions would be ceded a narrow strip of territory to the Red Sea on condition (a subtle Laval touch) that no railway should be built on it to compete with the French-owned line from Addis Ababa to Djibouti. Moreover the sacred city of Aksum, already occupied by the Italians at the time of the Hoare-Laval conversations, would be returned to the Emperor.

The terms of the proposed compromise were ignominious, but not so ignominious as the débacle of the French and British policy a few months later, or as the collective surrender of the League to the policy of brute force. The fact that subsequently the Emperor might have been gratified to retain even a fraction of his kingdom was not appreciated then, and in any case would not lighten the moral responsibility of the statesmen who calmly negotiated the heaviest bribe ever offered in history to buy off an invader. The opinion of the entire world was shocked and revolted. British opinion, both Conservative and Opposition, was outraged at the proposals. A storm broke over the heads of the government, and in particular over the head of the Foreign Secretary.

The government took refuge behind the transparent and timorous pretext that owing to the week-end absence of most of its members from London, Sir Samuel Hoare had not been able to consult his colleagues. Sir Samuel Hoare gallantly faced his accusers and admitted his guilt. Generously he took the entire responsibility for the British share of the agreement upon his own shoulders. He said that real pressure could be brought upon Italy only by the application of the oil sanction, and it had not been found possible to obtain agreement to apply this. Failing this essential weapon against the aggressor, he and M. Laval had used their best efforts to discover a basis for a settlement. Neither of them liked the terms, but they were forced to be realists in a realist world. And he ended his speech—he had already resigned from the office—by a homily upon the need for states members of the League to honor their obligations under the Covenant. Without greater co-operation between the sanctionist states, collective security would vanish and the League would be disrupted. And with these words, uttered to a House suddenly become sympathetic on the realization that the disgraced Foreign Secretary had possibly been more sinned against than sinning, Sir Samuel Hoare left the Foreign Office to the enterprising and eager spirit of Mr. Anthony Eden.

§ 5

Ten years earlier an even younger Captain Eden, recently arrived in politics *via* Eton and the Guards, had figured among the immediate entourage of Sir Austen Chamber-

EDEN

lain. Geneva saw in him then merely one more of those tall, slim, black-coated, striped-trousered, modest, industrious, brief-case-bearing, Foreign Office officials who stand behind the chair of their chief at the League Council table, like feudal vassals at a feasting. Captain Eden was agreeable, handsome, blond-haired, with good shoulders and a friendly blue eye, a pleasant young Guards officer's fair mustache, and that unmistakably and invincibly British air of wearing the world's troubles lightly and shaking them off as a dog shakes off water. He had been born under a friendly star, for there has been no British Foreign Secretary at thirty-seven for well over a hundred years. The fates had given him, in addition to reasonable wealth and good looks, a talent for languages, a quick intelligence and a fair share of imagination. But fortunate as he had been in gaining the friendship and confidence of Mr. Stanley Baldwin, and in having the succession to the Foreign Office opened to him thus prematurely by the misfortunes of Sir Samuel Hoare, it cannot be said that he had not qualified for the post.

Few British Foreign Secretaries have served so long or so useful an apprenticeship. No British minister since the foundation of the League has been more assiduous in his attendance at Geneva. As Parliamentary Secretary to Sir Austen Chamberlain, then as Under-Secretary of State for Foreign Affairs, and finally as Minister for League Affairs, Mr. Eden had shown industry, tact, ardor and intelligence. He brought his brilliant talents to the department of state, which during the last administration of Mr. Baldwin was destined to be most continuously and most anxiously tried. For some weeks during the long Abyssinian crisis, he seemed to have assumed the rôle of an European St. George fighting the Fascist dragon. The Abyssinian tragedy had become his own. He seemed to be engaged in a personal duel with Mussolini at once for the independence of Ethiopia and for the honor of the League. At the height of his influence at Geneva, he was rewarded by daily orgies of vituperation in the Fascist press, the burning of his effigy in the streets of Rome, and, what was more remarkable, the daily adulation of the Labour and Liberal opposition organs in Great Britain. When his efforts failed, and he perforce had to acquiesce in the collective surrender of the League, he saw himself censured and denounced in all the countries and by all the parties which had enthusiastically acclaimed, but which had not supported, his single-handed contest with the Italian dictator.

Mr. Eden had been swept into the Foreign Office on the crest of one of those waves of righteous indignation and vague idealism which occasionally sweep through Great Britain, and which overthrew Sir Samuel Hoare. Temperamentally he was well-fitted for the rôle of crusader. He was young enough to be rendered indignant by injustice, and not experienced enough in disillusion to be cynical about it. Moreover he had the healthy Guardsman's contempt for the military qualities of the Italian. He had also more than a trace of the eighteenth-century Tory squire's contempt for the political parvenu. On the famous occasion of his visit to Rome to meet Mussolini he returned to the British Embassy from the great Sala della Mappamondi in the Palazzo Venezia with a single eloquent phrase in description of the Italian dictator: "He is not a gentleman." In the mind of Mr. Eden the words had the final quality of political epitaph. But as events showed it was not Mussolini's epitaph that came dangerously near being written, but his own. For snobbery in statecraft is even more fatal than vanity.

The interview between the two men was conspicuously unsuccessful. Mussolini resented Mr. Eden's youth, his English arrogance, his height, his good looks, his social background. The class memories and instincts which made him immediately cordial to former Socialists like Pierre Laval and Ramsay MacDonald urged him to a mistrust and a hostility no less instinctive in the presence of Sir Eric Drummond and Mr. Anthony Eden. Yet Mr. Eden's disdain of Mussolini was not entirely inspired by snobbishness. The Foreign Secretary had previously met Hitler in Berlin, and Stalin in Moscow, and their encounter had been cordial in each case. Doubtless in Mussolini's case there was a greater incompatibility of type and temperament. Moreover, there was not between them the mutual assurance created by the feeling of political and military equality as between their respective countries. Hitler and Stalin both represented great Powers. In Rome the young minister of a great Power met for the first time the experienced leader of a second-class Power afflicted with the modern itch for world empire.

Bravely as he acquitted himself, he cannot be fairly said to have emerged unscathed from the ordeal. For once the Imperial mantle of Britain had not served to preserve youthful if scarcely immature shoulders from the blows of a jealous, scornful and challenging adversary. Traditional British foreign policy had encountered a new historic enemy in its path, but Eden was not to triumph over Mussolini as Pitt triumphed over Napoleon. The new Grand Alliance, infinitely more ambitious and more powerful, an almost universal confederation of states, was less successful than the old. Eden was out-faced by Mussolini as Alexander, that earlier figure of a political Bayard, was out-faced, out-maneuvered, in love as well as in diplomacy, by Metternich. The times change, and the men. But history resembles itself and repeats itself.

§ 6

Mr. Eden's predecessor, it was said in his defense, had been betrayed by Laval. Before the Hoare-Laval peace terms had even been transmitted to him, Mussolini could reject them in safety, secure in the knowledge that the French Premier had given him *carte blanche* in Rome. Mr. Eden was betrayed partly by his own confident optimism, partly by the treachery or the hesitations of the other sanctionist states, but above all by Britain's own weakness. In reply to journalists at Geneva who suggested that the League had acted too late, and that Italy's prestige was at stake, Mr. Eden retorted: "And what about Great Britain's prestige?" But when the supreme moment came, Mussolini was ready to risk war to maintain his country's prestige and Great Britain was not. A war with Italy alone might have been envisaged without great apprehension, but the threat was not of an Anglo-Italian war, but a war in which Italy and Germany were equally engaged. The British navy might still retain command of the Mediterranean, and Great Britain stood in no great danger from Italy's air arm. But she was not so immune from the aerial attacks of Germany.

France would be fully engaged in protecting her own soil from invasion. Soviet Russia's great air fleet could at most secure Czechoslovakia, and defend the frontiers of the U.S.S.R. from the double attack which might be expected from Germany and Japan. Great Britain might be partly disarmed or partly destroyed before even she had begun to strike a blow in defense of the League Covenant and of invaded Ethiopia. London was in as imminent danger from German planes as Addis Ababa from the Italians. And if British statesmen had not been aware of the grave nature of the emergency, their colleagues of the French government were fully alive to the danger.

How precarious was their own position was seen in March of 1936 when Hitler's troops marched into the Rhineland, and for the first time in eighteen years German guns were pointed across the Rhine. M. Sarraut, then French Premier, declared angrily in a radio broadcast that France would not allow Strasbourg to remain under the menace of German artillery. But France did nothing and the guns are still trained on Strasbourg. It was not the loud challenge of Mussolini that revealed Britain's weakness, but the silent challenge of Hitler. Germany was the unknown factor in Europe during the Abyssinian crisis. She played a waiting game, and when the opportunity came, when the impotence of the League in general and of France and Great Britain to impose effective sanctions on Italy was revealed, she struck her blow in the Rhineland and struck it with impunity, since France, like England over Abyssinia, would not run the risk of a general war.

Mr. Eden's real enemies were in part the enthusiasts who encouraged him on, and the military and aerial and naval weakness of England which held him back. Great Britain suffered the blow to her pride and her prestige in silence, but the lesson had proved salutary. It may be doubted if any other British foreign minister will be encouraged to pursue a policy of force without the means to sustain it in case of need.

The curtain fell, appropriately enough in Geneva, on the last act in the Ethiopian tragedy. As the Italian forces approached his capital, the Emperor Haile Selassie appealed almost daily for the help of the League, for the oil sanctions which alone might check the advance of the invader. Meanwhile, oil sanctions proving a difficult obstacle to surmount, the League turned its attention to the negotiation of a truce. Baron Pompeo Aloisi, the bald Roman aristocrat who had represented Italy in the Manchurian and Abyssinian negotiations, returned from Rome in what was hopefully believed to be a conciliatory spirit to meet Señor Madariaga, the Spanish Chairman of the League Sub-Committee on Abyssinia, in the room of the Secretary-General. But the hope proved illusory. Mussolini scornfully declined the assistance or even the discreet scrutiny of the League over any peace negotiations. He would talk peace with the Emperor alone. A few days later the army of Marshal Badoglio entered Addis Ababa and the Emperor took refuge in flight to Palestine. There was no longer any occasion for peace negotiations. Ethiopia had been conquered by the sword, and on the night of May 9, 1936, Mussolini proclaimed the King of Italy Emperor of Abyssinia in succession to the dethroned and fugitive Haile Selassie.

But the supreme affront to the League had yet to come. It was delivered during that memorable Assembly of 1936 when the self-exiled Emperor, unsurpassed in the dignity of his bearing and the Shakespearian pathos of his utterances, appeared on the tribune to make his final appeal for justice, and a group of Fascist journalists in puerile and

MADARIAGA

ignoble protest attempted to heap public scorn on their defeated adversary. Even the circumstances of Haile Selassie's appearance before the League were not without humiliation for some of the great Powers. It had been decided by the foreign ministers of France and Great Britain that now that the Italian conquest of Ethiopia was a *fait accompli*, and Italy had formally annexed the ex-Emperor's territory, the recognition of a delegation representing the defeated régime in Ethiopia would be a needless provocation to the aggressor Power. The champions of the defeated policy of idealism had suddenly become realists of the most persuasive kind. Moreover, even the government of the Socialist, Léon Blum, had persuaded the Radical professor Gaston Jeze, that to return to Geneva as the adviser and official representative of the defeated Emperor would be to convince Italy that France was secretly supporting the cause of Haile Selassie.

The Emperor thus found himself abandoned by the sanctionist states, deserted by his habitual delegate at Geneva, and faced with the decision of the Credentials Committee of the League on which the great Powers were predominant, that his delegation could not be admitted since Ethiopia was no longer an independent and sovereign state. In his extremity the Emperor telephoned to his former American adviser, the late Everitt Colson, who had been attached to Haile Selassie's court for some years as financial counselor, and was now gravely ill of a mortal heart affection in the neighboring city of Evian. Despite the formal prohibition of his physicians, Colson left his bed, hurried to Geneva, and summoning all his energy, resource and moral courage, rallied the small powers in Geneva to the defense of the victim of Italy's war of conquest. The result of this gallant and self-sacrificing gesture of a dying man was to evoke a belated but spontaneous protest from the Assembly. The intrigue of the great Powers was defeated. The report of the Credentials Committee was rejected so far as Abyssinia was concerned and the Emperor's delegation was admitted to the League. It only remains to be said of this last-minute revolt of the little nations, in sympathy with the victim of a great Power's aggression, that it was magnificent, but it was not war.

Chapter XXII

ALBERT THOMAS AND THE I.L.O.

§ 1

WITH the single exception of Clemenceau, the late Albert Thomas was the most remarkable Frenchman of the Great War. If he had been born a century and a half earlier, he would have lived in the history of the French Revolution in the immortal company of a Danton, a Camille Desmoulins, a Marat or a Robespierre. In the Third Republic he achieved a more modest success by becoming Minister of Munitions during the World War, and at its end, the first Director of the International Labor Office.

He was born in a Paris suburb in 1878, the son (like the French essayist and novelist Henri Béraud) of a baker, who jealously scrutinized the duration of the weekly lessons in Latin given to his precocious offspring by a young Paris student, and grudgingly counted out the few francs with which they were remunerated. In his early twenties he became passionately interested in the doctrines of French socialism and syndicalism, studied trade union problems, and founded a trade union weekly, *La Revue Syndicale*, which he edited until 1910. In that year he came under the notice of the great Socialist, Jean Jaurès, and was invited to join the editorial staff of the Socialist newspaper *L'Humanité*. When the war broke out his talent for organization, his energy, industry, eloquence, and above all, his knowledge of industrial conditions, secured his appointment as Under-Secretary of State for Artillery and Munitions, and later in the war a separate department was created for him, and he was appointed Minister of Munitions. In that capacity he made frequent journeys to London and made the acquaintance of Mr. Lloyd George, whom he captivated by his humor, energy and common sense. In 1917, on the outbreak of the first Russian Revolution, he was sent to Russia at the head of a French mission, half political, half military, to bolster up the tottering military machine in Russia, and revive the waning enthusiasm of the Russian army for the cause of the Allies.

His British Socialist colleague, Arthur Henderson, had been sent to Russia on a similar mission by the British Cabinet, and Albert Thomas played a curious rôle in the complex drama which led to Henderson's recall from Russia and the celebrated incident when he was forced to cool his heels in impotent embarrassment "on the doormat" at 10 Downing Street. Henderson afterwards claimed to have been fully covered, for all he did in Russia, not only by the secret instructions he carried from London to act as the envoy of the British government, and if necessary to supersede and dismiss the British Ambassador in Petrograd, Sir George Buchanan, but also by a mysterious telegram sent by Mr. Lloyd George to his friend Albert Thomas, a telegram which Thomas afterwards gave to Henderson. This was the document referred to by the indignant Labour leader after his resignation from the War Cabinet, when he intimated that he proposed to vindicate himself fully before the House of Commons. He was induced to desist from this complete vindication, and to refrain from divulging the contents of the telegram to

Thomas, by the late Lord Balfour, then Foreign Secretary, who wrote to Henderson that the telegram was a Cabinet document and could not be divulged without special permission of the King.

In Russia, Thomas found himself in the characteristic Slav atmosphere of revolutionary fervor, confused idealism and semi-religious, semi-patriotic mysticism which so marvelously harmonized with his own half shrewd, half mystical nature. This French revolutionary, born out of his time, threw himself with passion and with delight into the birth-throes of the new democratic Russia. In Kerensky he saw a natural demagogue like himself, part statesman, part evangelist. In almost delirious enthusiasm for the sacred cause of democracy, as impersonated by the Allies, he drove up and down the Russian front, delivered a score of speeches daily, haranguing thousands of bewildered Russian infantrymen, fresh from the trenches, in mudstained and torn uniforms, many of them without rifles or ammunition, listening with feelings compounded of ennui, incomprehension and amusement to this gesticulating, black-bearded Frenchman who in the heat of his eloquence tore off his collar, opened his coat, and perspired in torrents, although his speeches were delivered in the open air and the temperature was twenty degrees below freezing-point. Many of them took him for a priest, by reason of his hirsute appearance, his effusive embracing of officers, his solemn benedictions of the men.

His speeches were composed of a curious mixture of Karl Marx, the Declaration of the Rights of Man, Liberty, Equality and Fraternity, and the collective propaganda of the Allies against Prussianism. When the communicative enthusiasm of speech and applause had waned, Thomas

would genially explain his technique of revolutionary ora-
tory to a cynical and slightly bemused spectator. "I do
not," he said on one occasion, "deceive myself as to the
merit of my eloquence, nor do I put myself to any trouble
for the benefit of these moujiks. The greater part of my
speech, all the paraphrases of Karl Marx—except for the
adaptations rendered necessary by the circumstances of the
time, the holy war against capitalist militarism in the name
of social justice, etc.—I hand out to them exactly as I hand
them out to my Socialist audiences at home in Belleville
or Ménilmontant. The curious thing is, and it is humiliating enough for any speaker, that the Russian troops, who
do not understand a single word of what I say, since the
translation is given in one piece at the end, applaud at
exactly the same places as the Socialist comrades in Paris.
There is something in the accent, gesture or the look of
an orator which provokes applause. Eloquence is physical
not mental. Nevertheless, the solitary phrase which excites
enthusiasm during the translation of the interpreter is my
reference to the future League of Nations."

§ 2

This was in 1917. Two years later the black-bearded
and fiery pope of Kerensky's infantrymen, with the cynical
tolerance of Clemenceau, the friendly support of Lloyd
George, and the cordial approval of Wilson, had become
the head of one of the most novel and influential of the
creations of the Treaty of Versailles, the organization based
upon Article 23(a) of the Covenant of the League of Nations, charged with the securing and maintenance of fair
and humane conditions of labor for men, women and children. The autonomous International Labor Office was

THOMAS

equipped, like the League itself, with a Governing Body or Council, and an annual Conference or Assembly. It was the Allied governments' reply to the revolution of Lenin and Trotsky. Through it Albert Thomas, the French Kerensky, vaguely promised to accomplish, by discussion, palliation and reform, what Kerensky had failed to achieve in Russia and the second Russian Revolution had accomplished by violence.

It mattered little to Thomas that the governments represented on his Governing Body, no more than the employers sitting thereon, intended his cherished organization to be used for the promotion of a mild form of socialism. If the brilliant son of the Paris suburban baker had learned his eloquence in the school of Jaurès and Déroulède, he had also learned diplomacy and statecraft in the school of Machiavelli, Lloyd George and Clemenceau. He journeyed incessantly about the world, visiting capital after capital, haranguing statesmen and workmen, bankers and trade unions officials, seductive, persuasive, his vivid brown eyes twinkling behind the mild, scholarly, gold-rimmed spectacles, his small white hands caressing eternally the thick masses of his rich brown-black beard. He went to Moscow, to Shanghai, to Peking, to Washington. Before the League was fairly launched, his International Labor Office had already begun its semi-independent existence.

Soon it had achieved greater universality than the League itself. Germany was an early member. The United States joined in 1934. Brazil and Japan, which resigned from the League, continued to adhere to the sister organization. The latter country actually agreed, under friendly persuasion from the I.L.O., to publish a decree raising to the age of eight years in the case of boys and ten years in the case of girls the age at which children might be employed in factories, and prohibiting the use of damp underground cellars as textile factories and carpet-weaving sheds. A more substantial industrial victory claimed by Albert Thomas was the establishment of the eight-hour day, although for domestic reasons this convention was never ratified by some governments, including that of Great Britain.

§ 3

The League of Nations had to wait sixteen years for its peace palace on the lakeside at Geneva, and even then it was but half finished. The International Labor Office was installed in a sumptuous building of its own on the shores of the Lake of Geneva in two or three years. No setting seemed more incongruous for labor organization. No background seemed more richly suited to the genius, the physical aspect, the restless personality of its first Director. The building has the superficial appearance and a good deal of the structural plan of a Greek or Spanish monastery. No man looked more like an abbot of a Greek Orthodox monastic order than Albert Thomas. He lived happily and luxuriously in his cell, the walls of which were lined with precious woods from the Orient and adorned with etchings by Goya and other masters. His desk gleamed a dark red, but not so darkly and richly as the warm tints in his curly hair and beard. He sat there like a prince of the Church enthroned in purple, and above him and around him his assistants of many nations compiled reports of hours and wages and industrial diseases and the accidents incidental to industry and the lighting and sanitation of factories and the evasion of the Plimsoll regulations in shipping and coolie labor, and tuberculosis in textile mills and hookworm in India, and a hundred other topics.

The League Secretariat, Council and Assembly, temporarily housed in a transformed hotel and its annexes, in a glass conservatory and a Calvinist conventicle, might lament their discomfort and insecurity, but Albert Thomas lived snugly in his exotic nest, among the tapestries given him by France and Belgium, the stained-glass windows of Germany, the paneling of Holland, the parquet floors, the murals, the painted ceilings, the wrought ironwork, the spun glass, the libraries of choice books, the statuary, the engravings donated by Canada, India, Australia, Czechoslovakia, Italy and other nations, by the Carnegie and Rockefeller foundations, by trade unions and by individuals, in response to his repeated importunities.

For Thomas begged shamelessly and almost insolently. He wandered from country to country asking or demanding alms. He presented his annual budget to the Financial Commission of the League with a magnificent effrontery which resisted all criticism. Storm after storm broke upon his head, but he emerged smiling, undaunted, more self-confident than ever. His extravagance was censured, his own salary (at one time, at the height of the French currency inflation, it was said to equal that of the President of the French Republic) was called in question, the salaries of his staff aroused comment, and, above all, the considerable private fund placed at the disposal of the Director for disbursements which were not revealed to the Financial Commission, but which were strongly suspected to include subsidies to certain Continental trade union officials. But Thomas refused to retrench, and declined to explain. Before and during each Assembly of the League, each annual conference of his own organization, he made his diplomatic reconnaissances of the terrain. He was a superb diplomatist. His personal influence at Geneva was greater than that of the Secretary-General of the League, his colleague and in some ways his rival. His activities were not limited to industrial matters. He was an itinerant French ambassador-at-large, independent of governments, diplomats and foreign office officials, but with his own curious means of access to the men in power in all countries.

§ 4

He died suddenly, at the zenith of his physical and mental powers, sitting at table at a café in the center of Paris, during one of his many mysterious journeys from Geneva. His death had an important and entirely unforeseen effect on the secretaryship of the League of Nations, which was soon after relinquished by Sir Eric Drummond. If Albert Thomas had survived the resignation of Sir Eric, the new Secretary-General would almost certainly have been British, and the present British Minister to China, Sir Alexander Cadogan, had already been privately elected for the job. As it was, Thomas was succeeded as Director of the International Labor Office by his British Deputy-Director, the modest, genial and athletic Harold Beresford Butler, a former Assistant-Secretary of the British Labour Ministry and a fellow of All Souls'. Since Great Britain could not reasonably claim the principal posts in both organizations, the succession to Sir Eric Drummond went to a Frenchman, M. Joseph Avenol, the present Secretary-General.

Chapter XXIII

THE THREE ORDERS OF THE WORLD STATE

§ 1

WE have traveled far from the concept of the Grand Alliance of Alexander, or the secret article of Kant, and farther still, it may be, from the concept of Smuts and Wilson and Cecil. If the League of Nations is not an association of monarchs, as Alexander planned, neither is it an association of peoples, as Smuts and Wilson dreamed. Nevertheless the peoples are represented at Geneva: a vast invisible audience, ultimately the real arbiters of the League's destiny. For of the three orders which comprise our new World State in embryo— the statesmen who represent the governments of the world; the Secretariat which represents the first international civil service, and the journalists who create and reflect world opinion—it is the journalists and not the ministers who are the real representatives of the peoples.

§ 2

The heroic days of the League are past, but it still possesses a curious fascination for the world's newspapers and their correspondents. Geneva is the first laboratory to be created for the manufacture of world opinion. During meetings of the Council and Assembly between four and five hundred journalists assemble in the town. Over a hundred resident correspondents are permanently assigned to the reporting of the League's activities. The one solitary American of the early days has become a dozen. And since the League's foundation over one thousand individual newspaper editors or correspondents have made at least one visit to Geneva. No other international organization has ever been the object of so much sustained attention and interest. No other international body has given so many privileges to journalists. The reason is evident. The League owes its very existence to the large body of opinion in all countries only too painfully interested in the preservation of even the most inadequate machinery for promoting peace. Albert Thomas, evoking cheers from the war-exhausted battalions on the Russian front, was not the only war-time discoverer of this universal sentiment. In Germany and Austria, in the neutral countries, in the United States, on the silent veldt of General Smuts's South Africa, the same vague craving for a new world order based on established peace made itself felt. Even today, after the failure of many experiments in international co-operation, the name of the League still has power to excite feelings of regret, of hope, of desire, or of resentment in the hearts of mankind. Even in Nazi Germany, where the Liberal and the Socialist press had disappeared, a League of Nations journal survives. Geneva, like Oxford, has become the home of lost causes.

The newspaper colony is less picturesque, less naïve, hilarious and orgiastic than it was in the brave days when the war was still a vivid memory, when Allied military missions, plebiscite control officers and financial commissioners, and other affiliated organs of the Peace Conference still industriously explored the outlying countries of Europe. When the Near East was in turmoil, typhus was raging in

Poland and Bolshevism in Russia, and Geneva opened its gates to the first Assembly of the League of Nations in an almost carnival gaiety. Now that the old Hotel Victoria is no longer an annex to the Assembly, and has become the headquarters of the Oxford Group, the British, French and American correspondents who once sat at their type-writers in the gloomy bedrooms of that well-named estab-lishment are dispersed all over the town. Some of them have ranged farther afield. Henry Wales, a famous corre-spondent of the *Chicago Tribune*, who with Wythe Wil-liams of the *New York Times* and the assistance of Mr. William Shearer of the United States steel interests, suc-cessfully fought the battle of the Three Power Naval Con-ference in 1927, is now a scenario writer in Hollywood. Edwin L. James, another old habitué of the Victoria, is now managing editor of the *New York Times*, and his newspaper is now represented in Geneva by the able and popular Clarence Streit. Lincoln Eyre, a brilliant corre-spondent of the defunct *New York World*, and the hero of the midnight incident on the lake recorded in an earlier chapter, died prematurely, as did the genial and talented George Adam of *The Times* of London.

A new generation of Geneva correspondents has sprung up, like the new generation of Geneva statesmen. Few veterans of the early years survive. Among the Frenchmen there are the scholarly Saint Brice of the *Journal*; Jules Sauerwein, once foreign editor of the *Matin* and now of *Paris-Soir*; André Géraud, better known under his pseudo-nym of Pertinax, the celebrated commentator of the *Echo de Paris*; Ludovic Naudeau, the French war correspondent, of *L'Illustration*; and Marcel Pays of *Excelsior*. Of the half-dozen great German journalists who went with Theodore Wolff into exile when Hitler came to power, the most talented, Georg Bernhardt, once editor of the *Vossische Zeitung*, now represents the organ of the German anti-Nazi refugees in Paris, the *Pariser Tageszeitung*. The British correspondents are a group which swells from the small and strictly professional nucleus of non-Assembly days, headed by Mr. H. J. Daniells of *The Times*, to a heterogeneous crowd in September, which includes Mr. Wickham Steed, Mr. Wilson Harris of the *Spectator*, the reverend Welsh gentleman who writes for *Y Cymru*, one retired army colonel, the lady correspondents of *The Schoolmaster* and the *Bournemouth Times*, Sir John Harris of the *Christian World*, and Sir Alfred Zimmern of the National Labour *News-Letter*, and Miss Sylvia Pankhurst on behalf of the quaintly named *New Times and Ethiopian News*.

The dean of the British correspondents is Robert Dell, of the *Manchester Guardian*. Mr. Dell gained a brief wartime distinction by being expelled from France, during the premiership of Clemenceau, for having sent to that newspaper a message describing one of the secret sessions of the Chamber of Deputies. He was authorized to return to France during the Herriot administration in 1924, and subsequently again became Paris correspondent for the same journal. He has since become the most prominent and the most picturesque of the correspondents in Geneva. Candid and courageous, an instinctive critic of all in authority, witty and occasionally provocative, Dell is held by diplomats in some awe and by his colleagues in respect and affection. His high, piercing voice is heard on the most incongruous occasions, raised in astonishment, in protest or in reproof. He is entirely devoid of caution or discre-

tion. During the war, when the spy-mania was at its
height in Paris, and pacifists and *défaitistes* were denounced
as public enemies, the unmistakable shrill accents of Robert Dell were overheard one day in a crowded underground
train, informing an embarrassed companion that "Caillaux
says . . ."

It was this stalwart and irrepressible veteran who sprang
to his feet in great excitement and indignation to protest
to Mr. Anthony Eden, as President of the League Council,
that Herr Greiser, the leader of the Danzig Nazis, had
thumbed his nose at the journalists as he left the Council
chamber after the insolent heel-clicking and saber-rattling
incident of 1936. Mr. Eden replied prudently that he
had not noticed the gesture, and that ended the matter.

During the year which witnessed not only this minor
journalistic incident, but also the major affair of the Italian
correspondents and the exiled Emperor of Abyssinia, the
press tribunes at Geneva were the scene of a third dramatic
gesture when a Czechoslovak press photographer of Jewish
origin committed suicide by shooting himself with a re-
volver. He died, he said, in protest against the failure
of the League.

§ 3

The newspaper correspondents represent one order, and
that not the least important, of the three estates of the
world organization at Geneva. The other two estates are
composed of the visiting statesmen and diplomats, the
periodical delegates to Council or Assembly, and the Secretariat. Of the three, to borrow the terminology by which
the various categories of seats on the League Council are
known, the members of the Secretariat alone are perma-

nent. The newspaper men are semi-permanent. The delegates, subject to the whims of dictators or democracies even more capricious than newspaper editors, are merely temporary. The Secretariat now numbers more than six hundred officials, both men and women. To such proportions have grown the members of that intimate luncheon party in the Bois de Boulogne whom we saw at the beginning of this study. Sir Eric Drummond's first lieutenant in the early days of the League was M. Jean Monnet, a member of a well-known French firm of brandy-distillers. In January, 1923, when M. Monnet decided to leave the League to look after his own affairs, and in particular the interests of French cognac, he was succeeded as Deputy Secretary-General by another Frenchman, M. Joseph Avenol, who in 1932, at the age of fifty-three, succeeded to Sir Eric Drummond as chief permanent official of the League.

Sir Eric had been a permanent official of the British Foreign Office. M. Avenol had been a permanent official of the French Treasury. The difference between the outward aspects of their careers helps to explain many temperamental differences between the two men. M. Avenol had not greatly desired his first appointment to the League of Nations. Like most Frenchmen, he hated residence abroad. He had gone reluctantly to London during the war as financial representative of the French government. He had gone reluctantly after the war as financial expert and delegate to the successive reparations and other international conferences at San Remo, Hythe, Spa, Boulogne, Brussels, Cannes and Genoa. He had aided in the financial restoration of Austria. And in 1923, when he went to Geneva, he went on the understanding that he would

AVENOL

be concerned exclusively with financial and economic questions. He still dislikes foreign travel, but he is incessantly *en voyage*. He has been frequently sent in the interests of the League to Central and Eastern Europe, to Canada and even to the Far East. In his Geneva days Sir Eric Drummond was also almost continually traveling in Europe.

Sir Eric was considered aloof and unapproachable by his staff. M. Avenol cultivates an ease and simplicity of manner, which nevertheless does not succeed in gaining him any greater popularity than was enjoyed by his predecessor. Hitherto he has not shown any marked originality in his decisions, or in his handling of staff questions. He went to Rome to urge the Italian government's early return to Geneva after the League had condemned Italy for the aggression against Abyssinia. He was snubbed by Mussolini, but unlike Mr. Eden, did not complain that Mussolini was no gentleman. In his long career as a minor and then as a major functionary of the French Ministry of Finance, M. Avenol learnt to exercise patience under the caprices of statesmen. One of his most original characteristics, for a Frenchman, is his horror of loquacity. He is little given to speaking, even at his own dinner-table. In committees or in staff conference his longest speech does not exceed three minutes in duration. Physically he looks the part of Secretary-General more thoroughly than his predecessor. In Geneva, Sir Eric Drummond wore soft collars and gray tweed on almost all save formal occasions. His manner was limp, melancholy and almost apologetic. M. Avenol is bald, wears horn-rimmed spectacles or rimless eyeglasses, starched collars and black clothes, has a precise, searching look, and a precise, clipped, functionary's speech. It is difficult for him to be anything but formal, and his attempts at informality betray this instinctive difficulty. With Sir Eric Drummond one felt that he had just wandered into his office from the lochs or grouse moors of Scotland. The heather was in his clothes and the native burr was on his tongue.

§ 4

Two Under Secretaries-General were originally appointed to assist the Secretary and Deputy-Secretary-General—an Italian, the Marquis Paulucci di Calboli Barone, a suave, popular and gallant diplomat famous for his hospitality; and a Japanese, the plump, smiling Mr. Sugimura, a giant physically, with the face and muscles of a Japanese wrestler. When Germany was admitted to the League a third Under-Secretary-General was added, in the person of Herr Dufour-Feronce, a former Leipzig merchant of French Huguenot origin. When Russia entered the League a fourth post was created for the short, dark, neurotic M. Rosenberg, a shy but courageous Russian diplomat who was a Soviet press attaché at the Conference of Genoa in 1922, was later sent on important missions to China and Afghanistan, and in September, 1936, after a short spell of activity as Under-Secretary-General at Geneva, was appointed Soviet Ambassador to the Spanish Republican government in Madrid. After the resignation of Japan and Germany one of the vacant Under-Secretaryships was given to a Spaniard, Señor Azcarate, who courageously resigned his safe and financially secure post at Geneva to represent his government in London at a time when Madrid seemed likely to fall at any moment into the hands of General Franco, and both Germany and Italy had diplomatically recognized the Spanish insurgents.

Other League changes in recent years are the replacement of the brilliant Pierre Comert, the original head of the Information Department, and now chief of the press section of the French Foreign Ministry in Paris, by a former Dutch journalist, M. Pelt; and the transfer of another Geneva veteran, the American Arthur Sweetser, from the information section to the political section of the League. Mr. H. R. Cummings, who was for many years the British member of the information section, is now Director of the League of Nations Office in London. The complex and exhausting details of the press arrangements at Geneva are still in the capable hands of Miss Vera Ward, who was the first woman to be appointed on the Secretariat, and whose service dates back to the London days of the League in 1920.

§ 5

Such are, in brief, the character, the history, the personalities and the composition of the League of Nations. It is, after all its failures, its disappointments and its defects, a highly perfected machine such as the world has never before constructed. It is a very complete microcosm of a superstate, a world government in miniature, with its Secretary-General and Under-Secretaries, its eleven sections embracing all the activities of the universe—Political, Legal, Financial and Economic, Reduction of Armaments, Transit and Communications, Mandates, Administrative and Minorities, Social, Health, Intellectual Co-operation, and Information—its diplomatic envoys, health missions, reforming zeal, waterways committees, refugee commissioners, currency experts, anti-slavery, anti-narcotic, anti-traffic-in-women-and-children organizations. It has enormous research departments, a colossal library, a radio station at Prangins, diplomatic immunity and freedom from Swiss income-tax. It has the most remarkable and in many ways the most efficient civil service in the world, a truly international staff, and a very novel and very sincere international spirit among members of that staff. And lately it has acquired, when its political fortunes seemed at their lowest ebb, an impressive palace in concrete, marble, glass and steel, fronting on the lake of Geneva and the mist-covered peak of Mont Blanc, a palace in whose foundation-stone were sealed in 1929 copies of the Covenant of President Wilson in French and English, the names of all the states then adhering to the League (Japan and Germany had not yet withdrawn), copies of the history of the League translated into all the languages of the States members, and specimens of the coins in currency in each of those states.

This Palace of the Nations will have been completed for the Assembly of September, 1937, and will have cost in all over 28,000,000 gold francs (at present rates about £3,000,-000 or $15,000,000). Like the organization of which it is to be the enduring monument, it has known a series of vicissitudes. As far back as 1926 the architects of the world were invited to submit plans for the building, which was then destined to rise on another site than that of the present palace, on land acquired by the League on the actual shores of the lake. From the 377 plans sent in two were chosen, both by official architects, a Frenchman and a Swiss. Prudently the League Committee invited the two to submit a revised plan in collaboration with three other architects—a Frenchman, an Italian and a Hungarian.

In the meantime the situation had changed. A Rockefeller gift of $2,000,000 for the endowment of a library permitted the Council to envisage a larger building than had originally been contemplated. More land was needed, and the League acquired it by exchanging its own site on the lake shore for another and larger site, the Parc Ariana, owned by the City of Geneva. The plans of the committee of five architects were repeatedly revised at the demand of the Secretariat. They were provisionally approved in 1928, and after fresh modification had been suggested were finally passed by the League Council and Assembly in 1929, when the foundation-stone was laid. Actual construction was not begun, however, until 1931, and the shell of the vast building was not completed until 1933. Three years later the Secretariat abandoned the old Hôtel National and took possession of its new offices in the Palace of the Nations. In the interval one of the original architects, the Frenchman Nénot, had died. He did not live to see the League flag flown from the masthead of an architectural monument whose only rival in size, costliness and impressiveness is Louis the Fourteenth's Palace of Versailles.

The façade of the principal building, that which is turned towards the lake and Mont Blanc, is a quarter of a mile long. The area covered by the entire palace is, roughly, equal to that of the Palace of Versailles. No single national style or period of architecture has been closely followed in the plan of the buildings, but if the choice of materials and the detail of the design are modern, the general effect is Roman. Without making any invidious comparisons as regards the beauty of the palace, it may be conceded without prejudice that it corresponds to the modern demand for functional design, and that in conception, size and utility it is not unworthy of the grandiose aims of the Covenant itself.

§ 6

In this new and impressive setting the members of the League Council met for the first time in September, 1936. Their council chamber, for public sessions, might have served for the solemn debates of the ancient Senate in Rome. By an ironic coincidence, the walls of the chamber had been decorated by the great Spanish muralist Sert, at the expense of the Republican government of Spain. At the very moment when the Council took their seats for the first time under the heroic compositions in which the struggle of mankind for liberation from tyranny, intolerance and injustice is commemorated, General Franco was beginning his long assault on the republicans in Madrid, and the legions of Germany and Italy were being landed in the ports of Spain as in the sixteenth century the legions of Spain were landed on the coasts of the Netherlands, and were launched against the coasts of England.

In September, 1937, the Assembly of the League met for the first time in the great new Assembly hall which is one of the principal features of the Palace of the Nations. Those of its members who witnessed the early meetings of the League may compare with reasonable pride the setting of the League of 1937 with that of 1920. Instead of the bare, stuffy conventicle of the Salle de la Réformation, the lace curtains and outmoded furniture and speaking parquets of the old League's ante-chambers in the Hôtel Victoria, the modern Assembly confers in a hall of gleaming wood and glass and metal, of soft lights, of conditioned air, of studied acoustics. About it are the rich furnishings offered by the states members: the President's chair and desk in rare Australian woods; a bronze plaque with a citation from the speeches of Simon Bolivar, the Liberator, from the South American Republics; Gobelins tapestries from Austria; carved panels by Eric Gill from Great Britain; a bronze statue from Greece; mural paintings by the Mexican Communist, Diego Rivera; a wrought-iron portico from Luxemburg; a President's chair in woods from the island of Samoa; rare carpets from Persia; and finally, a bronze group by the American sculptor Paul Manship to the memory of Woodrow Wilson, the founder of the League—the gift not of the Democratic administration of the United States but of a private philanthropic body, the Woodrow Wilson Foundation.

§ 7

The handful of survivors from 1920—graceful little Paul Hymans, the white-haired Belgian, the suave Greek Politis, the Swiss ex-President Motta, the Roumanian Nicolas Titulescu—may look upon this tardy magnificence of the Geneva scene with a melancholy tinged with irony. The last-comers to the League, the envoys of the Union of Socialist Soviet Republics, may gaze upon it with justifiable complacency. In this modern temple of the new religion of peace but one spectator is lacking, a representative of that other and more ancient universal institution, the Church of Rome. A papal legate, possessed of the spirit of paradox and endowed with the historic sense, might see in this late flowering of the League a curious analogy to the history of his own great Church. In the case of the one, as in the case of the other, a teacher had arisen in a distant country, in a time of universal trouble and confusion of spirits. In each case the teacher had found followers, had preached a world religion, had been betrayed and had died abandoned by his friends. In each case a Church had been founded in the name of the dead prophet, had arisen to its greatest glory through the zeal of men who knew not the Founder, had known its saints, its martyrs, its zealots and its heretics, had suffered and been derided of men, had itself condemned and excommunicated, had been poor and was now rich. And in each case the people from whom the teacher had sprung, and in whose name he had founded his Church, would not enter therein, but denied him and all his works.

BIBLIOGRAPHY

In addition to a large number of official publications of the League of Nations, for the opportunity of consulting which the author expresses his thanks to the officials of the Information Department of the League, the following works have been found useful:

Robert de Traz: *De l'Alliance des Rois à la Ligue des Peuples*. Paris, 1936.

Max Beer: *The League on Trial*. London, 1932.

A. Lugan: *L'Esprit public aux États Unis après la Guerre*. Paris, 1926.

Antonina Vallentin: *Stresemann*. Paris, 1931.

Saint Aulaire: *Génève contre la Paix*. Paris, 1936.

René Benjamin: *Les Augures de Génève*. Paris, 1929.

Raymond Escholier: *Souvenirs Parlés de Briand*. Paris, 1932.

Norman Hillson: *Geneva Scene*. London, 1936.

Louis Eisenmann: *Édouard Benes*. Paris, 1934.

Léon Bourgeois: *L'Œuvre de la Société des Nations*. Paris, 1923.

Valentine Thomson: *Briand, Man of Peace*. London, 1929.

George Glasgow: *Continental Statesmen*. London, 1930.

Theodor Wolff: *Through Two Decades*. London, 1936.

Henri Béraud: *Men of the Aftermath*. London, 1929.

William Plomer: "General Smuts" (in "Great Contemporaries"). London, 1935.